WHOSE MISSION, WHOSE ORDERS?

WHOSE MISSION,

WHOSE ORDERS?

British Civil-Military Command and
Control in Northern Ireland, 1968–1974

DAVID A. CHARTERS

McGill-Queen's University Press
Montreal & Kingston • London • Chicago

ISBN 978-0-7735-4926-5 (cloth)
ISBN 978-0-7735-4927-2 (ePDF)
ISBN 978-0-7735-4928-9 (ePUB)

Legal deposit second quarter 2017
Bibliothèque nationale du Québec

Printed in Canada on acid-free paper that is 100% ancient forest free
(100% post-consumer recycled), processed chlorine free.

This book has been published with the help of a grant from the
Department of History at the University of New Brunswick.

McGill-Queen's University Press acknowledges the support of the
Canada Council for the Arts for our publishing program. We also
acknowledge the financial support of the Government of Canada
through the Canada Book Fund for our publishing activities.

Library and Archives Canada Cataloguing in Publication

Charters, David A., 1949–, author
    Whose mission, whose orders? : British civil-military
command and control in Northern Ireland, 1968–1974 /
David A. Charters.

Includes bibliographical references and index.
Issued in print and electronic formats.
ISBN 978-0-7735-4926-5 (cloth). – ISBN 978-0-7735-4927-2 (ePDF). –
ISBN 978-0-7735-4928-9 (ePUB)

    1. Great Britain. Army – Political activity – History – 20th
century – Case studies. 2. Civil-military relations – Ireland – History –
20th century – Case studies. 3. British – Northern Ireland – History –
20th century – Case studies. 4. Northern Ireland – History – 1969–1994 –
Case studies. 5. Great Britain – Military policy – History – 20th century.
I. Title.

DA990.U46C48 2017   941.60824   C2017-900185-X
                                                C2017-900186-8

This book was typeset by True to Type in 10.5/13 Sabon

To the late Dr Dominick "Toby" Graham, MC, PhD,

Soldier, Scholar, Inspiration, Mentor, and Friend

Contents

Acknowledgments

I am grateful to the staff at the United Kingdom National Archives, the Imperial War Museum, and the Liddell Hart Centre for Military Archives, King's College, London for permission to cite documents held in their collections. Their efficiency and cheerful assistance also has been greatly appreciated. Staff in both Document Delivery and Microforms at the Harriet Irving Library, University of New Brunswick, were also very helpful. At UNB, I owe a debt of gratitude to the vice-president academic, the vice-president research, and the dean of arts, and to the History Department's James K. Chapman Fund for the financial support that made publishing this book possible. My colleagues in the Department of History and the Gregg Centre for the Study of War and Society were consistently encouraging and supportive. In particular, the Network for the Study of Civilians, Soldiers, and Society provided very useful feedback on one of the chapters, and Dr Marc Milner read an early draft of the full manuscript and several revised chapters. As always, his comments were insightful and constructive. My thanks go to Jacqueline Mason, my editor at McGill-Queen's University Press, first for "talent-spotting" my work at the 2015 ISA conference, and second for skilfully shepherding the manuscript through the review, editing, and production processes. I am grateful as well for Barbara Tessman's very thorough and thoughtful copy-editing. My family deserves praise for putting up with my prolonged absences on research trips and the many long, late hours I spent sequestered with my computer. Finally, I owe a debt that can never be repaid to my mentor, the late Dr Dominick "Toby" Graham, who started me down the path to this book nearly fifty years ago. I regret only that it took so long to get here, and that he is not here to see the final product.

Abbreviations

ACDS	assistant chief of the defence staff	DOE	defence operations executive
ACP	aid to the civil power	DOIC	Director of Operations Intelligence Committee
AUS	assistant undersecretary		
AUS (GS)	assistant undersecretary (general staff)	DOPC	Defence and Overseas Policy Committee
AVRE	armoured vehicle, Royal Engineers	D/OPS	director of operations
		DS	Defence Secretariat
BAOR	British Army of the Rhine	DUS	deputy undersecretary
CBF	commander British forces	FCO	Foreign and Commonwealth Office
CDS	chief of the defence staff		
CGS	chief of the general staff	GOC	general officer commanding
CINC	commander-in-chief		
CLF	commander land forces	GSU	Government Security Unit
CMR	civil-military relations		
CO	commanding officer (of a military unit)	HMG	Her Majesty's Government
COSC	Chiefs of Staff Committee	HO	Home Office
CSC	Cabinet Security Committee (of the Northern Ireland government)	HQ	headquarters
		HQNI	headquarters, Northern Ireland
		IG	inspector general
DASD	director of army staff duties	IRA	Irish Republican Army
D/DOP	director, defence operations and plans	IS	internal security
		ISC	Intelligence Sub-Committee (of the JSC)
D/INT	director of intelligence		
DMO	director of military operations	JIC	Joint Intelligence Committee

JSC	Joint Security Committee	RUC	Royal Ulster Constabulary
JSIW	Joint Services Interrogation Wing	SB	Special Branch
L/O	liaison officer	SDLP	Social Democratic and Labour Party
MA	military assistant		
MILO	military intelligence liaison officer	sitrep	situation report
		SLO	security liaison officer (MI5)
MO 4	Military Operations 4		
MOD	Ministry of Defence	SOP	standard operating procedures
MP	member of Parliament		
NATO	North Atlantic Treaty Organization	SPA	Civil Authorities (Special Powers) Act
NICRA	Northern Ireland Civil Rights Association	SSD	secretary of state for defence
NIO	Northern Ireland Office	SSNI	secretary of state for Northern Ireland
OD	operational directive		
O group	orders group	UDA	Ulster Defence Association
I PARA	1st Battalion, the Parachute Regiment		
		UDR	Ulster Defence Regiment
PAC	Public Accounts Committee	UKLF	United Kingdom Land Forces
PD	People's Democracy	UUP	Ulster Unionist Party
PIRA	Provisional Irish Republican Army	UV	Ulster Volunteers
		UVF	Ulster Volunteer Force
PM	prime minister	UVM	Ulster Vanguard Movement
PR	public relations		
PUS	permanent undersecretary	UWC	Ulster Workers' Council
		VCDS	vice-chief of the defence staff
PWO	Prince of Wales' Own Regiment		
		VCGS	vice-chief of the general staff
ROE	rules of engagement		

Denis Healey, secretary of state for defence, 1964–70. (Courtesy of Alamy
Limited)

Reginald Maudling, home secretary, 1970–72, shown meeting with soldiers in Belfast, July 1970. (Courtesy of Alamy Limited)

William Whitelaw, secretary of state for Northern Ireland, 1972–73.
(Courtesy of Alamy Limited)

General Sir Peter Hunt, chief of the (army) general staff, 1973–76. (Courtesy of Alamy Limited)

Roy Mason, secretary of state for defence, 1974–76. (Courtesy of Alamy Limited)

James Callaghan (right), former home secretary, 1967–70, shown here with
Prime Minister Harold Wilson. (Courtesy of Alamy Limited)

Lt. Gen. Sir Harry Tuzo, general officer commanding and director of operations in Northern Ireland, 1971–73. (Courtesy of Alamy Limited)

Merlyn Rees (left), secretary of state for Northern Ireland, 1974–76, with Prime Minister Harold Wilson (centre) and Stanley Orme, minister of State for Northern Ireland, in April 1974. (Courtesy of Alamy Limited)

Lord Carrington, secretary of state for defence, 1970–74. (Courtesy of the North Atlantic Treaty Organization)

Lt. Gen. Sir Frank King, general officer commanding and director of operations in Northern Ireland, 1973–75. (Courtesy of Victor Patterson)

Lt. Gen. Sir Ian Freeland, general officer commanding and director of operations in Northern Ireland, 1969–71. (Courtesy of the Imperial War Museum)

Field Marshal Sir Michael Carver, chief of the (army) general staff, 1971–73, and chief of defence staff, 1973–76. (Courtesy of the Imperial War Museum)

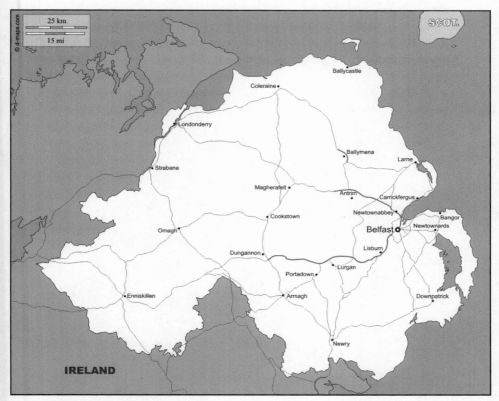

Northern Ireland

WHOSE MISSION, WHOSE ORDERS?

Introduction

WHAT THIS BOOK IS ABOUT

This is a study of British civil-military relations (CMR) – the command and control relationship between politicians and generals – during the first six years of Britain's longest war: the thirty-year conflict in Northern Ireland. The key question explored in this book is, who ran that war – the politicians or the generals? This question leads to several more that require answers. How did they reach decisions, and how did they handle disagreements over policy, strategy, and operations? What do such negotiations tell us about British civil-military relations in the larger sense? How do findings with respect to CMR in Northern Ireland conform to or differ from the prevailing CMR theories? Is theory a useful tool for understanding British CMR? And finally, was this a CMR success story or a failure?

By the standards of the major wars of the twentieth and early twenty-first century, the Northern Ireland conflict was very long but very small. Between 1969 and 1998, 35,669 shooting incidents and 10,412 explosions claimed the lives of 1,832 civilians, 1,117 members of the security forces (army and police), and 526 insurgents (republican and loyalist), for a total of 3,475 fatalities.[1] Some 42,304 people were injured, 27,274 of them civilians.[2] For Britain and for Northern Ireland, however, these numbers were significant. One estimate suggested that an equivalent victim-to-population ratio for Britain as a whole over the same period would have amounted to 100,000 dead.[3] Moreover, these figures, of course, do not take into account the psychological toll on individuals, families, and communities: parents losing children, children growing up without parents, those traumatized by physical injury, and communities divided by walls, wire, and watchtowers.[4] Nor do they take into account the financial costs: losses to the Northern Ireland economy over thirty years, costs to repair damage to infrastructure, and the costs of deploying thousands of soldiers in the province for three decades.[5] The prolonged and repeated deployment of many major units imposed considerable strain on the British Army. It taxed the army's ability to train, to plan, and to meet its obligations to the North Atlantic Treaty Organization (NATO).[6] The Northern Ireland conflict may have been a small war, but the human, material, and financial costs were enormous.

In many respects the conflict resembled those Britain had engaged in during the withdrawal from empire. Just as in Palestine, Malaya, Kenya, Cyprus, and South Arabia, it confronted an aggrieved population and civil unrest that morphed into insurgency, guerrilla warfare, and terrorism and that increased in lethality over time. British countermeasures also followed a familiar pattern: riot control, searches for arms and insurgents, raids and roadblocks, detention without trial, covert intelligence operations, and information warfare.[7] And, as had happened in most of those earlier conflicts, the outcome was not a clear cut victory or defeat. The Provisional Irish Republican Army (PIRA) – the leading insurgent group – was forced to abandon its goal of unifying Northern Ireland with the Irish republic by force, but Britain had to grant Sinn Féin (the PIRA's political arm) a share in political power as the price of peace.[8]

That said, the Northern Ireland conflict differed from its post-imperial predecessors in two crucial respects. First, the conflict took place within Great Britain. The British could not simply haul down the flag, board their troops on ships and planes, and abandon the territory to its fate. The province had been self-governing since 1922 and was responsible for public security until Britain imposed direct rule in March 1972. However, the British government bore ultimate constitutional, legal, political, and economic responsibility for Northern Ireland, just as it did for Scotland, Wales, and for England itself. The people of the province were British citizens. They voted in national elections, and their elected members sat in the House of Commons. Even if it wished to do so, Britain could not wash its hands of the province and its problems.

Second, unlike the steaming jungles of Malaya or the barren wastes of South Arabia, Northern Ireland was close by and accessible. When "the Troubles" broke out, as bombs went off and people died, the British press was right there. The violence of the day appeared on the television news that night. The conflict was right in the face of the British people and their political leaders; it could not be overlooked or ignored. Events that might have received minimal or no coverage had they happened in some remote colony were front-page news when they occurred in Belfast or Londonderry. Many nightly newscasts in Britain opened with the words "Last night another soldier ..."[9] Thus, perceptions of the first half-decade of the Troubles would be shaped by stark images: British troops fighting British citizens on the streets of British cities.

These two factors – responsibility and visibility – complicated the British government's handling of the Ulster conflict. At no time could the government in London fully distance itself from the conflict and leave policy and decisions mostly in the hands of a distant colonial governor. Every decision it made in the political and security realms with respect to the conflict in Ulster had to be considered within the context of British law, British domestic politics, and British public opinion. Although the Protestant-dominated government of Northern Ireland (seated at Stormont) retained responsibility for law and order until 1972, Britain was obligated to provide the troops that allowed Stormont to exercise that function in the conflict. So the British government could not escape responsibility for how the troops were used in the province, even if Stormont's autonomy frustrated London's ability to exercise complete control over how they were employed. Likewise, the security measures British troops had used with near impunity in the colonies came under close, constant, and critical scrutiny by the news media when they were applied in Ulster. So, decisions taken in cabinet committee (or by Stormont) one day could have a direct impact on the lives of British citizens and soldiers in Northern Ireland the next day and on public opinion and the political standing of the government the day after. Thus the British government's power was at once both absolute in theory and highly constrained in reality. If ever there was a British war that was "too important to be left to the generals," this was it.[10]

Finally, decision making was shaped in part by the conflict itself, which – as discussed later in this introduction – was a dynamic, not a static, phenomenon. It was not the same conflict in 1974 that it had been in 1968. And while deliberations in London invariably took time to result in a decision, events on the ground often forced the pace of the decision-making process. The result of all of these interactions was almost always less than ideal; more often than not, some degree of compromise was the order of the day. So, even when the effects of the security forces' actions were not outright disastrous, they often seemed to fall short of expectations.

Thanks to the visibility of the conflict, we know a lot about what happened on the streets of Northern Ireland. The daily news coverage allowed journalists and scholars to generate an extensive body of literature on the conflict and on its participants even before it came to an end.[11] But little of their writing examined the civil-military command and control decision-making processes that lay behind what happened on the streets.[12] They cannot be seriously faulted for this oversight. The deliberations of the British cabinet and its committees, their interactions with the Northern Ireland government, and the dialogue between the politicians and generals on how to handle the situation took place behind closed doors. These remained closely held state secrets until the opening of the official archives on the conflict commencing in 2000 and the 2010 release of the report of the official inquiry into the 1972 Bloody Sunday massacre. Access to these sources has begun to shed light on the decision-making processes, generating a second wave of scholarly literature.[13]

Even so, the picture of the policymaking and decision making that shaped the British Army's actions on the streets of Northern Ireland remains far from complete. This book is an attempt to fill gaps in that picture. Using original sources to answer the questions posed at the start of this introduction, it represents the first full-length scholarly analysis of the civil-military command and control process for the formative period of the conflict, 1968–1974.

In his 2003 study of the conflict, *Britain's Long War*, Peter R. Neumann attempts to answer the central question about the political control of the army's actions in Northern Ireland. He says first that the consensus on the army's role was weakened by "Westminster's tendency to remove itself from the execution of the military instrument, which meant that the government exercised less political control of the security forces than necessary."[14] He then asserts that "there was a tendency to delegate controversial security decisions from Cabinet or ministerial level to other actors or institutions who were thought to judge a particular question on a purely technocratic basis. By doing so, the government avoided responsibility, it distanced itself from events in the province and protected itself from accusations of partisanship."[15]

What Neumann is suggesting is a relatively clear division of responsibilities, akin to the military concepts of "mission orders," "directive control," or what the Germans called *Auftragstaktik*. Under this approach, a senior military commander sets the mission to be achieved and assigns the forces and other resources needed to subordinate commanders, leaving it to them to decide how best to achieve the goal.[16] Applying this model to Northern Ireland as Neumann sees it, cabinet defined the goal to be achieved by the army: "to reduce the level of violence to 'an acceptable level' ... which allowed the primacy of constitutional politics to be re-established."[17] It then left it up to the army, the senior ranks in the chain of command, the Ministry of Defence (MOD), and departments such as the Northern Ireland Office (NIO), to choose and apply the means to bring about that goal without further interference from cabinet.

This observation by a serious scholar of the conflict cannot be dismissed out of hand. Yet, the evidence presented in the chapters that follow suggests that the politicians did not – as Neumann contends – delegate "controversial security decisions" to the army and Whitehall (although they did defer to Stormont on the issue on internment). Nor was civil-military command and control simply a matter of the politicians giving orders and the army following them blindly. Rather, between the politicians and the generals there was a constant dialogue on political ends and military means.

They did not always agree. The army proffered its advice, but political considerations usually predominated. This meant that the army's efforts to turn political objectives into viable military operations were subject to frequent and direct political influence, sometimes down to the tactical level. Likewise, the army used its professional expertise – input that the politicians needed – and its access to the political leaders, as well as the respect accorded to its senior officers, to influence the political decision making that shaped its mission and tasks. Moreover, the politicians and generals did not reach their decisions in isolation from the rest of government. The senior ranks of the civil service, in particular the Prime Minister's Office, the Home Office, the MOD, and the NIO played a role in shaping the debates. They provided vital information, policy options, and procedural guidance to the decision makers, both civilian and military. While this multiplicity of players may have served as a check on rash decisions by the army and its political masters, some critics assert that it represented "fractured and ineffectual civilian control" that "facilitated a return to primordial military thinking," which led the army to rely heavily on repressive methods.[18]

Although Parliament did not play a direct role in decision making, neither could it be ignored. If only to protect its electoral mandate and reassure its own backbenchers, the government had to explain to parliamentarians why it took the decisions it did and how it was dealing with their impact. Being accountable to Parliament in this way is a litmus test of CMR in the Westminster system.

Consequently, this book reaches a conclusion that is at odds with Neumann's and that of other critics. Far from removing itself "from the execution of the military instrument," the government exercised a great deal of political control over military operations in Northern Ireland in the period under study. That is not to say that it always exercised such control effectively or wisely. Moreover, what is striking about the army's role in this process is its dualistic nature: at once both thoroughly professional in the execution of its mission and politically engaged in the process that defined it. In this regard its behaviour is consistent with the character of the army described by historian Hew Strachan in his 1997 book *The Politics of the British Army*, the premier full-length history of British CMR. Strachan asserts that "armies are self-evidently political institutions."[19] He then goes on to demonstrate persuasively that since the end of the seventeenth century the British Army has been both professional *and* politically active.[20] I will argue that the British system of civil-military command and control generally, and with regard to Northern Ireland in particular, cannot be explained by any single CMR theory. Such an argument calls into question the utility of theory as an explanatory tool for the British experience.

WHY ASSESSING CMR THEORY IS IMPORTANT

The study of CMR examines how societies and governments manage their relationships with their armed forces. The literature on this is now extensive, encompassing and bridging the disciplines of history, sociology, law, and political science.[21] Traditionally, the field – dominated by American social sciences – has focused on developing theories and models to explain those relationships. In particular, scholars have focused on the central, fundamental challenge of democratic CMR: how to limit the ability of the armed forces to use their coercive power to influence or to intervene in domestic politics. The civil-military relationship is fundamental to the functioning of democracy; getting it right matters. And when things go wrong, understanding why matters even more. If it is important to understand the balance between political and military objectives in the case of foreign wars, it is even more so in the case of internal conflicts, where decisions and military actions will directly impact the citizens and the functioning of a liberal democratic state. Maintaining public order is normally the responsibility of the police, whose powers are limited and are governed by legislation specific to their role. So, if the police cannot deal with a public order crisis, and the government feels compelled to call out the troops to do so, then managing effectively the CMR balance takes on enhanced importance.

In a mature liberal democracy, the civilian political leaders and the military leadership each have their particular responsibilities and competences: governance versus military operations. But the relationship between them is not one of equals. In his pioneering book *The Soldier and the State*, CMR theorist Samuel P. Huntington reminded his readers that, in a democracy, elected civilians retain supreme authority; election by the population grants them legitimate power to govern.[22] The military has no comparable authority or legitimacy in that domain; its principal role is to defend the state against external threats. What it does have is the means to use violence in a highly organized fashion on a large scale, something the civilian authorities lack. These authorities may need to rely on those means to serve national interests, but they – or the political structure in which they operate – must also keep the military in check to ensure that its monopoly on the use of force is not misapplied in a way that threatens the democracy itself.

That goal might be achieved easily if the military were used only abroad in support of foreign policy objectives, although even in that sphere the process of defining strategy, deciding missions, and allocating resources requires a complex interaction between civilians and soldiers. But ideally the politicians leave the conduct of operations overseas to the military professionals who have the expertise and competence to plan and direct them. However, when the military is used in an internal security role – such as that conducted by the British Army in Northern Ireland – the lines between civilian and military power and responsibilities become blurred. By its very nature that role inserts the military and its capacity to use force into domestic politics. Likewise, politicians may insert themselves into the handling of such operations because the political implications of internal military actions are too serious to be left to the military alone. While the outcome of a major conventional war is unlikely to be decided by the actions of a single soldier, the same is not necessarily true in internal security or counter-insurgency operations. A misstep by a single soldier can have significant political effects; hence the concept of "the strategic corporal."[23]

If that corporal on a street corner in Belfast is a "strategic" asset, then the politician, who along with the military defines the strategy and military means to be used to achieve national goals, has a direct, abiding interest in the actions of that corporal. The military may understand why political leaders feel they have a legitimate interest in influencing military actions at that level, but that does not preclude the fact that they are likely to resent any intrusion into their sphere of professional competence. Thus, military internal security operations do not just contain the potential for civil-military friction and conflict; they challenge the fundamental basis of democratic civil-military relations. How a state weathers such a situation will say a lot about the maturity of that relationship. The evidence presented in this book indicates a high degree of maturity in British CMR but also shows that even a highly developed system can be strained by the stressful and unpredictable character of internal security operations.

HOW THIS BOOK WILL MAKE ITS CASE

Through a series of case studies, this book will analyse British CMR in Northern Ireland. After an opening chapter that explains the "machinery of government" – the structures and processes of civil-military command and control – the book examines seven decision-making cases between 1968 and 1974 in which CMR figured prominently. The first of these concerns operational policymaking and decision making in the months preceding the deployment of troops, as the government and the military attempted to grasp their legal and constitutional responsibilities for keeping the peace in the province. The remaining six examine CMR and decision making with reference to specific events: the major deployment of troops in August 1969; the internment operation of August 1971; the Bloody Sunday massacre in January 1972; the imposition of direct rule in March 1972; Operation Motorman in August 1972; and the Ulster Workers' Council strike of May 1974. The place of each of these events on the trajectory of the Northern Ireland conflict will be discussed below. The conclusion draws together the salient points about civil-military decision making that emerged from the individual cases to discern and explain commonalities and discontinuities. These will include: the role of committees; the influence of senior civil servants in setting agendas; and the importance of personalities, both civilian and military, in decision making. The civil-military patterns displayed in the cases will be tested against a number of CMR theories to determine if any of them can explain why the civil-military relationship worked the way it did.

Although chapter 1 does not relate to a single event, but rather spans the entire period under study, several salient points illustrate the importance of the machinery of government. The first of these is the division of responsibility for security between London and Stormont.[24] That fact would bedevil intergovernmental relations, policy-making, and operational planning from August 1969 to March 1972. The second was the lack within the British government of any formal structure that exercised responsibility for and oversight of Northern Ireland affairs in that period.[25] There was, moreover, no Northern Ireland policy; prior to the events of 5 October 1968, discussed in chapter 2, the province simply was not on anyone's radar. London's attention was focused on Britain's economic problems and on foreign policy crises.[26] Thus, it was singularly unprepared for the conflict that emerged between the autumn of 1968 and the summer of 1969. So when the conflict broke out, the absence of policy, and the power of the prime minister and cabinet to make decisions, put a premium on personalities, experience, and leadership styles. That chapter draws attention to the differences in these between the Labour and Conservative governments over the period. Likewise, the absence of policy, and the rapid escalation of violence in 1969, thrust the army onto centre stage; it became the primary instrument for managing the crisis. Chapter 1 explains the army's capabilities, its professional and politi-

cal roles, the command structure, the role of the secretary of state for
defence, and the ability of senior civil servants in the MOD to constrain
the pace and scope of policymaking and decision making.

Finally, chapter 1 makes clear that civil-military command and
control was not a logical, linear, top-down process commencing with
direction from the prime minister and finishing with orders issued
through the military chain of command to that strategic corporal on
a Belfast street corner. Rather, the process was interactive, deliberative, and dynamic, involving constant, often prolonged, negotiation,
compromise, bargaining, and consensus building between the MOD,
cabinet committees, and senior civilian and military leaders. It was
not a system designed to reach decisions quickly. In fact, arguably, it
was not suited to managing a conflict at all. That said, as subsequent
chapters will show, those involved made it work in spite of its limitations. Furthermore, the relatively small number of people who
were part of the process conducted all of this work in secret. This
tended to limit options to current policy and to exclude the consideration of alternative policies or decisions. All of the foregoing suggests that the civil-military command and control process guiding
the British Army during the period under study defies explanation
by a wholly rational decision-making model or by any single theory
of civil-military relations.

THE CONFLICT AND THE CASE STUDIES, 1968–1974

This section explains the transformation of the Northern Ireland conflict over the 1968–74 period and situates each chapter within that
period and process. It highlights the relevance of key arguments to the
particular stage of the conflict addressed in each chapter and enhanc-
es our understanding of the influence that the conflict's constantly
changing character exerted on decision making in London and in
the province.

It must be acknowledged at the outset that attempting to identify
patterns of violence and to define temporal boundaries within this
conflict may impose an artificial sense of order on what was a fluid
situation. The boundaries between the different phases were not hard
and fast. So, what follows should be considered only an approxima-
tion of the conflict's shifting dynamics.

The first phase of the conflict opened in October 1968 and lasted until the spring of 1970. This period was marked by gradually escalating communal violence: clashes between Catholics and Protestants, and between demonstrators and police (the Royal Ulster Constabulary – RUC) and eventually the army. These clashes reached their apogee in August 1969, when their severity and the excessive use of force by the RUC prompted Stormont to request troops to restore order.

Chapters 2 and 3 are situated firmly within this phase. The first introduces readers to the conflict itself and provides a perspective on how the governments in London and at Stormont first responded to it. The scale and intensity of the violence in October 1968 caught the British government by surprise, forcing it to address the problems in the province it had long ignored and to consider how it might respond if the situation got worse.

This chapter also reveals a number of "disconnects" between London and Stormont: in their views on the causes of the crisis; in their prescriptions for conflict resolution; and in their responsibilities for public security. These are important because they complicated policy-making and decision making during the first three and a half years of the conflict. The evolving situation in the province pushed the British government to pursue two divergent and contradictory courses of action: to examine its obligations to provide military aid to the civil power (ACP) in Northern Ireland, and to engage in a desperate search for options to avoid doing so. In the end Prime Minister Harold Wilson's government realized it could not shirk its constitutional responsibility for the province. Because the crisis escalated gradually during this period, the civil-military decision-making process worked as intended.

The situation changed quickly and dramatically in the period covered in chapter 3: from spring through autumn of 1969. In mid-August, violent clashes in Londonderry and Belfast became so severe that the RUC (which itself was seen as part of the problem) could not contain them. In the space of forty-eight hours, two battalions of troops were deployed in the two cities. They separated the warring Catholic and Protestant populations, bringing about an immediate and dramatic drop in violence. Over the next few days three more battalions, a brigade headquarters, and supporting elements arrived in the province, marking the start of Operation Banner, a campaign that would last thirty years.

This chapter traces the debates that occurred before mid-August within the British government and between it and Stormont over the conditions under which troops might be deployed in ACP. Once the troops were in place, the two governments engaged in a prolonged struggle for control of the security forces, as Stormont remained responsible for law and order while London provided the troops that made public order possible. London put in place structures, processes, and people to ensure it had the final say. But the result was a bifurcated system in which Stormont retained control of the police for "normal" policing activity, while the general officer commanding (GOC) exercised control of them and the army for "security" operations. It was an unsatisfactory compromise, leaving the GOC answerable to two political authorities that did not always agree. This system, while awkward, was tolerable for the short term, since at that time no one expected the troops to be on the ground for more than a few months.

But Ulster's underlying socio-political problems remained unresolved, and its violent manifestations did not remain in stasis. For the first few months after August, Protestant gangs and rioters were the army's nemesis, while it enjoyed a relative honeymoon with the Catholic population, serving as its protectors. That began to change in 1970. The Irish Republican Army (IRA) split at the end of 1969 into the Official and Provisional factions. The latter planned to use violence, first to defend the Catholic population against the Protestant militants, and ultimately to force the British to withdraw from the North and allow reunification with the South.

Aware that the IRA was building its arsenal, the army tried to pre-empt its plans. In 1970 it conducted a series of arms searches that both alienated the Catholic population and convinced the IRA that it had to act to defend them. The IRA launched a bombing campaign in 1970, and in February 1971 began attacking the army. This phase of the conflict, characterized by rising terrorism and anti-terrorism operations, lasted until London imposed direct rule in March 1972.

This was the dynamic that brought about the internment operation that is the focus of chapter 4. Northern Ireland's Civil Authorities (Special Powers) Act legalized internment without trial, and that option was always on the table. The British general election of June 1970 had brought to power the Conservative Party, led by Prime Minister Edward Heath. Like Wilson, Heath sought unsuccessfully to

avoid a deeper engagement in the conflict, but it increasingly dominated his agenda. Internment was central to the debates over how to
manage the conflict, and it led to the most serious disagreement
between the politicians and the generals. In particular, by the summer
of 1971 the rising violence was undermining Stormont prime minister Brian Faulkner. A moderate unionist by comparison with his
rivals, he was being outflanked politically by more militant Protestants who demanded a tougher line against the IRA. This situation
presented Heath with a Hobson's choice: save Faulkner's government by imposing internment, or let Stormont collapse, and assume
governance of the province by direct rule. The generals opposed
internment on the grounds that it was unnecessary and would lead
to more violence. But, desperate to avoid the direct-rule option,
Heath chose to ignore the army's advice and authorized the internment operation. It was less effective than hoped, and the army's worst
fears were borne out. The level of violence in the province escalated
dramatically after internment.

Heath's refusal to follow the advice of his military advisers could
have caused a serious crisis in British CMR, but it did not. The army's
leaders had been asked for their advice; it was proffered but in the end
not followed. No officer resigned on a matter of principle. Nor did
they refuse to carry out the internment operation. It may not have
been sound security policy, but the army had no legal or constitutional grounds to refuse to implement the decision and did not do so.
Internment was a political decision and choice that clearly overlapped
both the political and military spheres of responsibility. But both parties respected each other's responsibilities and roles in their respective
spheres. Ultimately, the elected civil authority prevailed.

In the wake of internment, the rising violence brought about a cor-
responding shift in security policy, committing the army to a proactive counterterrorism program in those Catholic communities that
had become no-go areas for the security forces. So, relations between
the army and the Catholic population were at a nadir when Bloody
Sunday occurred. That tragic incident, in which the army shot and
killed fourteen civil rights marchers in January 1972, is the focus of
chapter 5. It makes clear that the army's preparations for the march do
not appear to have been shaped or driven by the new counterterrorism policy. Indeed, the whole tenor of pre-march planning stressed a
low-key approach to handling it, not a confrontational one. While the

planning for the march was solely in the hands of the security forces, there is nothing in the evidence to suggest that those plans were out of step with London's aims, which were to emphasize political solutions. What is important for this study is that Bloody Sunday cannot be explained as a product of confusion over or a breakdown of high-level civil-military command and control. Instead, it resulted from a failure of fire-control discipline at the lowest tactical level.

Like internment, Bloody Sunday could have led to a CMR crisis. The government had every reason to be angry at the army, whose actions had plunged it into a political disaster. Inside Ulster itself, the IRA stepped up its bombing campaign and its attacks on the army, while a new Protestant extremist organization threatened violence. Chapter 5 shows that in spite of all this the government averted a CMR crisis because it did not second-guess the tactical level of planning and conduct of operations. Nor did it rush to judgment and sack any of the officers in the chain of command. Instead, to distance itself from any charges of cover-up, it appointed a judicial inquiry into Bloody Sunday, while trying to ensure that this inquiry did not undermine the army's morale. This was a vital issue, since the army was carrying the heaviest security burden in Ulster. This government strategy was not an ideal solution, but it may have been the only workable one in the circumstances.

Bloody Sunday set the stage for the most significant political initiative up to that point in the conflict: the suspension of the Stormont parliament and the imposition of direct rule of the province in March 1972. This marked the start of the third and shortest phase of the conflict thus far, which involved a direct confrontation – both political and military – between the British government and army on the one side and the IRA on the other. Terrorism reached its apogee in this phase, while the army's role was in flux until it reclaimed control of the no-go areas in August 1972.

As explained in chapter 6, control of the security forces lay at the heart of the decision to impose direct rule. It was meant to resolve the conundrum that had been in place since August 1969, whereby the army was maintaining law and order in Ulster and was answerable to Westminster, but British ministers there had no responsibility for law and order in the province. That task lay within the domain of Stormont, at best a compromised democracy whose biased police force – the RUC – had been replaced by the army. The army welcomed direct rule, because it was no longer caught between two separate and conflicting governments. However, the new arrangement fell short of full unity of command. The GOC was still answering to two masters: to the new secretary of state for Northern Ireland (SSNI) and to his own uniformed superiors and cabinet minister – albeit all within the same government. Thus, it still left room for confusion and for disconnects between political goals and military means.

This issue becomes apparent in chapter 7. The SSNI, William Whitelaw, was a strong personality, determined to exploit the opportunity accorded to London by direct rule to explore political solutions. At his insistence the army adopted a less aggressive, "low-profile" operational posture to provide some incentive for the nationalists to enter into a political dialogue. It worked to a limited degree, leading to a temporary IRA ceasefire and a meeting between the SSNI and IRA leaders in early July. But, as expected, the talks did not succeed, and the IRA resumed its terrorist campaign, culminating in a series of deadly bombings in Belfast on 21 July 1972 that killed nine people and injured 130. In the meantime, the low-profile approach caused dissatisfaction within the army and the MOD. Because the proactive anti-terrorism program of 1971 had been abandoned, the low-profile mandate left the army unclear about the aim of its operations. This approach left the no-go areas in the hands of the IRA, and the army found its sources of intelligence drying up. Moreover, the army, the MOD, and Defence Secretary Lord Carrington felt that Whitelaw was making decisions without consulting them and was relying too much on the new Northern Ireland Office for advice on security policy that it was not qualified to provide.

Had this issue been allowed to fester indefinitely it might have become a serious CMR dispute. However, the collapse of the talks with the IRA and resumption of its terrorist attacks changed the mood in London and provided the opportunity the army desired to reassert its leadership on security policy. In fact, the army was proactive in this regard; on the very day of the IRA/Whitelaw talks, Headquarters Northern Ireland (HQNI) had started drafting a plan to occupy the IRA-dominated no-go areas. Ten days later, after a series of violent clashes between the IRA and the army, the Cabinet Office inserted itself into the process, drawing upon plans developed in 1971 in anticipation of violent opposition to direct rule. The complicated, and at times acrimonious, planning and decision making that ensued meant that ten more days elapsed between Bloody Friday and the launching of Operation Motorman, which in its final form was a compromise plan. Neither the politicians nor the generals got everything they wanted into the operational plan. Moreover, cabinet micro-managed the plan to use tracked armoured vehicles, as it wished to minimize their potential political impact. Whitelaw also insisted on issuing a warning, which removed the surprise effect. Nevertheless, Motorman achieved its principal objective: terminating no-go areas and restoring the army's freedom of movement within them. Violence within the province dropped dramatically thereafter and never returned to previous levels. Consequently, the operation is regarded as a major turning point in the conflict.

The next phase of the conflict covered in this book begins in March 1973 and ends in May 1974. It was characterized by a continuing decline in IRA violence but, more importantly, by a militant Protestant insurrection that inflicted a significant political defeat on Prime Minister Wilson, who returned to power in February 1974. Early in this phase, the reduced levels of violence provided an opening that the Heath government decided to exploit to create a lasting political solution to the conflict: a power-sharing government for the province. An all-party agreement was negotiated successfully at Sunningdale, England by the end of 1973, but the Ulster Unionist Party soon withdrew its support. This left its former leader Brian Faulkner in charge of the power-sharing executive while fatally weakening it. At around the same time, a general election brought Wilson's Labour Party back to power, but as a minority government facing a solid block of Unionists opposed to the agreement. When the government tried to bring about full implementation of Sunningdale in May 1974, militant Protestants, operating under the guise of the Ulster Workers' Council (UWC), launched a general strike. Within two weeks it brought about the collapse of the executive, and a return to direct rule.

Chapter 8 critically examines the enduring myth surrounding the army's role during the strike: that it disobeyed the government's orders to break it. Had this been true, it would have been the most serious crisis in British CMR since the Curragh "mutiny" in 1914. The official records, however, show that the government never issued such an order. Indeed, they indicate that it was the cabinet, not the army, that was reluctant to take on the UWC. Once given direction to act, the army did so with enthusiasm, arresting Protestant paramilitary leaders and delivering fuel to gas stations across the province. But these efforts came too late to alter the outcome of the strike. The army's efforts to clear its name traced the origins of the myth to disgruntled members of the executive, who fed rumours of army reluctance to act to a news media eager for a good story. Retold in many sources, it became the conventional wisdom.

SOURCES ON THE CONFLICT
AND ON CIVIL-MILITARY RELATIONS

For the decision-making processes inside the British government and the military, most of the sources cited are from official records held at the National Archives at Kew. Of these the most useful and extensively cited are those of the Cabinet Office and the Ministry of Defence. Records from the Public Record Office of Northern Ireland, accessed through the Conflict Archive on the Internet, provide insights from inside the Northern Ireland government. Together these official documents allow us to look "behind the green door" at the secret deliberations between the soldiers, politicians, and civil servants as they wrestled with difficult, indeed seemingly intractable, problems and tried to find workable solutions to them.

But it is important for the reader to be aware of two limitations of these sources. First, they are incomplete; not all records are available. Second, official records are often carefully written or edited in ways that present a rendering of deliberations that appears more collegial and straightforward than might actually have been the case. It is easy to miss nuances in the record that indicate serious disagreements, so the appearance of consensus can be misleading. Thus, any conclusions reached on the basis of these records should be treated with caution.

Having access to several collections of private papers has allowed me to explore some of the contentious issues and debates in greater depth, and to fill in some gaps in the official record. But the private papers of the two prime ministers in office at the time – Harold Wilson and Edward Heath – are not yet open to scholars. As a result, their personal reflections on these events and discussions are absent from this study. Regrettably, I found most memoirs and biographies of the key figures to be generally unhelpful.[27] The Saville Inquiry *Report* into the Bloody Sunday massacre was much more useful: the witness testimony and documents submitted shed a great deal of light on the structures and processes of decision making up to 1972.

For context and narrative of key events, I have drawn upon some of the scholarly and other secondary sources that constitute the now extensive literature on the Troubles. Thomas Hennessey, *A History of Northern Ireland*, is a solid survey of the province's political history. Useful studies of the nationalist opposition to British rule include Niall O'Dochartaigh, *From Civil Rights to Armalites*, which discusses the central role the Catholic community played in leading that opposition in Londonderry, and the reasons for its shift from peaceful to armed resistance. Ed Moloney, *A Secret History of the IRA*, and M.L.R. Smith, *Fighting for Ireland*, provide insights into the internal politics and military strategy of the IRA. I have drawn on some secondary sources that discuss the UWC strike, but none are wholly satisfactory. Scholarly studies of the military campaign based on original sources are now becoming more common. Peter R. Neumann, *Britain's Long War*, and Andrew Sanders and Ian S. Wood, *Times of Troubles*, are the pioneering works in this regard. Hennessey's *The Evolution of the Troubles* focuses on the crucial 1970–72 period. Martin McCleery's *Operation Demetrius and Its Aftermath* provides a new perspective on the internment operation. Newspaper reporting and parliamentary debates give some sense of the public perceptions of and reactions to those events, which the political decision makers had to take into consideration as they pondered their options.

What follows is not a comprehensive history of the Northern Ireland conflict to 1974. Moreover, the information from these sources do not yield stunning revelations of earth-shaking magnitude, requiring us to fundamentally rewrite the history of the conflict in the province. That said, I believe they leave us better informed about the complexity of the problems the politicians and soldiers faced, and about how and why they made the policies and decisions and took the actions they did. As the case studies will show, there were no ideal solutions, and the civil-military command and control decision-making process was inherently untidy.

This brings us, finally, to the literature on the study of CMR employed in this study. As already noted above, the only full-length study of British CMR – *The Politics of the British Army* – is the work of historian Hew Strachan. Unsurprisingly, it is largely atheoretical and thus does not fit within the canon of CMR literature, which is America-centric and rooted in the social sciences. I cite Strachan's work in chapter 1 and the conclusion, but for theoretical insights this study relies on the selected range of CMR writings cited below.

Primus inter pares is Samuel Huntington's work noted earlier: *The Soldier and the State*. Huntington wrote his book to address only the American civil-military relationship. He was concerned primarily about the rise of military influence in American policymaking during the Second World War and the first decade of the Cold War.[28] Nevertheless, his book has since come to be considered foundational in the CMR studies field, the touchstone to which all subsequent work in the field refers and defers, in particular those works that examine American CMR.[29] Huntington did not ignore the British experience, but he did not examine it closely, did not have access to original sources, and did not grasp the duality of the army's role.[30]

If that is the case, how might his work be relevant to this study? Central to Huntington's view of the military as a profession is his concept of "objective civilian control." By this he means that the government maximizes the professionalism of the military – its competence in the use of force – and makes it a tool of the state. Ideally, the professional military is apolitical and politically inactive: in his view, as a military becomes more professional it is less likely to intervene in politics. The antithesis of objective civilian control is its "subjective" polar opposite: a "civilianized" military that mirrors the state and is deeply embedded in politics as an actor in its own right or in cooperation with other political players.[31] The relevance of these two concepts to the British experience will be examined in the conclusion.

The early counterpoint to Huntington's thesis is the model advanced by sociologist Morris Janowitz, in his major work *The Professional Soldier*. Confronting the same challenges that animated Huntington – how American politicians should manage the rise of the military as a powerful institution and what its role in the Cold War should be – Janowitz argued that, as militaries became more professional, they would be more inclined to intervene in politics. Indeed, he felt that, given the changes in the military profession and the stakes involved in making national security policy in the Cold War, a more political role for the military was unavoidable.[32] This line of argument is relevant because it is in this "Janowitz school" that Strachan found the theoretical foundation on which to construct a challenge to the Huntington thesis.[33]

Strachan regards Janowitz's focus on the social composition of the British Army as a distraction. But in all other respects the two are on the same page. The army was (and is) both professional and politically activist. Its activism was not due to some malevolent intent but out of necessity. As CMR scholar Amos Perlmutter asserts, the army's activism arises both to protect its professional autonomy, and be-cause "it is a key partner of civilian politicians and bureaucrats in the formation and implementation of national security policy."[34] The civilian leaders *need* the army to be politically active because it has knowledge and expertise they require. Therefore, "senior generals are inherently predisposed to behaviour that can be construed as politi-cal precisely because their jobs employ them at the confluence of mil-itary and political power."[35]

This behaviour is consistent with what Peter Feaver calls the "agency theory" of CMR. He describes a battle of wills and wits between the principal (the civilian leadership) and the agent (the military) in which the former tries to ensure that its policies are enacted, while the latter either obeys or – if it disagrees with those policies – finds ways to delay or derail them and to assert its own agenda. Like Huntington, Feaver was writing with the United States in mind, and his "bipolar" model of civil-military power struggles sounds simplistic. But Strachan's work suggests that it might have broader relevance.[36]

Rebecca Schiff takes a different theoretical approach, but one that also may be relevant to the British experience. She argues that, where the work of Huntington and Janowitz emphasized the separation of the civilian and military spheres, with the former trying to assert con-trol over the latter, her "concordance" theory "highlights dialogue, accommodation, and shared values or objectives among the military, the political elites, and society."[37] She focuses on the cultural and insti-tutional conditions that prevent or promote military intervention in the domestic political sphere. Her main argument is that "if the mili-tary, the political elites, and the society achieve concordance on four indicators, then domestic intervention is less probable."[38] These indi-cators are: the social composition of the officer corps; the political decision-making process; methods of recruitment (conscription ver-sus voluntary enlistment); and military style (what the military "looks like," its professional ethos, and public attitudes towards it).[39] Con-cordance on these points occurs "in the context of active agreement, whether established by legislation, decree, or constitution, or based on longstanding historical and cultural values."[40] It may result in "a range of civil-military patterns, including separation, the removal of civil-military boundaries, and other variations."[41]

On the face of it, Schiff's theory has much to commend it in regard to examining British CMR in the context of this study. As will be shown in chapter 1 and discussed in the conclusion, Strachan's evidence leads him to conclude that – even if he doesn't use the term itself – there has been a concordance between the British Army, its political masters, and British society. The development of integrated control of the military, represented principally by the MOD and discussed in detail in chapter 1, "has emphasized the collaborative nature of the [defence] enterprise."[42] Civilians in the MOD increasingly identify with the services, in effect blurring the civil-military boundaries. During the Northern Ireland conflict the army was both a component of the machinery *and* an active participant in the processes that decided how to use it. These findings are consistent with Schiff's focus on the decision-making process and military style. Furthermore, Strachan's fundamental point – that the army's political role has been held in check by the political and social context in which it operates – is completely in line with Schiff's argument.[43] Thus, it is worth returning to Schiff's theoretical argument in the conclusion.

Of course, theories and generalizations about army behaviour do not tell the whole story. Indeed, a question we ponder in the conclusion is this: does CMR theory tell us anything about the British Army, British CMR, and the Northern Ireland conflict that history does not? And, if it does not, would this call into question the value of CMR theory itself?

This book will show that the civil-military relationship was more complex and nuanced than any one theory would suggest. It was dynamic and interactive. It played out through the machinery of government – the institutions, structures, and procedures that determine how governments and their armed forces carry out the tasks for which they are responsible: making security policy and enacting it. So, if questions about how and why command and control decisions were made are important, then it is here that we must begin our quest for answers.

1

The Machinery of
Civil-Military Command and Control

Neither government nor the military operate in a vacuum. Each is part of a network of connected, interactive structures and processes that turn policies and decisions into actions. The machinery of government includes cabinets, committees, legislative bodies, departments and ministries, civil servants, military commanders and their staffs, and a range of procedures used to make and enact decisions. This chapter attempts to explain the machinery of military command and control as it stood during the Troubles.

POLITICS AND LAW AND ORDER
IN NORTHERN IRELAND TO AUGUST 1969

Following the insurgency in Ireland in 1916–21, the island was divided into the independent Irish Free State in the south and the British-ruled province of Ulster in the north. Although Britain retained ultimate authority over the province, Ulster had been allowed to run its own affairs with relatively little interest or input from London. This suited both, as all British governments tended to regard Ulster as a distasteful problem, and Stormont, the seat of the Ulster government, likewise preferred to keep interference from London to a minimum. Under the Government of Ireland Act, 1920, the Northern Ireland government was established as a separate entity with powers devolving from Westminster. It had its own prime minister and cabinet, an elected bicameral legislature, and a civil service administering the usual range of public services. Defence and foreign affairs remained in London's hands. The prime minister of Northern Ireland in fall 1968 was Terence O'Neill, a politically moderate unionist who pursued modernizing and (under pressure from London) social reform programs until forced out in April 1969 by his own Ulster Unionist Party because his reform program was seen as a threat to Protestant hegemony.[1]

London's hands-off approach, Stormont's constitutional autonomy, and an electoral system that was gerrymandered in appearance if not in fact had allowed the Protestant majority to control politics, the economy, and social programs and to marginalize the Catholic minority. The latter were assumed to be in favour of unification with the Irish republic and thus were viewed as a threat to the state. The Irish Republican Army mounted several campaigns from the 1930s through the early 1960s to force reunification. All of them failed, but they reinforced both inherent Protestant fears and prejudices as well as the tendency to rely on the draconian Civil Authorities (Special Powers) Act (SPA) and a paramilitary police force, the Royal Ulster Constabulary (RUC) to keep order and to suppress challenges to Protestant hegemony. The overwhelmingly Protestant character of the RUC and its tendency to use heavy-handed methods again Catholic civil rights protesters in the late 1960s meant that Catholics did not see the police as impartial agents of law enforcement.[2]

Indeed, it was Stormont's control over law and order that would pose the most vexing challenge for the British government from 1968 to 1972. The Government of Ireland Act, 1920, gave the Northern Ireland government the authority to make and enforce laws. Up to August 1969, the province's Ministry of Home Affairs was responsible for public security policy and for the RUC. The SPA gave the minister of home affairs (and the RUC under his orders) powers nearly equivalent to martial law. Until forced out in December 1968 due to his public opposition to O'Neill's policies, the minister of home affairs was William Craig, a staunch anti-Catholic. He and his successors, and on occasion the inspector general (IG) of the RUC, reported to Stormont's Cabinet Security Committee (CSC), which had decision-making power over public security matters. However, Westminster retained control over the armed forces and military affairs in respect of the province.[3] Therein lay the division of responsibility for security that bedeviled command and control during the first two and a half years of the Troubles.

BRITISH GOVERNANCE AND NORTHERN IRELAND
TO AUGUST 1969

The term *division of responsibility* does not do justice to what was in fact a more complex array of intersecting and overlapping institutional responsibilities for Northern Ireland's security within the British government. But, at least at the outset, this complexity meant in effect that no single person or institution was responsible. "There was," Michael Cunningham writes, "no machinery for detailed parliamentary or executive scrutiny of Northern Ireland affairs."[4] The Home Office (HO) had formal responsibility for Northern Ireland but devoted little time to the province's affairs. Ulster did not even rate its own department within the HO; instead it was "relegated to the general department."[5] Unlike Scotland and Wales, Northern Ireland had no secretary of state, nor was there a separate cabinet committee on it until 1969. James Callaghan recalled later that, upon his appointment as home secretary in 1967, his first dispatch box contained nothing about Northern Ireland. He was not surprised by this, as the province was rarely discussed in cabinet, and the Home Office treated it as simply a minor routine responsibility.[6] There was no Northern Ireland policy. Moreover, because the very things that were the sources of dispute in the province lay outside the jurisdiction of Westminster, members of Parliament (MPs) were unable to raise questions about them.[7] So, in every respect the province was a political orphan. Thus, as the Troubles emerged in the fall of 1968, a variety of institutions in London had to scramble to understand their roles and stake out their turf in handling the province's crisis.

At the pinnacle were Prime Minister Harold Wilson and his cabinet. The prime minister is the chief executive of government. He or she chairs the cabinet, is responsible for the civil service, and is involved (nominally or directly) in appointing senior officials. The PM is head of the government party in Parliament, is the face of government to the nation and the world, and is expected to embody the interests of the nation as a whole. There is a scholarly debate over the power of the prime minister. Some argue that prime ministers have gained more authority either by force of personality, political acumen, or longevity in office. Others point out that cabinet committees now make policy or (more often) manage crises. Prime ministers can set agendas, dominate discussions, or make deals with specific ministers to meet departmental demands, but ultimately they must carry the cabinet and the parliamentary party with them. Of necessity this requires a mixture of persuasion, negotiation, and consensus building.[8]

All of these features were apparent in the Wilson government's efforts to deal with the Northern Ireland crisis. Wilson was not known as a dynamic leader – in that respect he was not dramatically different from most of his postwar predecessors. However, he was hard working and subtly skilful at imposing his will, particularly within cabinet and its committees.[9]

Labour had been in power for four years when disorder began to mount in Ulster in the fall of 1968. Until that time the government, beset by a severe economic crisis and distracted by a wide range of foreign policy issues, had paid little attention to the province. As chapter 2 will show, that neglect began to change in the wake of the violent attacks on civil rights marchers in October 1968 and a similar incident in January 1969. In February 1969 Wilson decided to create a ministerial committee on Northern Ireland to prepare issues for discussion in cabinet. It consisted of himself as chair, James Callaghan, Defence Secretary Denis Healey, Foreign Secretary Michael Stewart, Chancellor of the Exchequer Roy Jenkins, Lord President of the Council Fred Peart, Lord Chancellor Gerald Gardiner, and Attorney General Sir Elwyn Jones. Designated MISC 238, the committee held its first meeting on 26 February 1969. In addition, at the suggestion of Cabinet Secretary Burke Trend, a parallel committee of departmental officials was established to provide administrative and policy support to the ministerial committee. It is worth noting that, prior to becoming PM, Wilson had no experience with the military, although other members of MISC 238, including Jenkins, Healey, and Stewart, did.[10]

In June 1970 the Conservative Party won the national general election and Edward Heath became prime minister. Heath appointed Reginald Maudling as home secretary and Lord Carrington as defence secretary. The cabinet committee on Northern Ireland, which was renamed GEN 47, comprised Heath, Maudling, and Carrington, along with Foreign Secretary Sir Alec Douglas-Home, Chancellor of the Exchequer Anthony Barber, and Lord President of the Council William Whitelaw.[11] The composition was altered slightly when Britain imposed direct rule in March 1972. At that time Whitelaw became secretary of state for Northern Ireland (SSNI), adding a new position to the committee, which was renumbered GEN 79.[12]

Heath was an Oxford graduate, a veteran, and an experienced politician with previous cabinet service. He had served as leader of the opposition in Parliament from 1965 to 1970. Maudling was also an Oxford graduate, had served in Royal Air Force intelligence during the Second World War, and had held a number of cabinet positions during his political career. Carrington was a Sandhurst graduate and a decorated veteran, and had considerable parliamentary experience. Whitelaw was a Cambridge graduate and a decorated veteran, but had less senior parliamentary experience than his colleagues until he became lord president of the council in 1970. The one thing they all had in common was military service, albeit at relatively junior levels.[13]

Following the February 1974 general election, Harold Wilson returned to office for a second term as prime minister, albeit as head of a minority government. His new defence secretary was Roy Mason, and Merlyn Rees succeeded Whitelaw as SSNI. Wilson's ministerial committee was smaller than Heath's, consisting only of himself, Rees, Mason, Home Secretary Roy Jenkins, and Attorney General Samuel Silkin. Jenkins and Rees had some military experience, but Mason had none.[14]

THE MACHINERY OF MILITARY COMMAND AND CONTROL

As discussed in the next chapter, it became apparent as early as fall 1968 that the military might be called upon to provide aid to the civil power (ACP) in Northern Ireland; that became the case in 1969, and as a result the military became the primary instrument of London's Northern Ireland policy. This put the Ministry of Defence (MOD), the defence secretary, and the military chain of command at the centre of the Ulster problem and the efforts to resolve it. Indeed, the interaction of these three components with the political leadership is the centrepiece of this study. Thus, it is essential to examine them in some detail.

First, however, it is necessary to provide some background on the institution for which they were responsible and which they would order into action in Northern Ireland: the British Army. On the eve of the Troubles, it was about 200,000 strong, organized into divisions, brigades, regiments, and battalions.[15] The largest single portion of the army was assigned to the British Army of the Rhine (BAOR), Britain's land force commitment to NATO for the defence of western Europe. This consisted of three divisions deployed in Germany. Most of the remaining army units were stationed in Britain as part the United Kingdom Land Forces (UKLF) garrison. The Army Strategic Command, which was created in 1968 and was intended to provide additional units to the BAOR in the event of war, comprised one division, the parachute brigade, and the special forces. A handful of army units were deployed overseas in the few outposts that had survived the Labour government's decision – driven primarily by a financial crisis – to remove all British forces "east of Suez" by 1970. The largest of these deployments were at Singapore and Hong Kong.[16] The Northern Ireland garrison (39 Brigade), consisting of a brigade headquarters, two infantry battalions, and an armoured car regiment, was considered a quiet, pleasant backwater.[17]

The year 1968 was an unusual one for the army in more than one sense. Following the withdrawal from South Arabia in late 1967, it was the only year in the twentieth century that the army had not been engaged in active operations and not a single soldier had been killed in action.[18] As an institution the army also was wrestling with downsizing and reorganization, occasioned by the triple impacts of the "end of empire," the end of national service, and budget cuts. Financial restraint and fewer commitments meant force reductions. Famous long-standing regiments were being struck from the order of battle or amalgamated with others. Both fates were the subject of much consternation within the units concerned and in the press and Parliament.[19] And all of this was taking place against the backdrop of the larger defence reorganization discussed in this chapter.

The army was a thoroughly professional force in every sense. Since the end of national service (conscription) in 1962 it had been an all-volunteer force, and thus it was composed of soldiers who had committed their careers and lives to military service. It was "professional" in all aspects of the term, as used by political scientist Samuel P. Huntington. The army displayed expertise, responsibility, and corporateness – that is, it had specialized knowledge and skills in the management and use of armed force; it was performing a service seen as essential to British society; and its members were (and saw themselves as) a group distinct from the rest of society by dint of that expertise, and of careful selection, extensive training, unique rules, discipline, uniforms, and more.[20]

That said, it defied the Huntington model in one crucial aspect: its "political" nature. As noted in the introduction, central to Huntington's view of the military as a profession, embodied in his concept of objective civilian control, is his proposition that a professional military is apolitical and politically inactive. In his view, as a military becomes more professional it is less likely to intervene in politics. However, as noted, historian Hew Strachan rejects this position, asserting that armies are "political institutions."[21] His book demonstrates that throughout its history the British Army has been both professional *and* politically active.[22]

It is perhaps a testament to the British Army's very acute political skills that it has been able to sustain the myth that it is apolitical.[23] Although it has not attempted a coup since the time of Cromwell, it challenged the Asquith government's Ulster policy in 1914 (the Curragh Incident) and was implicated in the fall of his government during the First World War.[24] More frequently, however, over the span of its modern history it has used more subtle methods – in particular, what S.E. Finer calls "influence" and "blackmail" – to achieve its goals. It can promote its views through the normal constitutional channels open to it, through lobbying, and through the news media. For example, in recent times the chief of the defence staff (CDS) normally has been awarded a peerage, and in the Lords the CDS may speak freely on defence matters, even in opposition to government policy. Senior officers also can intimidate civilians with threats of resignation or non-cooperation, though actual resignations are relatively rare.[25] The Curragh Incident was exceptional in this regard.[26] As the following chapters show, the army has a voice, and with that voice comes political influence. This point brings us back to the structures designed to exert political control over the army.

The MOD, which was intended to combine and coordinate the work of all three services, had been established in 1946. Starting in 1964 it had been substantially reorganized, a process that was still underway as the Troubles started. The reasons behind the reorganization lie outside the scope of this study, but the results are relevant.

First, to maintain the fundamental principle of civilian control of the military, a civilian secretary of state for defence (SSD) headed the MOD and was the sole representative for defence matters in cabinet. Thus a civilian, rather than the military, exercised "complete and undivided responsibility for the formulation of strategy."[27] The military's role here was to provide informed professional advice to the secretary and the cabinet to aid policymaking and decision making.

The reorganization of the MOD and the creation of the defence secretary post coincided almost exactly with the election of the Labour
government, and Denis Healey was the first to hold the post. He remained in it until June 1970, when the Conservatives replaced Labour
as the government. It can be argued with some confidence that he was
"the right man in the right place at the right time." In fact, in *The Politics of the British Army* Strachan asserts that Healey was the most successful defence secretary until the mid-1990s.[28]

Healey brought to the position not only considerable political experience and acumen but also a substantial background in military
affairs, starting with his own war service in North Africa and Italy.
Throughout his political career he had specialized in defence matters,
serving on the councils of the Royal Institute of International Affairs
and the International Institute of Strategic Studies. He was energetic, a
master of detail, and an effective manager of his staff. He was determined that the secretary rather than the CDS should control defence
policy, and under his stewardship power on defence matters shifted
from the military back to the politicians. The creation of a unified-ser-
vice MOD had been a bruising experience for the armed forces, as the
individual services saw their power to influence their budgets and preserve their independent roles greatly constrained. Healey recognized
and exploited the tendency of the service chiefs to put the interests of
their services first, allowing him to "divide and rule" them. He further
centralized ministerial control in 1967, when he abolished the posts of
the three service ministers of state, replacing them with two (responsible for equipment and for administration). The services' voice in Parliament was reduced to undersecretaries, who had little authority over
the services and whose duties were limited largely to answering questions in Parliament.[29] That said, Healey had gained the respect of the
senior military commanders, and he represented them vigorously and
competently on the cabinet's Defence and Overseas Policy Committee
(DOPC)[30] and latterly on the cabinet committee on Northern Ireland.

Second, the reorganization streamlined the military chain of command. Overall command was vested in a single CDS, who would issue
orders to all overseas commands and also serve as the single source of
professional advice to the civilian authorities. The service chiefs of
staff would proffer their advice to the defence secretary and to cabinet
through the CDS, although *in extremis* they still had access to the PM
and cabinet.[31]

Sir Frank Cooper, formerly deputy undersecretary at the MOD and later permanent undersecretary (PUS) at the Northern Ireland Office (NIO), claimed in a 1992 interview that "in the early days there wasn't any political system of control of the military."[32] In the narrowest sense he was correct; there was no *direct* political control, since as Cooper himself explained, "no politician can give the military an order. It can give them a *direction*."[33] Only the uniformed chain of command can issue orders to the military, so cabinet would give direction on policy or preferred action to the SSD, who in turn passed on cabinet's wishes to the MOD and to the military. They would then turn cabinet's request into plans, orders, and operations.[34] With regard to major operations in Northern Ireland, guidance or orders flowed from the CDS to the army chief of the general staff (CGS) and then to the general officer commanding (GOC) Northern Ireland. The GOC in turn granted authority for minor, routine operations to his formation and unit commanders.[35] In the summer of 1970, when a third brigade joined the two deployed in August 1969, headquarters, Northern Ireland (HQNI) added the position of commander land forces (CLF), who was to be responsible for army operations. This left the GOC free to deal with "politico-military issues at the Government level."[36]

This process was meant to be relatively straightforward, but in reality it was complex. Because Stormont was responsible for law and order in the province until March 1972, its requests for military ACP introduced a second pole of political authority to which the military had to respond. This required negotiation between the governments at Stormont and London, and up and down the military chain of command, as is discussed in detail in subsequent chapters.

Third, all high-level military planning was conducted within the joint civil-military bureaucracy at the MOD. Thus, any proposed policy or action went through many hands in the MOD before it emerged as a finished product. This often slowed the policy- and decision-making process to a crawl. But it also may have served as a check on potentially rash decisions.

On the military side the Chiefs of Staff Committee (COSC), comprising the CDS, his vice-chief, and the heads of the three services, was responsible for the full range of military duties from operations and planning to procurement and relations with allied forces. It was also the voice of the three services to the CDS and thus to the defence secretary and to the cabinet. Given the role of the CDS, Michael Howard regarded the COSC as something of an anachronism within the modernized MOD: a repository of vested service interests. But it retained a central, controlling position in the policymaking process, which was as much bottom-up as top-down. Franklyn Johnson called it one of the authoritative arenas (which included cabinet and the DOPC) "in which negotiation, compromise and delay find their place as policy is made."[37]

The senior positions in military leadership usually changed every two to three years. The position of CDS rotated among the services, and thus was held in succession during the period under study by Air Marshal Sir Charles Elworthy (until April 1971), Admiral Sir Peter Hill-Norton (to October 1973), and Field Marshal Sir Michael Carver (until October 1976). The army chiefs of the general staff were, in succession, Gen. Sir Geoffrey Baker (to April 1971), Sir Michael Carver (to July 1973), and Sir Peter Hunt. The third senior position in the military command triumvirate was the GOC Northern Ireland, the post held first by Lt. Gen. Sir Ian Freeland (to February 1971), followed by Lt. Gen. Sir Harry Tuzo (March 1971–February 1973), and Lt. Gen. Sir Frank King, who held the position until August 1975. All of the above were long-service professional military officers who had seen wartime and postwar command and staff service at home and abroad.[38] Thus, they had experience of working with civil servants and politicians, and this gave them two potential advantages when dealing with the latter. First, because some cabinet ministers had no military experience at all, the generals had a near monopoly on vital expertise the politicians required to make effective decisions on military affairs. Second, cabinet ministers came and went frequently, so these senior officers and their military and civilian staffs usually were more familiar than were their political masters with the process and procedures for making and implementing defence policy.

The CDS and the COSC were supported by several key offices and staff whose jobs were to turn policy and plans into action and operations. The CDS's central defence staff was responsible for overall current and future defence planning and operations. It included officers assigned to direct operations, policy, requirements, intelligence, personnel, and logistics, each area supported by its own small service and civilian staffs as well as the chiefs of staff secretariat. The Defence Operations Executive (DOE) provided the link between the cabinet and the MOD for handling current operations. At the direction of cabinet through the defence secretary, the CDS would issue operational orders through the DOE, and the service chiefs would in turn issue orders to the units under their command. Supported by the DOE, the defence operations centre coordinated service operations on a routine and emergency basis. The defence signals staff was responsible for all MOD communications, while the defence intelligence staff provided intelligence support for operational decision making. The defence secretariat fused ministry and service civilian administrative staffs to support the chiefs of staff and the PUS.[39] The reorganization of the MOD increased the influence of the civil servants in the policymaking and decision-making processes, in part because of their long tenure in their positions.[40] Their management style favoured constant "feedback, negotiation, and compromise, both vertically and laterally among departments."[41]

The most senior civil servant was the permanent undersecretary, responsible to the secretary of state for the overall day-to-day administration of the MOD. Sir James (Ned) Dunnett held the position from 1966 to 1974, having served previously in the ministry of labour. The PUS was co-located with the defence secretary, the CDS, and the service chiefs of staff, and sat with the CDS on the official committee that supported the DOPC. The PUS's department comprised two second PUSs (for Administration and Equipment) and eight deputy undersecretaries (DUS), five in "functional" roles and three representing the services. In Howard's view the PUS bore the major burden of policy decision making on behalf of the defence secretary with the help of the DUS (Policy and Programmes). The latter worked with the assistant CDS (Policy) and represented the permanent undersecretary on the COSC.[42]

Each of the DUSs supervised a number of assistant undersecretaries (AUS), and at that point in time much of the administration and policy work fell to those assigned to the specific services. Howard writes that it was at this level that the civil service and the military interacted most directly and where friction between the two was most likely to occur. The job of the AUSs was to see that such friction did not occur. It was perhaps for this reason that the service AUSs did not report to their DUSs but rather to the DUS (Policy and Programmes). Sir Frank Cooper held that post from 1968 to 1970.[43]

Sir Arthur Hockaday served as AUS (General Staff) for the army from 1969 to 1972. His testimony to the Bloody Sunday Inquiry shed light on the intricate relationships that governed the use of the armed forces. As AUS (GS) he was part of the CGS management team, which also included the vice-chief of the general staff (VCGS), the director of military operations (DMO), the director of army staff duties (DASD), and the brigadier general staff (intelligence), a three-star, two two-stars, and a one-star, respectively. As the senior civil servant at the pinnacle of the army's command structure, Hockaday was granted the equivalent of two-star rank. Until he moved to the Cabinet Office in 1972, he was at the centre of military decision making, and he appears frequently in the document record. His successor was Derek Stephen.[44]

Initially Hockaday had two Defence Secretariats working under his direction: DS6 and DS7, responsible respectively for the "politics-military aspects of Army Operations (including at first Northern Ireland)" and for the structure and deployment of the army. Late in 1971 the MOD established a new DS (10) to deal exclusively with Northern Ireland. Over time, and especially after the introduction of internment in August 1971, Hockaday devoted more of his time to Northern Ireland matters, "leaving DS6 and DS7 to some extent to run themselves."[45]

The role of AUS (GS) in his view "was all about the military and the civil service working closely together and, where appropriate, providing joint submissions to the Secretary of State for Defence for relevant decisions to be made."[46]

Hockaday's equivalent on the army side was the DMO, Maj. Gen. Ronald Coaker, who held that position from 1970 through 1972. But, Hockaday says, Col. Harry Dalzell-Payne, the head of MO 4 – the general staff branch responsible for Northern Ireland – did most of the day-to-day work on the army in the province, and it was Dalzell-Payne with whom he worked closely.[47] However, MO 4 did not exist in 1968–69, so its role will be discussed later.

The intelligence community also provided input on the policymaking and decision-making process on the growing crisis in Ulster. According to Christopher Andrew's authorized history of MI5 (the security service), in November 1968 Home Secretary Callaghan asked the head of the service (Martin Furnival Jones) for a threat assessment on the prospects for IRA violence in the province. This request put the service in an awkward position, as (like the rest of the government) it had devoted few resources and had paid little attention to Irish issues, and thus had no sources of its own; it normally relied on the RUC. Nevertheless, a month later MI5 provided Callaghan with a prescient assessment. It set the IRA threat against the wider backdrop of unionist/nationalist mistrust that was leading to violence in the province, and

it was deeply doubtful about the prospect of resolving the root causes of violence. Alerted by the dire assessments from MI5 and prompted by the cabinet secretary (Burke Trend), the Joint Intelligence
Committee (JIC) – the senior intelligence assessment body
in the government – established an Ulster Working Group in April
1969.[48] Its job was to maintain a watching brief on the province on
behalf of cabinet.

The silent partner in all of this was Parliament. According to Malcolm McIntosh, in British constitutional theory "Parliament is sover-
eign"; the power vested in it is absolute, and "no other body has power
over it." Its role is "to oversee the work of government."[49] The prime
minister and cabinet (and through them the armed forces) are
accountable for their decisions and actions to Parliament. But in practice it wields little power or influence over their decisions or actions,
because "there is no device in the British constitution which demands
that all Prime Ministerial or cabinet decisions shall be ratified by Parliament."[50] In a majority government, power resides almost unchallenged in the cabinet, or in the hands of the PM and certain cabinet
committees.[51] Parliament can ask questions, and has the power to
approve or defeat the budget (including that for defence), but defeat
of a majority government is unlikely.

In 1969, apart from the Public Accounts Committee (PAC), Parliament had no committee that scrutinized defence or military affairs
generally. The PAC was effective at examining defence *spending* on specific programs but had no mandate to look at policy or operations.
And it heard testimony only from senior civil servants, not from the
minister.[52] Nor did Parliament have a committee to examine Northern Ireland affairs. Ulster did have a voice there: a small contingent of
Unionist MPs, who could be expected to defend staunchly the Protestant hegemony and the right of Stormont to exercise its powers without interference from London. But they would find no allies in the
Labour government. So long as Wilson kept his cabinet and backbenchers on side, he was free to exercise policymaking and decision-
making authority almost unchallenged by Parliament. That said, he
made a point of keeping it informed.

Three points emerge from this maze of interlocking, interactive
structures and processes. First, the development of policy and the
making of decisions were not instantaneous. In his 1980 book *Defence
by Ministry*, Franklyn Johnson took the view that the more centralized

executive decision-making process that emerged from the reorganization of the MOD could "be expected to produce better, or at least faster
results."[53] As subsequent chapters will show, the document record
on civil-military decision making over Northern Ireland calls this
assumption into question. Crucial decisions entailed extended deliberations within cabinet and its committees, throughout the military
chain of command, and among civil servants in several departments.
These concerns, taken together with the prime minister's need to
build consensus within cabinet, the inter-service "bargaining" processes within the COSC, and the need to consult political leaders in the
North, make the often glacial pace of policymaking and decision making easy to comprehend.

Second, the government had less freedom of action to develop new
policies for Northern Ireland or for defence than the cabinet's power
might suggest. On Ulster, its hands were tied by Stormont's autonomy. Unless the British government was willing to assume full responsibility for running the province by imposing direct rule – a choice
both the Labour government and its Conservative successor sought to
avoid or postpone –it had few means to exert influence on Stormont's
decisions and actions. Over time the one political lever London gained was not of its own making: disunity within the unionist government. Yet, as will become apparent later, even here the tail could wag
the dog.

On defence matters, as Michael Howard points out, Labour (like all
governments) found that its ability to develop new policies and programs was hindered by an array of factors: pre-existing policies, bud-
getary constraints, and commitments that could not be abandoned
easily. Experienced civil servants working in collaboration with a
(sometimes) unified front of senior military officers could impose
constraints on the government's freedom to act in line with its preferred policies. Conservative by nature and tradition, the civil service
was disinclined to make drastic changes in policy or practice.[54] According to one civil servant, policy advice or policymaking meant
"coordinating current policy," not developing new policies.[55]

Consequently, policymaking and decision making was not the logical top-down process (from cabinet to the military) that the foregoing
structure might suggest. Rather, policies and decisions often were
shaped or reshaped from the bottom up through the deliberative, con-
sensus-building, bargaining processes within and between the MOD

and the cabinet committees just described. Former Labour cabinet minister Richard Crossman later remarked, "I was right to recognise the importance of cabinet committees." But he also stressed the influence of the parallel "official" committees of civil servants: "This often means that very often the whole job is pre-cooked in the official committee." He believed this approach was how Whitehall rendered the cabinet system "relatively harmless."[56]

Finally, it is important to recognize that all of this work was and is conducted in secret. In his critical study of British defence policy-making, Malcolm McIntosh addressed this issue at some length. He noted that "secrecy has a special place in defence decision-making."[57] There are sound operational reasons for military secrecy, but McIntosh regarded it almost as a Whitehall fetish that exceeds necessity: "The secrecy that surrounds cabinet decision-making pervades the culture of Whitehall."[58] He went on to add that secrecy creates insiders and outsiders; only insiders can be experts, "and only they can make decisions."[59] Even the decision-making process itself is kept secret. The result, he feared, is a closed loop that limits the number of participants in the decision-making process to a select few within the "permanent government" (that is, Whitehall) who share common values, goals, and ideas. Those with influence include military and civilians in the MOD. There is little input from outside this charmed circle. These practices tend to limit options to current policy and to exclude the consideration of alternative policies or decisions.[60]

All of the foregoing suggests that the reality of civil-military command and control of the armed forces in Britain at that time defied a wholly rational model or any single theory. While there was in theory a clear line of authority from the prime minister and cabinet to the military chain of command, in practice the decision-making processes were not linear. Rather they were interactive and dynamic, involving constant, often prolonged, negotiation, compromise, and consensus building. This was a reflection not so much of tension between the civilian political authorities and the military but of the nature and structure of British command and control of its armed forces. Even if civilian control was paramount, there was more than one locus of control: the prime minister himself, the cabinet committees, the defence secretary, the senior civil servants in the MOD, and the COSC. All of these were influential in making policy and in making decisions. But they also highlight the role of individuals, not just systems and structures.

So, the processes cannot be explained and understood solely as the result of a wiring diagram. Personalities mattered, and some were more influential than others, Healey being a case in point. But as the following chapters will show, once the army became enmeshed in the Northern Ireland conflict, command and control issues entailed complex, protracted intra- and interdepartmental (and, until 1972, intergovernmental) negotiations and difficult decisions that would put civil-military relations to the test.

2

Planning for Aid to the Civil Power, 1968–1969

In the standard narrative of the Troubles in Northern Ireland, British troops commenced security operations on 14 August 1969, when they deployed on the streets of Londonderry.[1] However, it was actually in late April 1969 that troops were first deployed on internal security duties in the province, protecting vital infrastructure from sabotage.[2] Moreover, discussions concerning the possible use of troops to maintain order in the province had begun five months before that. Politically difficult civil-military command and control issues lay at the heart of that process. This chapter will show that the British military's obligation to provide aid to the civil power (ACP) in Northern Ireland forced the British government, which hitherto had taken a laissez-faire approach to the governance of the province, to confront undesirable and difficult legal and political issues. Indeed, what emerges from the documentary record is a prolonged, complex, at times even agonizing policy- and decision-making process that focused as much on how to avoid committing forces to the province as it did on the implications of using them.

AUTUMN 1968: THE TROUBLES BEGIN

British involvement was prompted by the deteriorating political situation in Ulster during the autumn of 1968. By the 1960s the Catholic minority was not only fed up with discrimination and political marginalization but was mobilizing to take action to end it.[3] Inspired by the example of the American civil rights movement, the Northern Ireland Civil Rights Association (NICRA) had been formed in 1967, and

the following year it began to mount protest marches to demand political and social reform.[4] As demands for and protests in support of
reform increased, so too did state-directed violence aimed at preventing them. This contest came to a head on 5 October 1968 in an ugly,
public fashion that London could not ignore. When NICRA protesters
disobeyed a ban on their march in Londonderry, they were attacked by
the Royal Ulster Constabulary.[5] The force "punched, batoned and pursued civil rights demonstrators in a brutal and sickening display ... of
concerted violence."[6] It then attacked uninvolved bystanders, who
responded by throwing stones at the police. Several days of rioting followed. In *From Civil Rights to Armalites* Niall O'Dochartaigh says the
organizers of the march had intended to force a confrontation, but
they were totally unprepared for the RUC's disproportionate response.
In fact, the interactions were more complex than this.[7]

As bad as it was, the event might have passed almost unnoticed
in London but for two factors. First, as Thomas Hennessey and Ed
Moloney point out, the events on the day were televised, and the
images shown on British television had a dramatic impact locally and
in Britain as a whole.[8] Second, in his article on the event, Simon
Prince asserts that it "disrupted the internal balance of power" in the
province, and as a result "many state and non-state actors turned to
violent strategies."[9] One of those bloodied by the police was local
Labour MP Gerry Fitt, who was understandably outraged by their
behaviour. He told reporters, "I will ask for an inquiry into the whole
political set-up here. A policeman hit me on the head, and as I was
falling he hit me again. I saw boys, aged 17 to 19, being brutally
assaulted. I want the strongest possible action against those responsible ... You cannot sweep this under the table any longer. The people
who are second-class citizens because of their Roman Catholic reli-
gion have had enough."[10] Fitt was not alone in his outrage. Other
Labour MPs who witnessed the clashes sent a report to Home Secretary Callaghan and then had a meeting with him.[11] The Londonderry branch of the Labour Party sent to Prime Minister Wilson a
telegram that read in part, "The calculated brutality of that body [the
RUC] shocked and horrified all those who saw it. We assert that they
set out deliberately to beat the people of Derry – *the working class people* – into submission."[12]

The attack on Fitt, and the telegram's direct reference to the working class, meant that the growing crisis touched Britain's governing

party directly. Questions were raised immediately in the House of Lords and later in the Commons.[13] The Manchester *Guardian*, a newspaper normally sympathetic to Labour Party policies, was openly critical of Wilson's laissez-faire approach to Northern Ireland's problems, which, it felt, allowed the province's government to ignore his posturing.[14] As if to confirm that view, Northern Ireland prime minister Terence O'Neill and William Craig, the Stormont minister of home affairs, responsible for the RUC, insisted that the police had acted with restraint, and therefore no inquiry was needed.[15] As a result, the government in London could not ignore the emerging crisis. Two days after the violence, Wilson invited O'Neill to London for talks.[16] However, a month would pass before the two men met.

O'Neill, accompanied by Craig, met with Wilson on 4 November. While conceding that dealing with the disturbances and the circumstances that gave rise to them was Stormont's responsibility, and that he would prefer to find ways to resolve these problems informally, Wilson said there was growing sentiment in the House of Commons in favour of intervention by Westminster. While this may have exaggerated the tone of sentiment in the House, he added that if events delayed progress towards liberalization, the position of his own government on the issue might become untenable and a more radical solution sought. When the discussion turned to the events of 5 October and the question of an impartial inquiry into them, Craig rejected the idea and offered a vigorous defence of the police. Wilson summed up by re-emphasizing that all of these issues lay within the competence of the Northern Ireland government, but they could not be shrugged off by Westminster, which ultimately had supreme authority. According to Wilson's memoir, he also hinted that continued financial support for the province – at a time of fiscal restraint in public expenditure – depended on the good will of the parliamentary majority. The implications could hardly have been lost on O'Neill. In the House the next day, Wilson repeated his warning about the consequences of either failure to reform or the overthrow of O'Neill by more extreme elements in his party.[17]

If the events of 5 October accomplished anything, they had made it clear to Wilson and his cabinet that the traditional arm's-length approach to administering Northern Ireland was no longer viable. Christopher Farrington argues that, through a cycle of mobilization by nationalists, ineffective state responses, and counter-mobilization by Protestants, the province was sliding into conflict.[18] The RUC itself told Stormont that, without political efforts to defuse the emerging crisis, "the law and order situation could get completely out of control."[19] So, Britain could not simply wash its hands of the matter. Constitutionally, it was responsible for Northern Ireland. The question now confronting the Wilson government was: what did that imply?

AID TO THE CIVIL POWER: CONCEPT AND PRACTICE

Britain's authority over the province included a responsibility to provide troops (if requested) to be used in aid to the civil power, a practice dating back several centuries and burdened with controversy. Under the common law, "it is the duty of the military, at the request of the civil power, to take whatever steps the military deem necessary to maintain order."[20] Conceived in an era when there were no organized police forces, ACP allowed local governments to call upon the army (regular or militia) to suppress political violence. Troops usually were used to keep clashing groups apart, thereby to restore "the King's Peace." As early as the eighteenth century, ACP practice had established a number of basic operational principles: that the troops must act in a non-partisan manner, not taking sides among the disputants; that they should use only the minimum amount of force needed to restore order; that they would always operate as formed units under the orders and command of their officers; and that ultimate authority to decide to deploy and to recall them lay with the civil authorities.[21]

The last two principles are of greatest importance to this study, as they lie at the heart of command and control and civil-military relations in internal security operations. They establish the central dilemma and tension of ACP: who decides what to do at the crucial moments on the ground, and who is responsible for those decisions and their consequences? These questions inform the purpose of this study – to determine the extent to which the civil authorities controlled or influenced the conduct of operations, and how much latitude the army had to conduct operations according to its professional judgment. This final point was very significant, as what constituted "minimum force" was not specified in military law or doctrine; it was left to the judgment of the military commander on the spot.[22] This could place officers in a difficult moral and legal position, facing possible prosecution if they used either too much or too little force.[23] As such, it was not a task that armies relished. Nor was it popular with civilians.

Once civilian police forces came into being in Britain, ACP began to recede as a common practice in the domestic sphere. Britain continued to employ it to suppress disorder in its colonies, although after the Amritsar Massacre (1919) the practice was constrained somewhat even there.[24] But it was retained as a course of last resort in Britain and the dominions. In Canada, for example, the Quebec government requested troops in ACP from the federal government to provide additional security following two terrorist kidnappings during the 1970 October Crisis and again to help contain and defuse a First Nations insurrection during the 1990 Oka Crisis.[25]

KEY QUESTIONS:
OBLIGATION AND CONSULTATION

The ACP issue was raised in regard to Northern Ireland on 14 November 1968 by Eddie McAteer, leader of the Nationalist Party in Northern Ireland. His query had been prompted by a news report on 23 October that the commander of HMS *Sea Eagle* (the Royal Navy base in Northern Ireland) had said that his personnel would be "pleased to assist in any way with the maintenance of law and order in Northern Ireland."[26] This comment may have referred only to providing temporary accommodation to RUC members deployed from elsewhere in the province. However, it was sufficiently ambiguous if not provocative enough to cause Wilson to ask that "full consideration" be given to the question of whether British military forces could be used to assist in dealing with civil disorder in Northern Ireland. He felt that the MOD must be given some guidance on the matter: "we must know where we stand. I am not so much concerned about what Stormont might ask, as what our reply would be. The Ministry of Defence must know the answer ... The Home Office cannot leave the situation in this degree of uncertainty."[27]

In response the Home Office convened a meeting to discuss this question on 20 November. K.T. Nash, AUS (Policy), and Air Commodore Alasdair Steedman attended for the MOD. They pointed out that service instructions and regulations regarding ACP were no different in Northern Ireland than in the rest of UK. They explained the common law obligation and the minimum force principle. Therefore, they said, if the military in Northern Ireland received a request for assistance from "a responsible level" (which they took to mean a police officer in charge or a senior government official), it was required to provide such assistance. The Home Office lawyer agreed. But there was one "grey area" that plagued officials for some time after this. Service regulations required that military commanders who receive such a request first inform the local commander-in-chief (CINC) and the MOD. But if immediate action was absolutely essential, the regulations said that the commander concerned could initiate action and then notify the CINC and the MOD.[28] The meeting did not address either what "informing" consisted of or what the implications were of acting before informing. At the end of the meeting the HO proposed that it would draft a "Note by Officials," consult MOD about the content, and submit it to the home secretary.[29]

In the meantime, the GOC Northern Ireland, Lt. Gen. Sir Ian Harris, submitted a report on the security situation in the province. That report led the vice-chief of the general staff (VCGS – Lt. Gen. Sir Victor FitzGeorge Balfour) to send a message saying that if, as GOC, he got a request for ACP, Harris's response should be governed by the pamphlet *Instructions on Internal Security in the United Kingdom in Peace* (issued 29 March 1968).[30] This was the standard guidance document for providing ACP in the UK.

The MOD received the HO draft note by 5 December, and Nash spent some time editing it for accuracy and to remove what he regarded as "unsuitable" phrases, such as "armed force" and "suppressing a riot," which would give a "misleading mailed fist impression" of the role of the military.[31] Such changes, of course, raise several questions: what did Nash think the army's role would be if it did not include suppressing a riot? Why would they be deployed if armed force was not needed? In an aside to J.F. Mayne (assistant private secretary to the defence secretary), Nash noted with some prescience that the HO's role in this problem with respect to Northern Ireland might be less than it thought. But, he said, "I don't think this is the moment to say so."[32]

The problem lay in the thorny issue of authority. First, the HO had authority for law and order in Great Britain, but not in Northern Ireland. Second, the HO could not direct a local authority in the UK *not* to request military help, and the MOD could not refuse a legitimate request. If the military became involved in ACP in the province, the two secretaries of state could advise the prime minister as to whether the military ought to be told to stop such involvement. However, Nash wrote, everyone involved knew they would be breaking the law if they did issue such an order. He said he would raise this point with the Home Office if the defence secretary wished, but he could foresee that it would lead to a long discussion. He predicted that the Home Office might be quite unwilling to weave this topic into the existing note because it might reveal how "unofficial" its interest in the Northern Ireland situation really was.[33]

In his reply, Mayne expressed concern that there were no regular channels for consultation between the Northern Ireland government and the MOD, and that the military might be asked for assistance before the defence secretary was consulted. He felt sure that Healey wanted assurance that this would not happen. Mayne added a handwritten note at bottom of the page saying that the CGS (Gen. Baker) had sent a signal to the GOC, "severely limiting his freedom to act on his own initiative." Baker's message said that the GOC was to refer to the MOD unless it was "humanly impossible" to do so.[34] Sent on 6 December, the message emphasized "the *great political sensitivity* of this subject," and hence the importance of referring to the MOD if humanly possible "before *repeat before*" acceding to any request for use of troops in ACP.[35] In this instance, the CGS had demonstrated his awareness of the difficult political position of the military and took a proactive approach to managing the problem.

Thus, it is clear that, months before troops appeared on the streets of Northern Ireland, the implications of using troops in ACP there was exercising the minds of senior officers, government officials, and the political leadership, including the prime minister. Mindful of the potential political fallout that could follow from any use of the military, the civil servants and politicians were determined first to grasp their legal obligations in this regard, and second, if possible, to limit the military's ability to act without their approval. But what emerged from these preliminary explorations was a political and legal minefield: if it received a legitimate request, the military's hands were tied – it had to respond. And it might have to do so whether or not the ministries and ministers had been consulted or even if they did not approve. Subsequent meetings and correspondence only served to confirm the worst fears of a government that abhorred the growing violence in the province and viewed the prospect of using the military there with grave apprehension. The lengths to which it would go to avoid a wholesale military commitment would become apparent in the months ahead.

Apparently dissatisfied with the advice received to that point, Secretary Healey decided that he wanted a "properly considered legal view" from Attorney General Elwyn Jones regarding the legal and constitutional position of the armed forces in Northern Ireland if they were called upon to provide ACP there. He wanted to know two things: first, were they automatically bound to give such aid in all circumstances? Second, what were the proper legal and constitutional forms of consultation between the Northern Ireland government and Westminster over the whole question of maintaining law and order and using troops to do so? In addition, he wanted the CDS (Air Marshal Elworthy) to tell him what provision could be made, consistent with political requirements and military effectiveness, to ensure that there was consultation between the GOC and the MOD before troops were committed, and what instructions the MOD had issued to govern how military resources would be used if Stormont asked for them.[36]

Three days later Elworthy sent a detailed memo to Healey. He confirmed what had already been established: the military's obligation to provide ACP, and to use only reasonable force, with the judgment as to what constituted such force left to the military commander on the scene. The request for ACP was to come from the civil power in writing (or be confirmed in writing as soon as possible), and the military authority who received the request was to refer the request to the MOD and to his superior commander, *except* if the situation – in the opinion of the commander on the scene – required immediate action. But, Elworthy noted, *there was nothing in law* to compel a military commander at *any* level to seek permission before answering a request for ACP. In fact he would be wrong to do so if the delay was likely to worsen the situation or prejudice the success of his action. The GOC had certain legal obligations that could not be inhibited or changed without changing the law.[37]

So, the CDS could not assure Healey that consultation would precede action. However, Elworthy felt confident that any disturbance serious enough to require troops was likely to be a matter of national concern, and that it was unlikely that an officer would be so cut off from higher command that he would have to act without guidance. Given the legal constraints governing ACP, Elworthy believed that no further action could be taken on the consultation issue. The GOC might have to act without it, since failing to do so would put him in violation of the law. And if the MOD instructed him to refuse a request, the legality of that instruction would be open to question.[38]

Elworthy explained that the army had a general instruction (noted above) outlining the circumstances in which troops might be called out. It stated that when a request was received from the appropriate authority as defined in the *Queen's Regulations*, in cases of immediate danger a commander was to take such action as he felt was needed and then inform the MOD. Otherwise he was to inform the MOD and command headquarters immediately. The instruction drew officers' attention to the common law, the *Manual of Military Law*, and the *Queen's Regulations*. The GOC has also issued instructions to his forces, noting that while a request normally would come to him from Stormont or the head of the RUC, it might come in exceptional circumstances from an RUC district inspector to a local commander. Except in an emergency it would be forwarded to the GOC. He noted as well that, because the RUC was an armed force, troops would be armed as well, since the situation that a commander faced was likely to require use of, or a threat to use, force. The CDS closed by noting that military commanders at all levels were well aware of the problems associated with ACP. They saw it as an unpopular and thankless duty that all would be reluctant to undertake unless it was "absolutely essential."[39]

Mayne followed up the CDS's memo to Healey with his own, suggesting that whether the military would provide ACP to Northern Ireland was not a legal but a political question.[40] In this respect he seems to have dismissed too easily the military's legal obligation. But his concern was focused on the position of the secretary of state, noting that he would be "especially vulnerable" if action were taken in ACP without his full approval. He challenged the CDS's view that the consultation issue was closed, on the grounds that, regardless of what the law said, it did not make political sense. To drive home the point he reminded Healey that the RUC was an armed police force. So, if the military were called in because the situation was or was about to become beyond the RUC's control, "the situation would be, to say the least, politically fraught."[41] He finished by suggesting that if the secretary concluded that prior consultation was a necessary condition of providing ACP, then he should meet with the CGS, CDS, and legal advisers to discuss ways to ensure consultation without violating the law.

The following day, Attorney General Jones weighed in. He had seen the CDS's memo and agreed with his statements of law, confirming the military's obligations. The fact that control of the armed forces was a reserved power of the UK Parliament and government, and that law and order was the responsibility of Stormont, did not affect the military's common law duties, which were no different in Northern Ireland than in the rest of the UK. However, he did acknowledge that it created political problems. Jones felt it was very important that a commander should consult higher authorities if there was time to do so, but also felt it would be a mistake to issue instructions forbidding commanders from taking action without direction from higher authority. In a case of extreme emergency it would place commanders in an impossible position. He felt that the CGS's instruction to the GOC to refer to the MOD "if humanly possible" before acceding to a request was appropriate. The attorney general was careful to draw distinctions between legal and constitutional theory and likely practice. The notion that the MOD would lose control of troops once they are used in ACP in Northern Ireland was, in his view, theoretically true, but the arrangements in place made this unlikely. Moreover, Stormont's responsibility for law and order made moot any question of *legal and constitutional necessity* for consultation, but he was certain it would happen.[42] The CDS agreed with Jones's note but felt there was need to further clarify the meaning of "consultation." Did it entail seeking advice, requesting instruction, or just the passing of information? In his view, if time was of the essence in a grave situation, then it could only be the latter.[43]

E.K. Stopford (DUS Policy) advised the defence secretary that the issue of political risk was a matter for the home secretary to consider, since it was not the MOD's responsibility to make political judgments for which it is not qualified.[44] Prior to sending the agreed version of the note to the prime minister, Mayne – apparently ever mindful of the need to protect his political masters – queried Healey as to whether he wished to accept the advice provided by his various officials or wished to indicate to the PM that such advice might fall short and whether, therefore, "he wishes to safeguard his political position, if necessary at the risk of giving instructions to the GOC Northern Ireland that run counter to the Common Law."[45] In a handwritten note at the end he wrote: "I think you will accept the CDS's ... *in principle*."[46] But Mayne's hint that the PM could protect himself by putting the GOC in a legal bind was not the last extraordinary idea advanced on this matter.

On 17 December Healey gave Wilson his reply to the questions the PM had raised on 19 November. The defence secretary deferred to the views of both the CDS and the attorney general regarding the legal obligations of the military and the issue of prior consultation. He also accepted Stopford's point that the issue of political risk should be left to the home secretary. Healey closed by suggesting that there was need for some new machinery of government that would facilitate urgent consultation to approve instructions to the GOC if Stormont requested troops in ACP, and if it was practicable for the GOC to refer the request to MOD. He suggested setting up a committee with representatives from the relevant departments.[47] The following day Cabinet Secretary Sir Burke Trend discussed the machinery issue with Sir Philip Allen (PUS at the Home Office). They agreed that if the MOD received a request from the GOC, it should contact Allen immediately and he would arrange as soon as possible the necessary consultation with the appropriate ministries.[48]

Two days later Home Secretary Callaghan told the PM that he agreed with the attorney general's position. He felt law and practice would have to cater to emergencies. Situations might range from having enough time to convene a prepared ministerial meeting to having to respond at an hour's notice on a Saturday night. Callaghan did not favour creating a formal committee. If time allowed, officials would meet; if not, cabinet ministers – or an individual minister – would have to rely on their appraisals as time permitted.[49] Wilson's response to this advice does not appear in the records I have seen. But the case studies will show that there was time for some consultation in almost every case.

CONTINGENCY PLANNING: INTERVENTION OR WITHDRAWAL?

Before the discussions over ACP could resume, the British government received another brutal reminder that this issue was not merely academic. Starting on 1 January 1969 People's Democracy (PD), a student group more radical than NICRA, carried out a march from Belfast to Londonderry in defiance of pleas from both nationalist and civil rights leaders. PD deliberately chose its route to pass through several Protestant areas: provoking a confrontation with militant Protestants would suit its political objectives. These included radicalizing the Catholic working class, and possibly bringing about the fall of Stormont as well as a British intervention. The group achieved only the confrontation. At Burntollet Bridge on 4 January the several hundred marchers were attacked by an organized group of some 200 militant Protestants, including off-duty members of the B-Specials (the Ulster Special Constabulary). The militants attacked the marchers with clubs and stones, yielding televised "images of peaceful marchers with bleeding skulls assaulted by Protestant bigots."[50] The previous day there had been a major clash in Londonderry, where a crowd of Catholics besieged a large group of militant Protestants in the Guildhall. O'Neill, obviously feeling pressure from within his party, condemned the PD march as a "foolhardy and irresponsible undertaking."[51] He condemned all those who took the law into their own hands, but also took care to praise the police for their "restraint."

That this happened should not have come as a surprise after the events of 5 October. As noted earlier, in December, MI5 – at Callaghan's request – had produced an assessment that warned the British government about the sources of and prospects for violence in the province.[52] Nevertheless, the Burntollet clashes and related rioting in Londonderry and Newry had a direct and sobering impact on the ACP discussions. During a parliamentary committee meeting in late January the home secretary mentioned "in an off-hand way" that it was not beyond the realm of possibility that O'Neill's government might be replaced by one headed by hard-liner Craig, who then might ask for military assistance to maintain law and order. Callaghan then mused that in such circumstances the British government might have to consider imposing direct rule. Defence Secretary Healey hastened to point out to Callaghan that this was not a matter that could be considered on an ad hoc basis at the time it arose. The home secretary agreed that contingency planning would have to begin immediately, and the HO advised the MOD that it would initiate discussion on this issue shortly.[53] In the meantime the PM tried to reassure Ulster MPs that Britain remained committed to the principle of non-interference in the constitutional responsibilities of the province.[54]

It was against this backdrop that representatives of the Home Office and the MOD began a series of exploratory meetings on contingency planning for ACP in Northern Ireland. Discussions followed two tracks: with and without direct rule. It was the prospect of direct rule that caused most concern. At that point it was contemplated only if a reactionary Stormont government emerged, leading to large-scale disturbances and a request for troops. Otherwise, military ACP might be required to deal with a single serious riot or a series of disorders that were beyond the local authorities' ability to control.[55]

By early February the parliamentary counsel had prepared the first draft of a bill to suspend Stormont temporarily and vest executive power in the governor of Northern Ireland. Following discussions with the HO the MOD had drawn up five scenarios that could lead to the use of troops. These ranged from minor disturbances that the RUC could handle with little or no military assistance to a "worst case" in which the British government decided to impose direct rule and was opposed by a Northern Ireland government that refused to quit office, thus creating a situation of open rebellion. Based on his discussions with the GOC, the CGS felt it was unlikely that any faction within Stormont would let the situation deteriorate to the point where Westminster would have to take over governance of the province. Healey sent the scenarios to Wilson, alerting him to the possibilities and noting that the MOD was giving priority to reinforcement planning anticipated in the third (mid-range) scenario: widespread riots. This decision proved to be fortunate, because it was this scenario that most closely anticipated the events that occurred in August 1969, in terms of both the nature and scale of the violence and the military measures required to contain it.[56]

In late February Wilson decided that a small ministerial committee on Northern Ireland should be established to prepare issues for any discussion in cabinet. In addition, Burke Trend suggested to Sir Philip Allen (the Home Office PUS) that they should consider creating a parallel committee of departmental officials.[57] The ministerial committee, designated MISC 238, first met on 26 February 1969. It noted that the RUC and the military were working together for the first time, though no details were given. The ministers focused mainly on how to keep the O'Neill government on the reformist path, but also considered options if the situation worsened, including direct rule or granting outright independence.[58]

In the months that followed, the British government sought to increase its understanding of the situation in the North. This was a logical and necessary step, but one that started from a position of weakness. Up to this point British intelligence had devoted little attention and few resources to Irish issues and thus had no sources of their own. For information on the security situation in the province it was totally dependent on the RUC, which it did not regard as reliable. To remedy this, the Joint Intelligence Committee (JIC) established in April 1969 a Working Group on Northern Ireland. Its primary customers would be the ministerial and official committees.[59] The group had barely come into being when events in the province forced Britain to act.

The most politically significant event was the resignation of O'Neill as Northern Ireland prime minister on 28 April, five days after winning support of his party for electoral reform to guarantee "one-man, one vote." He had been undermined first by opposition to reform in unionist ranks even within his government, which had resulted in a split majority in the February general election, and then by a series of sabotage bombings, which will be described below. The new Ulster PM was James Chichester-Clark, who vowed to continue O'Neill's reformist program. But he would be doing so from a weakened political position.[60] And even before the universal suffrage vote, Harold Black, secretary to the Northern Ireland cabinet, had been directed to ask the Home Office what the attitude of the British government would be towards the use of troops "for law and order enforcement" in the event of political violence in the province. The British government replied in early May, explaining the legal basis underlying the use of troops in aid of the civil power and stating that it could not give "any secret pledges of military assistance."[61]

Nevertheless, contingency plans had been made in the spring to reinforce the province if necessary, an eventuality that arose more quickly than had been anticipated. Protestant extremists associated with the Ulster Volunteer Force (UVF) bombed power and water utilities five times between 30 March and 26 April, crippling Belfast's water supply. In a deliberate effort to undermine O'Neill and his "liberal" agenda, his unionist political opponents attributed the attacks to the IRA.[62] The Northern Ireland cabinet asked the British government for military ACP to protect vital points from further sabotage. Wilson, Callaghan, and Healey met on 21 April and agreed to the request. Troops from the Northern Ireland garrison (39 Brigade) were deployed, but guarding many widely dispersed installations quickly used up most of its forces.[63]

So, when the UVF carried out more sabotage attacks after 21 April, Stormont sent a second request for troops. By this time the RUC and the garrison were fully stretched protecting sixty-five vital points, with few reserves left to patrol the border areas, which were seen as vulnerable. Border patrols had always been part of the garrison's role but, given political sensitivities, the GOC asked the MOD for permission to conduct such operations if requested. The DOE referred the matter to the defence secretary. Forwarding to the secretary the military case for agreeing to the request, the DOE suggested on 24 April that Healey propose to the PM that the relevant ministers meet as soon as possible. The ministerial committee agreed on 25 April to a temporary reinforcement of Northern Ireland by one additional battalion (the 1st Battalion, Prince of Wales' Own Regiment – 1st PWO), which began deploying that day. However, after meeting with the CGS, VCGS, VCDS, and other senior officials, Healey asked the GOC for evidence from the police of the nature of the threat to the border areas and to be prepared to provide an appreciation of the need for border patrols as soon as the Stormont made a request for them. In any case, intergovernmental consultation was to precede any further requests.[64]

In this instance there had been time for consultation at the highest levels of the British government, and it appears that all concerned followed the agreed procedures. But the rapid sequence of requests showed how quickly the situation in Northern Ireland could change and how easily it could consume large numbers of troops. Healey's closing request to the GOC suggests that he was wary of Stormont's motives and rightly suspicious of the evidence they used to justify their requests for troops. He was not prepared to simply "rubber stamp" their every demand. And in the weeks to come the Wilson government would search in vain for ways to avoid a deeper commitment.

In the meantime Wilson encountered some opposition in cabinet not only regarding the implications for London of committing troops to Ulster but also about his procedures for handling the crisis there. In his *Diaries of a Cabinet Minister* Richard Crossman claims he was frustrated by Wilson's reluctance to discuss the crisis in the full cabinet, leaving it in the hands of the ministerial committee. On 24 April Crossman demanded some discussion of the crisis in cabinet. When Wilson said London was legally bound to deploy troops to preserve law and order in Northern Ireland, Crossman asked him what "law and order" meant. "Does it mean whatever the Royal Ulster Constabulary ... define as law and order?"[65] Crossman felt Wilson prevaricated, leaving him infuriated, but later the PM mollified him by appointing him to the committee.[66]

In spite of such concerns, the commitment kept deepening in incremental steps. On 25 April the official committee learned that the RUC had told MI5 that its Special Branch was "overwhelmed," and had asked the security service to second an officer to it. At the suggestion of the ministerial committee, MI5 posted a security liaison officer (SLO) to RUC headquarters on 29 April. Under the same guidance the army also posted there a military intelligence liaison officer (MILO). The two men found the branch in a parlous state. The tiny HQ staff was headed by a new officer untrained in Special Branch work. Branch officers in the counties did not report to RUC HQ but to county police chiefs, who might or might not forward their reports. The branch lacked a system for collating reports, its sources on the IRA were suspect, and it was not watching Protestant extremists. At the urging of the CGS (Gen. Baker), who also found the intelligence system in the province inadequate and insisted that it be put right, Chichester-Clark met in mid-May with the SLO, who was blunt in his criticism of the intelligence situation and of the RUC in general. MI5 eventually established a small full-time desk to cover Irish affairs, and sent a small group to work with the RUC. However, as late as fall 1969 the Irish desk in London comprised only two relatively junior staff, who soon became buried by an information overload that – at the time – yielded very little useful intelligence.[67]

It wasn't just the Northern Ireland Special Branch that was falling short in the intelligence field. Crossman felt that cabinet lacked adequate political intelligence to deal with the situation. Callaghan, supported by Wilson, reportedly resisted the notion of collecting more political intelligence on the province, as he was "seeing Chichester-Clark every day." But Healey came to Crossman's defence, saying, "we shall [be] as blind men leading the blind if we have to go in there knowing nothing about the place."[68] The need for better intelligence was a recurring theme in policy discussions on the Troubles.

At the ministerial meeting on 29 April, Callaghan highlighted the dilemma facing the British government. Those present agreed that once the situation had become so grave that lives were in danger a request for troops could not be refused. But committing troops to put down disorder meant that the British government would assume responsibility for seeing that a reform program was carried out. And if the request for ACP was brought about by Stormont's use of the RUC's paramilitary B-Specials against civil rights demonstrators, such a situation could lead to legislative action, bringing Britain closer to direct rule. The British government's options were few; disengagement from the province was impractical, and granting independence to Ulster could not be contemplated for a number of serious political reasons. So long as Northern Ireland remained part of the UK, the British government could not escape the political consequences of having to guarantee law and order there.[69]

Nevertheless, the government persisted in seeking alternatives to what it feared could become an incremental, open-ended commitment to providing troops in ACP. According to his authorized biography, Wilson "cast around for any alternative, however far-fetched." That apparently included floating "a proposal to evacuate the Protestants from Northern Ireland."[70] What he expected Britain to do with a million displaced (and undoubtedly angry) Protestants was not explored. A cabinet meeting on 7 May yielded an equally dramatic suggestion: that Britain consider pulling all of its troops out of the province *before* they were committed to ACP. The basis for this proposal was the curious notion that the obligation to provide military ACP did not apply to the British government itself but only to any of its armed forces stationed in the province, in their capacity as citizens (who had special means at their disposal). Once those forces withdrew that obligation would lapse. But this notion was challenged in cabinet. The British government could not allow anarchy to prevail in Ulster, and the prime minister noted that Britain could not simply "wash its hands of Northern Ireland affairs."[71] In short, the British government accepted some responsibility for law and order in the province. Yet, cabinet asked the defence and home secretaries to consult and to produce a paper on the possibility and the implications of pursuing the withdrawal option. The paper, to be pulled together by a working group representing all the interested departments, was to cover the military, political, legal, and constitutional implications. In a memorandum to the secretary of the COSC, Arthur Hockaday of DS6 at the MOD predicted that the paper would show that the government could not carry out its responsibilities without either leaving troops in Ulster or being prepared to send them back after a withdrawal.[72]

Hockaday circulated on 16 May a draft cabinet paper on the implications of a complete withdrawal of all military forces from Northern Ireland. It said that while army line units could be moved out within a week, redeploying the remaining 10,000 service personnel, civilian employees, and dependants (who would require immediate temporary housing), along with stores, equipment, vehicles, and ammunition, could take about three months. The paper also noted that a withdrawal would have a significant negative impact on the Northern Ireland economy, which was already weak.[73]

But the crux of the problem was political. In the absence of extreme action by the Northern Ireland government, it would be difficult to justify a withdrawal. In fact, such a move might bring about the very actions it was intended to prevent, or it could lead to greater disorder. The Irish government might seize the opportunity to assert its claim over the province. In the event of serious violence or collapse of government, British troops might have to return to restore order. If so they would be redeploying in conditions that would be operationally and logistically less favourable, and the scale of intervention required might be considerably greater, than if troops had remained in place and were able to respond quickly.[74] Hockaday had highlighted the central contradiction implicit in the idea of withdrawing British forces from the province. Constitutionally, Ulster would remain part of the UK, and with that came Britain's obligation to provide troops in ACP.

Healey responded a few days later, noting that if withdrawal were intended to show that the British government would not allow its troops to be used as "agents of a regressive regime," it would be hard explain their withdrawal at a time when Stormont was pursuing more liberal policies. Furthermore, he noted that if the Northern Ireland government's policies did become more regressive, then a withdrawal of British forces would be seen as abandoning the Catholics, instead of using the presence of troops to deter violence and protect the minority. Britain would be roundly condemned for such an act.[75] A week later the HO lawyers advised that they could not be certain the ACP obligation would lapse if troops were withdrawn.[76] In short, all concerned had reached the same conclusion: because the British government was responsible for maintaining the integrity of Northern Ireland as part of the UK, its obligation to assist Stormont in maintaining law and order was inescapable, whether or not troops were actually based there.[77]

In any case, by this time the die already had been cast: the first troops had been deployed. The obligation had been accepted implicitly and acted on before the debate was over. For the next few months the government would try to limit its liability in Northern Ireland. That effort collapsed when public order in the province deteriorated dramatically in August 1969 and troops had to be used on a large scale to contain communal violence. From that point on, the British government and the army were forced to turn legal and political theory into practice in a chaotic and dynamic situation complicated by divided political authority over internal security.

3

Troops on the Streets, 1969

COMMAND AND CONTROL DEBATES, APRIL TO AUGUST 1969

Once the first troops had been deployed to protect vital points in the spring of 1969, the focus of concern shifted from questions of legal obligation to ensuring that the British government retained some control over how the troops would be used. For the reasons already noted this proved less straightforward than it wished. From August 1969 until March 1972 the army in Northern Ireland was subject to a bifurcated system of direction. Stormont was responsible for enforcing law and order, while London was responsible for the troops that allowed Stormont to do so. It was an unwieldy arrangement that caused frustration on all sides. So, even before the major deployments began, and continuing in their aftermath, British politicians became deeply engaged in managing security matters in the province and the army's role in them.

While London was anxious to avoid being drawn into the conflict, by April it confronted several unpalatable options. The "least unsatisfactory" of these, Defence Secretary Denis Healey told the cabinet committee on Northern Ireland on 21 April, was to continue to deal with the situation through Stormont. However, if troops were used against civil rights protestors he expected that there would be growing pressure on Westminster to exert control over the use of the troops. This, he felt, likely would lead to direct rule, the very thing London wished to avoid. However, if it refused a troop request under current arrangements, there was still nothing to prevent the province from calling in troops in aid to the civil power. In that case, the British government would not be able to make the provision of troops conditional on Stormont carrying out any reforms. Yet by acceding to Stormont's request, London would be implicated in all of its policies, even though it had no role in making them. Prime Minister Harold Wilson summed up the dilemma: "that both allowing the Northern Ireland Government to make use of troops as it saw fit and attempting to control their use would eventually force us to make a fundamental change in the constitution of Northern Ireland."[1] Nevertheless, the committee agreed to give the prime minister and the home and defence secretaries the collective authority to approve further use of troops even if full ministerial consultation was not possible.[2] The committee probably saw this as the only way to ensure some high-level political control by Westminster over the use of troops in and by the province if the situation changed rapidly.

Furthermore, at a meeting on 29 April the cabinet committee reversed its earlier position and directed the home secretary to advise Ulster PM James Chichester-Clark that London's willingness to provide troops was, in fact, conditional. Troops could not be used to support repressive policies; if they were, the British government would "have to consider the constitutional implications."[3] But since a troop request could not be refused even if the troops might be misused, this conditional willingness was more binding on London than on Stormont. The price of London exerting more control over the use of troops inevitably would be its greater involvement in the political direction of Northern Ireland. As Home Secretary James Callaghan put it in a paper for the committee on 1 May, the preferred course was to let the province sort out its problems by itself, but this would "always be subject to the need for us to intervene politically if we intervene militarily."[4] Wilson and Callaghan reiterated this point when they met with Chichester-Clark and his senior officials on 21 May. They stated that if Stormont requested troops to maintain order in the face of public disturbances, "very difficult political and parliamentary problems would arise at Westminster ... [and] would also create considerable difficulty for the Northern Ireland government."[5] The Northern Ireland PM could hardly have failed to notice that the veiled threat of British political intervention barely concealed London's deep anxiety about such a course of action.

According to Lt. Gen. Sir Ian Freeland, who in July had succeeded Ian Harris as GOC Northern Ireland, from June through August "a considerable amount of military/police IS [internal security] planning took place, but no overt preparation could be made until such time as, first, the Northern Ireland Government requested … troops to be deployed in Aid of the Civil Power, and secondly, Westminster agreed to the request."[6] This contradicts the assertion of Aaron Edwards that the RUC request for the deployment of troops in August came as "something as a surprise to Freeland."[7]

The first major step to prepare for ACP in Ulster was to clarify the military chain of command so that London was fully informed and in control. On 1 May the CDS advised the defence secretary and the GOC that the chiefs of staff had decided to "normalize" the chain of command for Northern Ireland. Under the new terms the GOC would report directly to the CDS (not through the CGS) on policy and major operational matters. Likewise, the CDS would represent the military in committee meetings on Northern Ireland.[8]

Second, Stormont and London agreed that they would consult before the former issued a request for troops, and if it did so the GOC was "under orders to seek prior instructions from the Ministry of Defence, *if humanly possible*."[9] Harking back to the discussions in late 1968, the final phrase presumably was inserted to give the GOC a little flexibility to respond quickly if widespread violence broke out and escalated rapidly.

Despite this clarification of procedures, preparations were hampered by the fact that the intelligence picture remained problematic. In late July the GOC told the CGS that Special Branch intelligence was still completely ineffective and unable to forecast trouble, thereby hampering planning. However, such criticism actually might have made things worse. In late July 1969 a dispute with the RUC inspector general over the SLO's reporting charter forced MI5 to move the SLO and MILO to an army office in Belfast, limiting their ability to advise Special Branch. MI5's director general, Furnival Jones, was not too worried that this move would reduce the flow of intelligence to the service, but the army felt it could impact its ability to conduct effective internal security operations.[10]

This move could not have happened at a worse time, as violence became more frequent and intense in July and August. Loyalist vigilantes began to appear on the streets of Belfast in July. Moloney writes that they claimed to be there to protect Protestant areas, "but in reality they were there to attack Catholic districts."[11] Their appearance coincided with the "marching season," during which Protestants paraded at various locations near Catholic areas, flaunting their contempt for the Catholics and their power over them. On 14 July Londonderry "experienced its first large-scale sectarian clashes."[12] That same day saw the first death from rioting: a Catholic man died in Dungiven one day after being hit by an RUC truncheon.[13]

As a result of the rising tempo of violence, Stormont made a series of requests to London, and the two governments consulted frequently. The first, made on 25 July, was for military helicopters to allow the RUC to conduct overhead surveillance of crowds. Considered at the ministerial level in London, it was quickly denied, at least in part because it could inflame an already tense situation.[14] Though not stated, it is likely that the MOD minister for administration (minister (A)) also turned down the request because it would directly involve the military in RUC operations over which London had no say. A second request followed shortly after, this time for military helicopters to transport RUC personnel. This was a less clear-cut issue. Since the police could be picked up and disembark discreetly at air bases, the task might be less provocative than flying directly over crowds and incidents. Furthermore, allowing the police to reinforce trouble spots quickly could help them contain violence and obviate the need for troops. However, the minister (A) regarded even this limited use of the military as unwarranted as long as the police were still in control of the situation. The DMO disagreed, arguing that the case for forestalling greater military action outweighed the political considerations. In the COSC meeting, the VCDS suggested that the military's case (presented in the DMO's brief) could be put more strongly to the minister (A) to bear in mind if the situation worsened, but this idea was rejected. In any case, the COSC conceded that the ministers were free to reconsider the helicopter issue if Stormont repeated the request. On 30 July the cabinet approved the minister (A)'s memorandum, and the GOC was notified.[15]

Rioting by Protestant gangs broke out again on 2–3 August in the Shankhill Road area of Belfast. Clashes between the police and the gangs eventually morphed into Protestant-Catholic violence. After an emergency cabinet meeting, Northern Ireland Minister of Home Affairs Robert Porter warned rioters that "the Government would not shrink from any action, however exceptional, to maintain law and order."[16] This threat prompted speculation in the press that Stormont might be about to call for military assistance to help quell the disorder, a decision that – a *Times* editorial warned – "could have grave consequences both for Ulster and ... the United Kingdom."[17]

The speculation was not wrong. On 3 August the Northern Ireland cabinet had initiated the process of intergovernmental consultation that would precede any request for troops. Harold Black, secretary to the Northern Ireland cabinet, contacted the Home Office, advising that with trouble continuing in Belfast the Northern Ireland government felt it might be approaching the point where the police might not be able to contain the disorder and it would be necessary to call in the army. But, at Home Office insistence, Ulster did not proceed with a formal request at this time because the GOC, after consulting with the RUC, concluded that the situation did not yet warrant it. Porter and the commissioner of police for Belfast later disputed the GOC's "optimistic assessment."[18] The following day Robin North from the HO phoned Black. In the course of their discussion North pointed out that while London had "willingly acquiesced" in the use of troops to protect vital points after the April bombings, any extension of that role to include riot control would require consultation between the two governments. He emphasized that if the troops were to be so used "they could clearly not be placed under the orders of the Northern Ireland Government."[19] North went on to outline the home secretary's view: that taking on such a role would force the British government to consider introducing legislation to provide temporarily for direct rule.[20]

This prospect was not being considered solely behind the closed doors of government. The press was discussing it openly and critically. In early August, *Times* reporter John Clare wrote that, "it has always been understood that if British troops were essential to bring back peace to Northern Ireland then the whole constitutional relationship between Stormont and Westminster would have to be considered."[21] An editorial in the paper that same day noted that the ultimate responsibility for "maintaining the Queen's peace" lay with Westminster, but using troops in Ulster would draw UK ministers more closely into handling the province's affairs, something neither government wanted. If a display of force calmed the situation, then Stormont could retain responsibility for public order, "with troops lending assistance ... and with continuous consultation with Westminster. At that stage any formal transfer of authority could be avoided. But that could not continue if troops were to become actively engaged in street combat."[22]

The mere hint that the British government might consider imposing direct rule brought about a flurry of activity. On the 5th Black met with North and Sir Philip Allen in London, and laid out Stormont's position in blunt terms. He said, first, that it would be unwise to impose constraints that might cause a delay in the request for troops, since such a delay might lead to a situation where more force was required to restore order. Second, he felt the British government was saying that, before requesting troops, Stormont should consider the consequences – which could include its own demise. Third, in those circumstances the Northern Ireland government would have to consider alternatives, including "putting armed Specials on the streets – with all the implications that that might carry for the deepening of the sectarian conflict."[23] Black also alluded to the possibility of an invasion of the province from the Irish Republic, a concern the HO itself had raised. Fourth, if disorder continued and increased, and there was no military intervention, Stormont would have to explain why publicly. Finally, he said that the British government should consider the possible consequences of imposing direct rule: "a frightening reaction by the Protestant community which could make anything that had happened up to now seem like child's play; a provisional government might be set up with extreme elements at its head and it is highly probable that wholesale sectarian strife would break out not only in the streets but in the factories."[24]

Although he finished on a conciliatory note, asking only that the same principles that guided ACP in the rest of the UK be applied to Ulster, Black clearly was "playing hardball."[25] He was resorting to threats – to "unleash" the B-Specials, or to leak the London-Stormont dispute – and was playing on London's worst fears: an invasion from the south, or a coup d'état by Protestant extremists. This ploy was a measure of Stormont's sense of desperation, but it also was a perfect example of the kind of political manipulation by Stormont that London was anxious to avoid.

The discussions ended with an agreement that the home secretary would write to the Stormont PM, laying out London's position, expressing understanding for Stormont's reluctance to call for troops except *in extremis*, indicating London's readiness to respond to such a request, but also emphasizing that gravity of taking this step, which would have to be explained to Parliament. Once troops were deployed, the two governments would have to consult about the next steps to be taken, and in the course of such consultations the possibility of direct rule – however remote – could not be ruled out.[26]

The following day Callaghan and Chichester-Clark conferred twice by phone, then the Ulster PM wrote to the home secretary to clarify the province's attitude regarding any request for troops. Failing to achieve such clarification, Chichester-Clark wrote, "would be to risk a most serious constitutional crisis with the gravest practical implications."[27] After reminding Callaghan that the British Army was Ulster's army too and thus that its role, including the ACP role, was no different there than in the rest of the UK, the Northern Ireland PM hastened to assure the home secretary that Stormont understood London's final authority over the armed forces. He added that his government also recognized that the British government would want to put in place arrangements to ensure that troops were not placed in situations they could not "influence or control" and to give itself a voice in the "law and order field." He believed this could be handled through normal government-to-government cooperation. Chichester-Clark then went on to say he was "appalled" to learn that London was contemplating the suspension of Stormont in the event that troops were deployed. He acknowledged that he had been reassured that this would not arise from a single, temporary use of troops and that London would seek greater control only in the event of a continuing deployment. Still, he felt that this put his government in an impossible position, forcing it to make a decision – whether or not ask for military ACP – "with a sword of Damocles hanging over our heads."[28] Callaghan was unmoved. He told the Ulster PM to assume that intervention would be "all or nothing."[29]

But Chichester-Clark's desperate plea prompted a hasty meeting with Callaghan two days later. The meeting addressed two major issues: the decision to use troops and the constitutional aspects of such a decision. The Stormont PM was concerned that if his minister of home affairs had to consider both the "law and order grounds" and the political consequences of asking for military ACP, that might lead to "undesirable" delays in requesting troops. The alternative, he suggested, was to use the B-Specials, "who were unpopular in certain quarters." Chichester-Clark stated explicitly that he "could not visualize the B-Specials being armed and used against large numbers of the population."[30] Once again, Stormont was resorting to not so subtle blackmail.

Callaghan asked the Northern Ireland ministers what they thought the role of the military would be in such circumstances. When Chichester-Clark said, a "normal internal security role," Callaghan replied bluntly that there was no such thing. He went on to chastise them for a casual approach to the use of troops to suppress disturbances, and warned them against thinking that they could be called in for anything less than as a "last resort in severely abnormal conditions."[31] While acknowledging the common law obligation and conceding that it was possible that troops might be used only once to deal with an isolated outbreak of "hooliganism," the home secretary said he felt that the conditions prevailing in Northern Ireland would lead to a continuing deployment. The Northern Ireland PM and his minister of home affairs hastened to assure Callaghan that they did not take the situation lightly, and that asking for troops would indeed be a course of last resort and "a very grave step."[32]

When discussion turned to the constitutional implications, Chichester-Clark asserted that, as the Government of Ireland Act, 1920 ensured that there could be no constitutional change without their consent, Protestants – even moderates – would regard any suspension of Stormont as a first step towards merger with the Irish republic, and that reaction to such a betrayal would be widespread and possibly very violent. Callaghan responded emphatically that the cabinet never intended such a merger. He asserted that the British public would not tolerate the use of troops without London being in control of the situation and of the policies that might affect the soldiers. While it had no desire to assume responsibility for Northern Ireland's affairs, the continuing use of troops would make political intervention inevitable. After all, if troops were needed to control crowds or riots on a continuing basis, then ordinary forces of law and order had already failed. And "a Government which does not control law and order was not a Government in the normal sense of the term. This was bound to have political and constitutional consequences."[33]

Callaghan agreed that the Northern Ireland ministers were right to believe that a "sword of Damocles" hung over them. If a situation of anarchy was developing there and troops were deployed, Stormont might lose its autonomy. Chichester-Clark asked for some clarification of the circumstances in which the use of troops would have such constitutional consequences, but Callaghan refused to be more specific beyond saying that it might arise from a continuing deployment of troops. The Stormont delegation then raised the option of a division of responsibility, with London taking over law and order only. In light of the likely Protestant reaction if Stormont were suspended, Chichester-Clark expressed hope that the Northern Ireland government could remain in being even if Westminster took control of law and order and exercised greater control and influence over other aspects of government. Callaghan was doubtful that London could limit its role to law and order only, but agreed that their advisers should examine the issue.[34]

The same day, the minister (A) met with the VCDS, VCGS, and other Ministry of Defence officials to consider these same issues. Presciently, he was concerned that once troops were committed it would be hard to withdraw them or to withhold them in future, and that it would be difficult to prevent the commitment from growing larger. Furthermore, since the military command structure directed responsibility back to the MOD, the British government inevitably would play an increasing role in Northern Ireland's affairs. "Before committing ourselves, therefore," he argued, "we should consider very closely what we would be letting ourselves in for beyond the short term."[35] Those at the meeting agreed that the MOD should send a letter to the Home Office stressing the need for the departments to consult closely "before any hasty decision was taken."[36]

But events on the ground forced Stormont's hand and, in turn, London's. Partisan rhetoric was being stepped up. On the 10th, former Northern Ireland opposition leader Eddie McAteer spoke at a Catholic rally, calling for "intervention of the Irish Republic if there was any further violence in Londonderry."[37] When asked if he meant Irish soldiers, he replied, "Not necessarily ... Anyone [from the republic]."[38] The *Guardian* newspaper berated the civil rights movement, saying it had "lost its way," and that "a depressing number" of its supporters were raising the partition issue, which was driving Protestants into the more hard-line organizations.[39] But it was the Apprentice Boys' march on 12 August that proved to be the tipping point – both for the conflict and for the army's role in it. In spite of efforts across sectarian lines to defuse trouble before the always provocative march began, Catholics in the Bogside area of Londonderry (Derry) prepared for the worst. On the day, stone throwing by Catholic youths rapidly expanded into three days of intense rioting in Derry that spread to Belfast, Coalisland, Dungannon, Newry, and Armagh.[40]

The violence that occurred in Derry became known as "the Battle of the Bogside." After initial clashes between Catholics, Protestants and the police, the RUC broke through barricades blocking entrance to the area; Protestant crowds followed the police into the area, smashing windows as they went. But Catholic crowds pushed the RUC back. Once a stalemate ensued, the police resorted to using CS gas, a tear gas never used before in the province, to keep crowds at bay. The police, who had not been trained in the use of CS, often fired the canisters directly at individual rioters. By morning the Bogside was enveloped in a cloud of gas. The Bogsiders resorted to hurling paving stones and petrol bombs. Even if the police believed (as they later claimed) that they were being neutral, it did not look that way to the Catholics, as Protestant civilian rioters blended into the RUC. On both sides rumours fed fear and stoked the violence. The first shootings, by the RUC, occurred on the 13th. The B-Specials were deployed in Derry on the evening of the 13th, but by the following day they had joined in the rioting rather than controlling it. The violence got worse on the 14th in Belfast as well, where Protestant crowds set fire to houses in Catholic areas. Exhausted and overwhelmed, the RUC resorted to using vehicle-mounted machine guns. Seven people were killed in the first two days, four of them shot by the RUC.[41]

If in the days immediately preceding the riots the British newspapers had largely ignored the rising tensions in Ulster, they gave it front-page treatment once the violence began. Lurid headlines (such as "Child Dies in 'Little' War") and dramatic photographs dominated their coverage.[42] And this was coverage neither the Stormont nor Westminster politicians could ignore.

Meanwhile, as violence grew in Londonderry, on the 12th Chichester-Clark called an emergency meeting of his cabinet, to be followed by an emergency session of the province's legislature.[43] He and his minister of home affairs, Robert Porter, requested that troops be moved to a base in the city and be placed on immediate notice to come to the support of the RUC. The 1st PWO was concentrated at this base but did not move onto the streets for two more days and not until several actions had occurred. First, Callaghan and Wilson met early on 14 August at RAF Station St Mawgan, Cornwall, in anticipation of a troop request from Stormont. The home secretary said that

he thought London would have to accede to it but that the troops'
role should be limited to restoring order in the specific area to which
they were deployed, after which they should be withdrawn as quickly
as possible, with law and order then being handed back to the RUC. If
a quick handover were not possible, some new arrangement would
have to be made. Wilson agreed.[44] So, political approval in principle
had been granted at the highest level even before the request was
received. But as a consequence of the decision of the cabinet committee in April, cabinet itself was bypassed. It played no role in the decision to deploy the troops, except to approve the decision retroactive-
ly, once the troops were already engaged.[45] Nor did Parliament play a
role, since it was on summer recess and was not recalled to deal with
the crisis.

Second, at about the same time, and at the request of Victor Stonham (HO minister of state), Roy Hattersley, the deputy secretary of
defence acting on behalf of Healey (who had been hospitalized), was
consulting with Lt. Gen. Freeland regarding the steps he planned to
take if asked for troops – a request that the GOC expected within the
hour. Freeland said the troops' first task would be to lift the siege of
the main police station in Derry, which had been nearly surrounded
by a large crowd. He hoped that with the troops protecting the station
the police would be able to disperse the crowd. However, he acknowledged that the RUC might not be up to the task and that the troops
would have to be used instead. Once that was accomplished he would
use troops to keep the factions apart. They would first use their riot
control equipment, including CS gas, but if that failed to achieve
results they would open fire after issuing a warning to the crowd.[46]

With the approval of the prime minister secured and interdepartmental consultation completed, it remained only for Northern Ireland to make a request. On the afternoon of the 14th, the inspector
general of the RUC did so to the GOC, who – as agreed – forwarded the
request up the chain of command. According to the *Times*, Callaghan,
who was flying back to London after his meeting with Wilson,
received the request from Stonham at the Home Office at 4:35 p.m.
via radio/telephone. Callaghan told Stonham to inform the Northern
Ireland government that troops would be deployed immediately.[47]
The Home Office issued a statement explaining Stormont's request
and London's response, and emphasizing that the troops would be
under London's control.[48]

TROOPS ON THE STREETS:
LONDON TAKES CHARGE?

Within an hour of the VCGS authorizing the GOC to deploy troops in
Derry if necessary, the GOC had issued the order for the 1st PWO to
move into the city. The battalion completed its deployment in little
more than an hour and the city quieted quickly.[49] A similar process
occurred in Belfast on the 15th with the same effect, although Robin
Eveleigh says the process moved more slowly. The commissioner of
police for Belfast issued his initial request at 4:30 a.m., but the Northern Ireland cabinet did not send its call to the HO until 12:25 p.m.
Although ministerial approval was issued from London at 3:10 p.m.,
the troops did not deploy onto the streets of Belfast until 6:30 p.m. –
and then at the wrong location, hours after factional shooting had
begun. They did not reach the correct site until 9:35 p.m.[50] The delay
in Belfast notwithstanding, Ulster's Catholic communities initially
welcomed the troops warmly, seeing them as a preferable alternative
to the RUC.[51]

After the request for troops in Derry had been received, the COSC
met to review the situation and to approve the dispatch of reinforcements. The contingency planning developed in the previous months
was put into effect, and over the next few days three more battalions
plus a brigade headquarters and its supporting elements deployed to
Northern Ireland.[52] Operation Banner, which no one at the time expected to become a forty-year commitment, had begun.

Although no one at the time could have predicted the duration of
the operation, the press immediately expressed concern about how to
terminate the mission and whether it could be done quickly. An editorial in the *Guardian* on 15 August warned that "the use of troops
will be attended with dangers that no one with any knowledge of
Irish history can have forgotten."[53] David Wood, writing in the *Times*
the same day, said that, "as always happens once troops are committed
there is no certainty how they will be disengaged. Everything depends
on London's assumption that they have been deployed to deal with a
local situation that will be of limited duration."[54] The following day
he wrote, "Ministers soberly realise that it is always easier to order
troops in than to bring them out in conditions of crisis."[55] An editorial in the *Times* on 15 August made the same points and concluded
that, "the probability is that the troops will be required in strength for

a longish period."[56] It went on to highlight the complicated arrangement under which the troops would operate: "The troops will of course remain within the military chain of command which terminates in Whitehall. They will not take their instructions from the present civil authorities in Northern Ireland; but in coming to the aid of the civil arm they will be taking part in operations ... which are the responsibility of those authorities."[57] The editorial concluded by stating emphatically that having troops for which London was responsible embroiled in a situation for which Stormont was responsible "is not acceptable."[58]

Official records do not indicate whether such opinions exerted any influence over the decision makers, but they clearly would have been aware of them and, indeed, were already wrestling with those very issues. Once troops were committed to the streets, and with the concurrence of Stormont, Westminster wasted little time in asserting its control over how they would be used. Prior to the deployment Stormont had three security committees: ministerial, internal security, and protective security.[59] On 15 August, on the advice of Ulster's minister of home affairs and the GOC, Chichester-Clark ordered the creation of a Joint Security Committee (JSC), which, at least initially, would meet daily, review the security situation, and issue instructions (presumably to the security forces). Initially, the JSC included the minister of home affairs as chair, members of the Cabinet Security Committee, the secretary to the Stormont cabinet, the army chief of staff from HQNI, the inspector general of the Royal Ulster Constabulary, the MI5 security liaison officer, and the county inspector of the Special Branch. However, on the 20th the Stormont cabinet agreed that the CSC members did not need to attend the JSC meetings.[60]

Creating the JSC was just the first step. On 18 August, after a meeting with his own cabinet that endorsed the decisions and actions already taken, Wilson met with Chichester-Clark at 10 Downing Street, following which they issued the joint "Downing Street Declaration." In it the Northern Ireland government affirmed that with reference to the deployment of British troops, it would take the views of the British government "into the fullest account at all times."[61]

To ensure that this would happen, London quickly dispatched two senior civil servants to conduct ongoing liaison with Stormont. Foreign Office official and former ambassador Oliver Wright was assigned to Ulster's Cabinet Office, and A.S. Baker to the Ministry of Home

Affairs. Based on the idea that Britain's new security role could not be separated from the social policies of the Northern Ireland government, Wright's role was two-fold: first, to suggest ideas for actions that Stormont could take to heal divisions in the province and, second, to warn London if Stormont proposed to take action that it would not approve, and to keep the latter informed.[62]

The declaration was accompanied by a separate communiqué that clarified the role and powers of the GOC with respect to security matters. It stated that he would

> with immediate effect assume *overall responsibility for security operations*. He will continue to be responsible directly to the Ministry of Defence but will work in the closest co-operation with the Northern Ireland Government and the Inspector-General of the Royal Ulster Constabulary. *For all security operations the GOC will have full control of the deployment and tasks of the Royal Ulster Constabulary*. For normal police duties outside the field of security the Royal Ulster Constabulary will remain answerable to the Inspector-General who will be responsible to the Northern Ireland Government.[63]

Appointing the GOC to be the director of operations in charge of all security operations was consistent with the British practice in most of its postwar counter-insurgency campaigns.[64] But at Home Office insistence he was also assigned one of its staff to serve as a civil adviser, presumably to ensure that security efforts supported London's political objectives.[65]

Nevertheless, at a meeting on 20 August Defence Secretary Healey and his senior military and civilian advisers (including the CGS, the DMO, and an Home Office official) agreed that the GOC needed a new directive based on the communiqué and the Downing Street Declaration. The Ministry of Defence and the Home Office would draft it and then show it to the Stormont government, but the latter's consent would not be required. They felt that the GOC would need greater freedom to use his forces than he'd had up to this point, and they would leave it to his judgment and that of his political advisers to decide which operations were large or sensitive enough to require prior consultation with Whitehall. But the directive would not spell out in advance how much discretion he had.[66]

In the event, the directive, issued two days later, was not quite the blank cheque the meeting with Healey had appeared to approve. In line with the communiqué, it stated that the GOC would have overall responsibility for security operations, which were defined as relating to internal and external security. These included the execution of operations necessary to counter action (whether covert or overt) aimed at subverting the security of the state, and the action necessary for the protection of life and property in case of actual or apprehended civil commotion.[67]

The GOC would be responsible to the MOD but would consult with the Northern Ireland government. In the event of any dispute, he was to refer it immediately to the British government. He was to keep the CDS fully informed. If time permitted, he was to seek guidance from the MOD on any matters he (or the British government officials in the province) felt had wider political implications or involved any major redeployment of forces. He would have full control of RUC for security operations only, and full control of the Ulster Special Constabulary (the B-Specials) including organization, tasking, deployment, and arms. He was to be free to use the B-Specials as he thought necessary, to stand down those personnel not needed, and to issue instructions to centralize their weapons. However, they were not to be used for riot or crowd control. Finally, in consultation with Stormont and the British government, the GOC was authorized to set up security committees or other machinery he deemed necessary.[68] So, the GOC had limited operational discretion. And until March 1972, when Britain imposed direct rule, his role and powers remained essentially unaltered and based on this directive. Although a new one was issued in 1971, it largely confirmed the status quo.

Finally, London sought to gain control of the information on which security force operations would be based. The army had entered the conflict with an intelligence deficit. During their 19 August meeting, Chichester-Clark and Wilson had agreed that the GOC would need "more adequate intelligence advice and Special Branch support."[69] The army's then current internal security operations practice, based on experience overseas since 1945, called for the creation of "a single centralized, integrated intelligence organization."[70] That was not achieved during the period under study, but the security forces took a number steps intended to better coordinate intelligence.

The first priority was to get the security and military intelligence liaison officers reinstated at RUC HQ.[71] Concurrently, along with the head of RUC Special Branch, they were appointed to the newly created Intelligence Sub-Committee (ISC) of the JSC. The subcommittee's role was to produce a weekly intelligence summary for the JSC and to consider issues such as protective security and methods for acquiring intelligence. But due to the already strained relationship between the branch and the liaison officers, and to the failure of the JSC to define its intelligence requirements, the ISC had ceased to function by early 1970. MI5 viewed this failure with considerable concern, and in May urged the immediate reconstitution of the ISC with a Cabinet Office representative in the chair and its terms of reference fulfilled.[72] Evidence suggests that the ISC was restored soon thereafter. However, it may have been superseded eventually by the Director of Operations Intelligence Committee (DOIC).[73]

The second and more successful step was to appoint a director of intelligence (D/INT). Two days after the 19 August meeting, the GOC told the CGS that he "would welcome a Director of Intelligence ... who would be answerable solely to him."[74] The matter was referred to the JIC. In early September Freeland told his commanders: "It is the intelligence of the security machine that is at present the weakest link." He said that a director of intelligence would soon join his staff, "and then all intelligence agencies will be coordinated correctly." He added, "We shall also ensure that we are all working off the same information rather than the fragmented efforts of the present set-up."[75] The D/INT (a senior MI5 officer) deployed to the province in early September. His terms of reference included responsibility for coordinating all sources of intelligence in the province, assessing and providing all-source intelligence to the GOC, disseminating material to the JSC and the JIC, and recommending to the GOC any improvements to the intelligence machinery. A concurrent directive to the GOC gave him responsibility for setting intelligence requirement priorities and implementing any of the improvements recommended by the D/INT to meet those requirements. The revised 1971 directive reaffirmed the D/INT's role in coordinating the work of military intelligence and RUC Special Branch.[76]

According to the D/INT who was serving in January 1972, his job, in addition to the tasks identified above, entailed overseeing a joint military/MI5 staff, liaising with Special Branch, and improving the branch wherever needed by providing training and assistance. He also chaired the DOIC, which met weekly to discuss (among other things) the intelligence assessment he had produced for the relevant period. But the D/INT later told the Saville Inquiry on Bloody Sunday that, when he first took up the post in 1970, "there was no established procedure for how I was supposed to operate."[77]

The establishment of the ISC and the appointment of the D/INT with a joint staff were certainly major steps towards an integrated intelligence effort. But they fell short of that goal, as army and police efforts remained separate and army-police cooperation was problematic. That said, it is important to acknowledge that in 1969 the violence consisted mostly of rioting; an insurgency had not yet emerged. Moreover, the army's presence in the province was seen as a temporary measure.[78] So, a more limited approach to intelligence organization probably made sense at that stage in the conflict.

Much to the relief of Stormont (and to that of politicians and officials in London) Westminster did not impose direct rule on Northern Ireland at this time. And the actions taken in mid-August 1969 fell far short of the "all or nothing" approach threatened by Callaghan earlier that month. Nevertheless, London did intervene politically as well as militarily and stripped away some of Stormont's power. But London's approach to command and control seemed to embody a contradiction. While it strove to ensure that it had a greater civilian political voice in security matters, it also came perilously close to giving the GOC an operational blank cheque. Even so, as will be shown below, the arrangements put in place in August 1969 did not end the struggle between Westminster and Stormont over control of security operations.

THE CHALLENGES OF
DIVIDED COMMAND AND CONTROL

Simply put, from August 1969 to March 1972 the Northern Ireland government retained responsibility for maintaining law and order in the province while the British government provided the troops that allowed it to do so. Thus, the army was directed by two civil powers: it acted at the request of Stormont but was accountable for its actions to Westminster.[79] Yet the situation was more nuanced and complex than this simple formulation suggests. As Arthur Hockaday explained in a 1971 memo, "The soldier acts under higher military authority up the chain of command as far as the Defence Council ... The Secretary of State [for Defence] is the Minister responsible ... to the Westminster Parliament for all matters relating to the Armed Forces ... The soldier has no responsibility to the Stormont Government, nor has the Stormont Government any responsibility for his actions. This is not affected by the fact that ... [Stormont] is the civil power ... which may call upon the Armed Forces for assistance."[80]

This arrangement would have been difficult to manage under the best of circumstances, let alone under those in Northern Ireland. In fact, as will be shown, the two governments did not always agree on security policy or on how the troops should be used. Thus for two and a half years the army was, to some extent, caught in the middle of a struggle over the power to dictate what happened in Northern Ireland. To illustrate the difficulties, it is worth comparing how Lt. Gen. Freeland explained his role and powers on two occasions separated by sixteen months.

In an interview with the *Times* in August 1969 Freeland said, "There is no question of policemen giving soldiers an order ... What they will do and how they will do it is dictated by me." Moreover, he said, "nobody in London could tell him where they [troops] should go on the ground."[81] The GOC might have been responding in part to an editorial in the Manchester *Guardian* a few days earlier in which the writer stated bluntly, "The first action of Mr. Callaghan's police advisor should be *to tell the GOC to order* this notorious force [the B-Specials] out of the trouble areas."[82] In light of this comment Freeland may have used the opportunity afforded by his *Times* interview to inform British readers about the boundaries between the civilian and military domains of control. He also remarked optimistically that "it is most unlikely that we would have to go to the politicians to resolve difficulties."[83]

Later, addressing the Army Staff College in December 1970, Freeland was more pessimistic about the problems of divided political direction. The government of Northern Ireland, he reminded his audience, was responsible for law and order in the province,

> but the Director of Security Operations (myself) and the Army, who are at present the main security arm, are not under their command. But the RUC are under Stormont although their securi-

ty operations as opposed to police work are coordinated by me. You can see therefore how easy it is for misunderstandings and complications to arise, particularly between the Director of Security Operations and the Chief Constable of the RUC ... These are not the only complications. Two ministries in Whitehall are involved in the security situation in Northern Ireland, the Home Office and the Ministry of Defence ... The Home Office is responsible for law and order, but it is the MOD who gives me my orders. Although on two occasions the late Home Secretary tried to give me orders on tactical security matters, once on the telephone and once in person![84]

Freeland does not specify when the home secretary tried to issue such orders, but his remarks indicate that he had less freedom of action and more political oversight from London than his earlier interview suggested. In fact, as early as August 1969 Whitehall was scrambling to clarify the respective roles of the various departments regarding that oversight. Prompted by a Home Office briefing on the B-Specials, Healey told Wilson in a 20 August telephone call that he was concerned that the HO was understaffed on the Northern Ireland problem and that he had offered an MOD official to assist them.[85] Clearly, he was trying to ensure that on security matters the British government spoke with only one voice: that of the MOD. Wilson reassured Healey that the MOD had responsibility for all matters relating to security in the province, and that the cabinet secretary (Burke Trend) had "sold" this idea to Sir Philip Allen at the HO, which would retain responsibility for general policy and political relations with Northern Ireland.[86] Nevertheless, the prime minister had his staff try to clarify the relationship between the MOD, the HO, and the Cabinet Office.

What followed was a fortnight-long exchange of messages and memos among senior officials that ultimately confirmed in writing what Wilson had told Healey on the telephone about the responsibilities of the MOD and the HO. The two departments had arrangements for daily consultation and coordination with each other (and with other interested departments). The final message also restated the authority granted earlier by cabinet to the PM and the defence and home secretaries to take any urgent decisions.[87]

In the interim, however, the process revealed the degree of confusion within the Cabinet Office about how those departments interacted on the Northern Ireland question. Sir Robin Hooper's memo to Sir Philip Allen on 22 August proposed that Allen would chair a committee of PUSs to deal with general policy matters, while an MOD official would chair an interdepartmental executive committee to address day-to-day operational issues. The Home Office operations room would be merged into a joint centre in the MOD.[88] Allen pointed out in reply that his committee (MISC 244) had been in existence for some time and comprised senior officials, not just PUSs.[89] Ned Dunnett (PUS to Healey) questioned the need for an interdepartmental committee to deal with daily operational matters, as existing means for consultation were working adequately, hampered only by a shortage of staff assigned to the Northern Ireland problem. Staffing the proposed committee would put an "intolerable burden" on both ministries without producing any advantages in the conduct of business. Since the HO Northern Ireland desk was being strengthened, the need for new formal machinery was obviated. By October it had two divisions (one for political and constitutional questions, the other for internal security) and a staff of sixteen working for Assistant Under-Secretary of State Neil F. Cairncross. Dunnett also pointed out that, although the HO did not have an "ops room," it did have permanent contact with the defence operations centre and was represented at DOE meetings when Northern Ireland was being discussed.[90]

The extent of Cabinet Office confusion over responsibility for Northern Ireland undoubtedly reflected a lack of experience that resulted from the practice of keeping Ulster at arm's length and allowing Stormont to run itself. That said, even if founded on ignorance, the Cabinet Office effort represented a necessary attempt to reconcile the need for a clear delineation of institutional responsibilities and autonomy with the need to ensure that the HO, MOD, and Cabinet Office worked together. In this sense it was not atypical of the Westminster style of policymaking and administration. If there appeared to be some reluctance or hesitancy to put new structures in place, it probably had as much to do with the hope that the situation would prove temporary (and that these procedures thus would prove unnecessary) as it did with the normal bureaucratic tendencies to protect turf.

If there was confusion at the highest levels of the British government about how to manage the security task in the province, there was great concern at Stormont. Even if its worst fears had not been realized, it was being marginalized to a considerable degree on matters that formerly had been within its exclusive remit. In his 1970 lecture Freeland expressed some sympathy for the government of the province: "Imagine the feelings of Northern Ireland Ministers, who are members of the Joint Security Committee chaired by the [Northern Ireland] Prime Minister, who know that they have got to persuade me about the desirability of any new policy that they want to effect, and then I may have to refer it to the MOD who then has to consult the Home Office – a very cumbersome chain of command which complicates my life ... It is surprising that this system of control does not lead to more difficulties than it does ... I see no alternative to the present arrangements whilst Stormont continues to govern."[91]

But he was less charitable after retirement. In a 1973 letter to former Home Secretary Callaghan he wrote that the Stormont ministers "resented strongly not being complete masters in their own house in the security field." Their members of the JSC "constantly griped at me and the Army during committee meetings and also sometimes at British Government policy. I longed for the British government to take complete control of security and provide a Minister as Chairman of the Security Committee."[92]

The griping may have been due in part to the fact that, in spite of its original mandate, the JSC actually played a minor role in security planning. According to Kenneth Bloomfield, then deputy secretary to the Stormont cabinet, the JSC "was a place where both security commanders and Northern Ireland ministers could exchange ideas about what they were thinking of doing. It was a forum for the exchange of views rather than an executive decision making body."[93] He recalled that "the serious decisions were taken privately by, for example, the [Stormont] Prime Minister, the GOC and the Chief-Constable. The JSC meetings would not have been a forum to discuss detailed security plans because there were too many people present."[94]

Brian Cummings, who served as principal private secretary to Chichester-Clark and later as private secretary to Brian Faulkner, confirmed Bloomfield's recollection, but clarified it on some matters of detail. He asserted that the JSC did exercise some decision-making power, but it was limited to matters that were the sole purview "of the civil power, such as law making and prison accommodation."[95] The Home Affairs Department or the Government Security Unit (GSU) would prepare papers on these subjects and send them to the JSC for approval.[96]

In that sense, the JSC made decisions about what, in a broad
sense, could be called security policy. However, it did not make
decisions on operational law and order matters. There the situation was different. As for operational law and order matters,
reports about the security situation were regularly tabled at the
JSC. Sometimes they were presented verbally, sometimes in writing. The committee would listen to the comments and/or read
the paper. The GOC would report that something was planned for
whatever date and that it would be dealt with in a certain way.
That would then be noted by the JSC. In short, decisions about
matters "on the streets" were made by the Army and the RUC and
reported to the JSC. I have no recollection of the JSC ever making
an executive decision about how an event should be policed – it
did not perform that function.[97]

If the memories of Bloomfield and Cummings are accurate then
the civil-military command and control arrangements put in place at
Stormont did not function exactly as planned. The JSC exercised less
oversight and direction of the actions of security forces – especially
the army – than was intended when it was created. The Ulster PM
and his security chiefs apparently made operational decisions behind
closed doors, not within the wider forum that the JSC was meant to
be. While the army did not have a completely free hand to operate as
it saw fit, it may have had more freedom of action than anyone in
London or Stormont had envisaged. As Freeland suggested in 1970, it
may have been that there simply was no alternative to the existing
practices. But there is some indication in the record for this early period that neither the government in London nor that in Ulster was
entirely comfortable with this arrangement, and that both sought to
change it.

Clearly there was dissatisfaction within Stormont, which pushed
back against some security policies imposed by Westminster. In the
months that followed the major deployment of troops in August 1969,
there emerged a multifaceted struggle over control of the police, which
illustrates the command and control problem. The fusion of control
of military and police forces embodied in the terms of reference for
the GOC-D/OPS had been proposed not by Harold Wilson but by
Chichester-Clark, with the agreement of the GOC and the head of the
RUC. At that time it was envisaged that this control would include the

administration and command of the police and of the B-Specials. Wilson felt this should be a short-term measure to ensure that any political opposition normally reserved for the police would not be deflected onto the army; the Stormont PM agreed.[98]

But, during the discussions that had preceded the Downing Street Declaration and the associated communiqué, agreement on these basic points had run into an immediate obstacle – the issue of disarming the B-Specials. The GOC favoured limiting their activities and placing their weapons under centralized control. Chichester-Clark thought that such a move would be inflammatory in the current climate. In view of threats from the IRA, "it would undoubtedly lead some citizens into taking the law into their own hands."[99] Wilson was unmoved by these arguments. He pointed out to Chichester-Clark that by proposing that the GOC take responsibility for internal security the Northern Ireland government was "in effect inviting the United Kingdom government to take responsibility for the actions of the B Specials, and their consequences. In the very serious situation ... it was essential to be clear about the authority that Lt. Gen. Freeland would be allowed to exercise over the B Specials, and over their arms."[100]

Wilson went further, invoking public opinion and suggesting that the British public would expect the disarming and possible disbanding of the B-Specials in return for the deployment of 5,000 troops. Under pressure as well from Secretary Healey, the Northern Ireland PM grudgingly accepted the idea that the B-Specials would no longer be used for riot control, but cautioned against the British government's preference for an immediate announcement to that effect. He felt that any change in their role "should be introduced gradually and with the minimum of publicity."[101]

During a break in the discussions, Gen. Baker (the CGS) had joined the British cabinet ministers as they wrestled with the command and control issue. After further discussion they concluded that Chichester-Clark's basic proposal was acceptable, provided that the Northern Ireland government agreed to an independent inquiry into the role, structure, and organization of the police and to the GOC's control of the B-Specials and "above all, central control of their arms."[102] While they clearly had some reservations, the consensus seemed to be that the proposal "could not put us in a worse position, so far as our responsibilities were concerned, than we were in now; and it would give the United Kingdom Government a measure of control and authority in

Northern Ireland which had hitherto been lacking."[103] Moreover, the GOC favoured the proposal. The ministers expressed concern that it would be difficult for the British government to defend a rejection of the proposal if the GOC's support for it became public. The British ministers clearly felt "boxed in" by the lack of viable alternatives and by the GOC's endorsement. Yet, once the meeting with the Stormont representatives had resumed, the British government's position prevailed, subject only to a brief delay in announcing the inquiry into the police (to allow the Northern Ireland PM to discuss it with the RUC IG).[104]

On 20 August Freeland had what Healey described as "a very difficult meeting" with the RUC. Getting the B-Specials out of the cities was not a problem. Most members actually lived in urban areas, and some would remain on duty in Protestant areas to prevent looting, but they were out of Derry and the Catholic areas of Belfast. The stumbling block was the issue of disarming them. A briefing – apparently by the Home Office – had given the impression that the objective was to disarm and disband them, which was causing concern. In fact, the intent was to change their role and control their weapons. Healey was inclined to deploy them along the border, although Wilson feared they might fire across it. Healey thought that the price of making progress on the issue might be to adopt "an attitude very sensitive to the position inside Ulster."[105]

Gen. Baker had met with Freeland the previous day in Northern Ireland. While Baker concluded that it was the RUC itself, not the B-Specials, who were responsible for most of the indiscriminate shooting at the height of the riots, their discussion focused mostly on the Specials. Baker felt that there would be no return to "normalcy" in the province until they were either disbanded or "fundamentally changed." The GOC was concerned that precipitate action, such as withdrawing them from border control, might lead to mutiny, with the Specials giving their arms to extremists or becoming such themselves. According to Healey the CGS conceded that dealing with the Specials would be "an extraordinarily delicate business" and would have to proceed cautiously. To resolve this problem Freeland favoured concentrating their weapons. As a first step in that process and at his instigation, the RUC had removed all Browning machine guns from RUC Reserve armoured cars.[106] Later that day Baker met with Chichester-Clark before a meeting of the CSC. The Northern Ireland PM agreed to centralize the B-Specials' arms. HQNI drafted a directive to this effect, the Northern Ireland government approved it, and the GOC promulgated it on 22 August.[107]

That should have been the end of it, but it was not. In late August the GOC's political adviser sent to the Home Office a draft memorandum from the Stormont cabinet that would give legal sanction to the GOC's relationship with the RUC and B-Specials. The adviser thought this was unwise because it would implicate the GOC (and through him, ministers in London) "in unpalatable decisions (and, no doubt, in any unpalatable incidents in which these forces may get involved)."[108] He also feared it would give "an air of permanence" to what everyone hoped would be a temporary situation. Moreover, there were doubts about the legality of this step. For all these reasons, the adviser's inclination was not to tamper with the existing arrangements, which, "however flimsy they may be in law, work well enough in practice."[109]

On 3 October Healey wrote to the CGS saying he was "surprised to learn" that fifty B-Specials were on duty doing "police patrol duties" in the Shankhill Road area of Belfast, albeit armed only with batons and "subject to stringent precautions."[110] While saying he did not question the GOC's judgment on tactical situations, he pointed out that government ministers had agreed in August that the B-Specials would be removed from the cities. They should not have been reintroduced without prior consultation or immediate notification. The home secretary was "extremely concerned" but was reserving his decision on whether the situation should be allowed to continue. Healey went on to note that he felt he was not being kept properly informed. He asked the CGS to "give some thought" to improving their lines of communication so that he could be fully informed of developments that might have "political repercussions, as they occur. The lines of communication exist and should be used."[111] He closed by saying that if the GOC needed more personnel to feed information back to White-hall he should be given them.

Gen. Baker replied the same day with a letter of apology. He conceded that his political master was correct and that this was not the only instance where communication had failed. The VCGS was currently in Northern Ireland and this issue of communications was one of the main reasons for his visit. By way of explanation Baker noted that Maj. Gen. Tony Dyball, then serving as chief of staff to the GOC, was constantly on call for meetings and negotiations. Such commitments were necessary but existed to the detriment of staff work, in particular the passing of information back to London. The CGS had brought this "unsatisfactory state of affairs" to Freeland's attention and he had promised to remedy it immediately. The CGS had also promised him more personnel if they were needed.[112]

As for the B-Specials, Baker explained that owing to disturbances the previous Sunday the GOC had required some additional manpower to ensure security in the Protestant "rear area" and had deployed the fifty B-Specials there. The CGS was at pains to emphasize that these particular personnel were not like the rural B-Specials, who were more akin to a militia, but were in fact trained in the police duties that special constables carry out in England. The GOC had agreed to their deployment under strict conditions: they were unarmed except for truncheons and were to act only as police on the beat, without any responsibility for riot control. They were also confined to a small area out of any contact with the Catholic population. Their presence freed up regular RUC to be used for crowd control in the Protestant areas that were experiencing disorder. Had the GOC not been able to use the B-Specials, he would have had to deploy more troops, which were needed elsewhere and which might have been less effective, as the army was "not popular at this time with more extremist Protestants."[113] The arrangement had worked so well that the GOC had agreed to continue it. There had been no objection from the Catholic community because they were made aware that this effort kept Protestant extremists away from them. Freeland felt that using the Specials in this way fell within the terms of reference of his August directive. Baker disagreed on this point and felt that at the very least he should have reported it earlier. But setting aside the "rights and wrongs," the CGS felt it had been "a useful and effective measure."[114] In closing, the CGS wondered if it had been wise for Home Office to withdraw its official from the HQNI sometime earlier, and whether it might be beneficial if the GOC and Oliver Wright were co-located.

Healey met later that day with Baker, the VCGS, and several other senior officials. The written record makes it clear that he "read them the riot act." Conceding that thus far "nothing had gone badly wrong as a result of the shortcomings in communication," the defence secretary nevertheless emphasized that he could no longer accept a situation in which the MOD was not informed immediately about important matters or consulted about issues that had political implications. He cited the B-Specials' deployment as a case in point. He also felt that he should have been consulted about a decision (taken at a JSC meeting on 29 September) to use tougher tactics in dealing with riots. Healey demanded a solution to the communication problem by the end of the day.[115]

Regarding the use of the B-Specials in the instance under scrutiny, Healey said he had found the CGS's explanation persuasive and was prepared to allow the practice to continue, subject to "very close and continuous review." He was not opposed in principle to the new anti-riot methods but was concerned about how the decision was implemented. Failure to settle on a standard approach to be used by all army units and agreed to in advance with the police adviser would cause a rift between the army and the police and thus between the MOD and the HO. Healey then addressed a statement by the GOC to a committee, chaired by Lord Hunt, that was looking into the future of the RUC. The secretary requested that in future any conversation of an official nature by senior officers outside HQNI should be recorded. The meeting agreed that communication between Oliver Wright and the GOC could be improved and that what the GOC really needed was a political adviser who could warn him of issues whose political implications might warrant consultation with London. Such an office also would improve communication with Whitehall generally. The Home Office was to be pressed to re-establish this position. Failing that, MOD would provide its own.[116]

It is clear from the foregoing messages and meeting record that there were two major sources of discord: the continued use of the B-Specials in a limited security role and the GOC's exercise of autonomy in decision making. From London's perspective the latter was the more significant problem. The former simply served as a catalyst for a dispute between the military and the politicians over command and control that actually revolved around the problem of communication.

The directive to the GOC had granted him some operational discretion, but it was not unfettered. Where operational decisions had political ramifications – and any use of the B-Specials was inherently political – the GOC was required to consult London. In this case he did not, and the defence secretary had every right to be annoyed and to assert his authority to make such decisions. But this communication

and consultation failure can be explained several ways without at-
tributing malign motives to anyone concerned.

First, the tempo of army operations imposed excessive demands on
the time of senior officers in Northern Ireland. They were making
rapid decisions to solve immediate problems. It was perhaps not surprising that they sometimes failed to consult with their political masters on issues the latter felt were politically sensitive. Getting the job
done was taking precedence over staff work.

Second, it may be fair to suggest that the unique character of the
conflict being fought on the streets of major cities in the UK left both
the army and the politicians in a position where the line between the
routine event or decision and the politically significant one was not
always obvious to either. All the more reason then, one might argue,
for the army to err on the side of caution and consult the politicians
more often. But Freeland was taking a generous approach to the interpretation and application of his directive, allowing himself more discretion in decision making than his civilian boss Healey thought he
should have. The defence secretary, for his part, was perhaps letting his
sensitivity to political problems get the better of him. The result was
a tendency on Healey's part to micromanage, even if only after the
fact. Finally, the unspoken subtext to Healey's disagreement with Freeland may have been a perceived need on the part of the secretary to
remind the GOC – and through him the Stormont representatives on
the JSC – that it was London that had the final say over security matters, and that it was London to whom he owed his loyalty.

In the aftermath of the meeting, an exchange of messages clarified
the issue of riot control tactics. The army explained that it was not
possible to apply a single standard method in every instance, and that
the police adviser (Mr McKay) had been consulted on this matter and
had agreed with the army's approach. This being the case, Healey
decided to let the issue rest.[117] In December, however, he decided to
appoint a senior official from the MOD to act as adviser to the GOC and
to serve as a point of contact for the defence secretariat.[118] This clearly was meant to provide a degree of direct political oversight of the
GOC's decisions and actions and an independent line of communication to Healey.

But the issue of relations with the police continued to trouble the
army. In mid-October Freeland wrote to the CDS, pointing out that
the new head of the RUC, Sir Arthur Young, felt that the directive

issued on 22 August gave the GOC too much control over the RUC. The
GOC noted that while he never issued orders to the police, in light of
efforts to recast the image of the force, he felt that anything that could
be done to get the police re-established as the primary law enforcement body and to boost Young's image as a reformer would be welcome. With the approval of Wright and McKay, he proposed an
amendment to the directive that he thought would "smooth over"
potential problems. The defence and home secretaries agreed and the
directive was amended so that the GOC as D/OPS was responsible, not
for full control, but for the "co-ordination of the tasking of the RUC,"
and only for "security operations."[119]

The issue did not end there. During a meeting with the home secretary on 18 November Chichester-Clark and his senior colleagues
suggested that, as the situation in Northern Ireland was returning to
normal, the position of the GOC in relation to the RUC should be
reviewed. They felt that his coordinating role was no longer necessary.
That claim raised the ire of the CGS, who saw it as a not so thinly dis-
guised attempt to change command relationships – and as a challenge
to the principle of unity of command. In a letter to Freeland in late
November 1969, enclosing notes of the conversation, Baker stated
emphatically: *"The principle that we must stick to is that at any one time
there can be only one security boss."* And until the RUC were back to
being "keepers of the peace" and the troops were in the background,
he added, *"that boss must be the GOC."* Furthermore, "I would never
agree to soldiers operating under command of the Inspector General."[120] Nor did he favour a system of dual command.

The CGS won the day, and the battle over command and control
subsided for the time being. But it was not over because, while Young
wanted to end military control of operations, he refused to allow the
RUC to engage in riot control duties in the army's place.[121] So, the
issues raised during the initial deployment would resurface frequently during the next five years.

That deployment had changed the political arena in another significant way. Remarkably, it was the one major change that no one
had raised during the cabinet, committee, or other meetings or in the
many memos and other communications. Perhaps it was so implicitly understood that it required no discussion. Simply put, because Parliament exercised ultimate responsibility for the armed forces, having
London ministries and ministers in charge of security in Northern

Ireland opened the door for parliamentarians to enter the security policy debate.

Silent partners no longer, they could and did ask questions that ministers had not been able to answer before.[122] After returning from the summer recess they posed questions and offered comments to the PM and his ministers on the use of troops, command relationships, security policy, and the future of policing in the province, including the fate of the B-Specials.[123] For example, on command and control one MP remarked astutely, "Dual control will not be easy. It will be a very delicate business, and we cannot hope that it will be effective very quickly."[124] Asked about the possible duration of the army's deployment, Secretary Healey was forced to concede that "this, I fear, will take a good deal longer than next winter."[125]

Engaging Parliament did not alter the policy- and decision-making process, which still lay in the hands of cabinet, its committees, the ministries, and the military chain of command. But forcing the prime minister and his cabinet members to respond to questions brought the process and its results partly out from the secret corridors of Whitehall and into the public domain. Now that troops were on the streets, in a very real sense Parliament was there looking over their shoulders.

4

Operation Demetrius: Internment, 1971

In the early hours of 9 August 1971, British troops launched Operation Demetrius: a massive detention operation intended to "decapitate" the IRA. They detained 342 people in the first twenty-four hours (and nearly 2,000 more over the next four years). However, the security forces quickly determined that their intelligence was flawed: fewer than 100 of those arrested that first day had any connection to the IRA, and 116 had none at all. The latter were quickly released. Meanwhile, the key leaders of the movement had evaded capture. Worse still, in the wake of internment the nationalist communities in Northern Ireland were angry and resentful, IRA recruiting increased dramatically, and violence escalated.[1] Catholic hostility to internment and to the security forces was then sharpened further by revelations that some detainees had been subjected to harsh interrogation techniques that bordered on torture.[2] The consensus is that interment was a political disaster that changed the nature of the conflict.[3] Even the army's official narrative of the Northern Ireland campaign describes Operation Demetrius as an "operational level reverse."[4]

What is intriguing about internment is that it was conducted *against* the advice of the force ordered to carry it out: the army.[5] As will be shown, both the general officer commanding and the chief of the general staff opposed it as being unnecessary. Yet, they carried it out as directed. This operation, more than any other single event in the Northern Ireland campaign up to 1974, exposed a sharp split between the army and its political masters over a significant strategic and operational decision. Politicians too were divided on the issue. Those in London were opposed, while the Northern Ireland government favoured it, largely to ensure its survival in power. Because Stormont was still responsible for security in the province, and London did not want to take on the task of governing the province, the former's views prevailed.

INTERNMENT:
A BLUNT WEAPON OF REPRESSION

Simply put, internment consists of detaining people indefinitely without charge and without due process of prosecution, trial, and conviction. In 1971 it was not a new method of conflict containment either in Ireland or in Britain's colonial experience. It had been used frequently in Britain's postwar counter-insurgency campaigns, generating mixed results and an abundance of controversy. In campaigns such as those in Palestine and Kenya, it yielded ugly (and not wholly undeserved) comparisons with concentration camps.[6] As such, it was seen as a symbol of the worst vestiges of colonialism.

Internment also had its own troubled history in the Irish context. The Civil Authorities (Special Powers) Act had legalized it as one of many repressive methods for maintaining law and order that were introduced in Northern Ireland to prevent a recurrence of the IRA.[7] Ironically, the Irish Free State/Republic also used it for the same reason.[8] Both governments had applied it with success in the 1950s to contain the IRA's "Border Campaign."[9] As one of the powers exercised under the hated SPA, internment long had the effect of cowing the Catholic nationalist population in the North into submission to Protestant dominance.[10] Within the nationalist community it was a deeply resented hot button that was likely to yield a violent response.

THE POLITICAL AND SECURITY CONTEXT

The context in which internment took place had changed in three significant ways from that of the period of the initial troop deployment. First, after a general election in June 1970 the Conservative Party took power in London, and Edward Heath became prime minister. Heath had not intended Northern Ireland to be a priority; he had intended (and tried) to focus on British entry into the European Economic Community. Like his predecessors he regarded the Irish problem with distaste and sought to avoid deeper involvement.[11] Home Secretary

Reginald Maudling apparently shared that view. Sir Frank Cooper, who had served in both the Ministry of Defence and the Northern Ireland Office, later opined of Maudling that, "I don't think he showed any signs of wishing to probe into the problems of Ireland ... and he thought that the less we got mixed up in it the better."[12] Similarly, former home secretary James Callaghan later criticized him for being "too laid back" to provide the kind of daily supervision Northern Ireland required.[13] While Callaghan's comments could be dismissed as partisan, his views together with those of Cooper lend weight to the reflections of Lt. Gen. Freeland. He later said that when the Conservatives took over he felt that they "took a long time to get to grips with the situation and I felt a lack of guidance rather than a letup in 'back seat driving.'"[14] Although there was no immediate change in security policy upon Heath's election, over the next year events forced the Ulster crisis onto his agenda, and security policy took centre stage.[15]

Second, the context was changed by decisions and actions of both the IRA and the army.[16] When the IRA split at the end of 1969 into the Official and Provisional factions, the latter committed itself to reasserting the primacy of traditional "physical force republicanism." It planned to use violence, first to defend the Catholic population against the Protestant militants, and ultimately to force the British to withdraw from the North and allow reunification with the South. It launched a bombing campaign in 1970, and in February 1971 began attacking the British Army. The army, aware that the IRA was building its arsenal with the intent of eventually attacking them, had tried to pre-empt them with an intensive arms search and curfew in the Falls Road section of Belfast on 3–5 July 1970. But the searches and curfew alienated the Catholic population and spurred the IRA to defend its base. The interaction of these opposing forces led to escalating violence in early 1971.[17] As the CLF, Maj. Gen. Anthony Farrar-Hockley, said at the time, the "battle has been joined with the Provisional IRA. It is not war but is definitely battle."[18]

The third way in which the context in Northern Ireland was changing was that this IRA activity exerted a negative influence on the government of Northern Ireland. Under pressure from his own Ulster Unionist Party (UUP), which in September 1970 passed a vote of no confidence in his law and order policies, Stormont PM James Chichester-Clark repeatedly asked the British government to take a firmer line on security issues, but London refused to do so. The UUP was also largely opposed to his reformist path. Unable to reconcile his party to the policies, Chichester-Clark resigned in March 1971.[19] He was replaced by Brian Faulkner, who, while claiming to support a reformist position, continued to give priority to increased security force action against the IRA.[20] This response was driven largely by the internal politics of the UUP. Just as it had for Chichester-Clark, these political considerations weakened Faulkner's position and limited his room to manoeuver. In an extended dispatch to Home Secretary Reginald Maudling on 11 June 1971, Howard Smith, the UK representative in Northern Ireland, noted that many unionists did not trust Faulkner and that they agreed with the charge by Ian Paisley (who, Smith said, had his own reasons for undermining Faulkner) that the Stormont PM had not defeated the IRA. In Smith's view this pressure from his own political base had led Faulkner to overemphasize security at the expense of reform. Yet, the more he talked about security (forgetting, in Smith's opinion, the wise advice of the military that it would be a long task with many "ups and downs"), the more his critics pointed to what they saw as inadequate results.[21]

Ironically, as Faulkner's options narrowed, so did those of the Heath government. In August 1971 it was confronted with a Hobson's choice: internment or direct rule. The former was seen at the time as the lesser of two evils. But as will be shown later in this study, it is clear (though only in retrospect) that the decision to approve the internment operation merely postponed the imposition of direct rule to a time when the conditions were much less to London's advantage.

THE COMMAND AND CONTROL CONTEXT

In April 1970 Chichester-Clark called Lt. Gen. Freeland in for a meeting to ask, among other things, whether he "felt in any way inhibited in taking decisions because of policy decisions or orders eminating [sic] from London."[22] The GOC denied any such limits and defended the army's refusal to take "aggressive action," which he thought would only make matters worse. The army could restore order, but maintaining the law was a police function. He felt that the army was a vehicle through which the RUC could "travel to 'public acceptability.'"[23] Robert Porter, the Stormont minister of home affairs, insisted that "wrong-doers" had to be apprehended. The GOC pointed out that the local population was protecting them, and that, consequently, the army was faced with a difficult choice: to pursue them or not. Doing so could risk causing a larger disturbance, which might yield negative publicity on television. Freeland returned again to the problem of policing. He noted that it would take time for the public to accept new police methods but that, once they did, the arrest of perpetrators would help the situation.[24] Freeland was not being wholly candid. As noted previously, he was constrained both by directives and political concerns from London.

In November 1970, some four months after the curfew and arms search in the Lower Falls area of Belfast had effectively ended the honeymoon between the army and the Catholic population (and brought about Porter's resignation),[25] Stormont and London revisited the issue of the army's powers and who had the authority to direct them. The discussion focused on the question of authority to conduct searches of homes for arms: did the GOC require ministerial approval before such a search could be launched? It was not an idle question, either politically or operationally. As the July searches showed, such operations could have significant negative political impacts. Yet, if the GOC had to seek approval for every search, his operational freedom of action would be seriously limited at a time when the IRA was starting to emerge as a threat.

In a 9 November letter to Sir Philip Allen at the Home Office, Arthur Hockaday at the MOD said that Allen had told him on the 6th that the home secretary had confirmed that, apart from unspecified "exceptional circumstances," no searches were to be undertaken without prior reference to *ministers* (presumably both the home and defence secretaries). This apparently was confirmed in a letter from the GOC to Chichester-Clark earlier that week. The GOC stated that the restriction had been imposed after the Falls Road searches in July.[26] Hockaday said the GOC was referring to the minutes of the 13 July meeting of the ministerial committee on Northern Ireland, to the effect that, "in view of the gravity of the political implications involved, the security authorities should not, without reference to Ministers in London, initiate any action to search for arms in the Bogside [in Londonderry] or re-establish civil control over the area."[27] Hockaday added that, in summing up, Heath had said that "the political implications of searches or other security operations in the Bogside, *or in any Roman Catholic areas*, were potentially so serious that no action of this kind should be taken without previous reference to Ministers in London."[28]

That position had not changed in the subsequent four months. An exchange of messages followed over the next several weeks, in which the HO, defence secretariat, general staff, the minister of state, and the defence secretary provided input on the matter.[29] The final result was a relatively brief note from Maudling to Chichester-Clark on 2 December 1970 that clarified the GOC's search powers. It said that he had discretion to search for arms or people "without prior authority" in cases where there was specific intelligence indicating arms would be found at a particular location or if objects had been thrown from the premises at soldiers. However, if the GOC wished to mount a major search he would be required to seek ministerial permission, as the ministers had to take responsibility "for authorizing action which might have far reaching effects on the total security situation."[30] If a major search was needed on very short notice, the GOC would have permission to conduct the search, but this was seen as a "remote contingency," since the time required to mount an operation would be sufficient to permit consultation.[31]

Following disturbances and consequent arms searches in the Ballymurphy area of Belfast in early January 1971, the home secretary felt compelled to clarify his position yet again, in the event that further searches in that area were deemed necessary. Small-scale searches (not exceeding twenty to twenty-five houses per night) would not require prior consultation, but larger planned operations would. At that moment he preferred that the latter be avoided unless there was a resumption of shooting at troops.[32] During a meeting in London on 18 January Chichester-Clark suggested that, subject to veto from London, Stormont should be permitted to tell the army what to do "in given circumstances," but Defence Secretary Carrington "turned him down flat."[33]

Three things are apparent from the discussions of November 1970 through January 1971. First, the political leadership in London was determined to ensure that it retained control of major security operations. Second, the leadership was explicit about the political reasons for doing so. Finally, these two points arose from the Catholic reaction to the Falls Road searches, which seems to have shaken the politicians' confidence in their control of the army.[34]

In a meeting on 26 January 1971, held at a time when violence was escalating in Ulster,[35] the COSC took note of the growing divergence between London and Stormont over security policy. Stormont wanted the GOC to be authorized to conduct more search operations. Lt. Gen. Sir Cecil Blacker (standing in for the CGS) observed that, "whereas the Army at present were trying to de-escalate the situation by playing it as quietly as possible ... the Northern Ireland government considered that a tougher line should be taken ... *This was a fundamental difference of view.*"[36]

The following month the COSC issued to the GOC a new directive, the timing of which suggests it was intended to remind him whence his authority derived. It stated that he was responsible to the CDS and, while he was to work "in closest cooperation" with Stormont, "in the event of any disagreement with the Northern Ireland Government you are *at once* to refer the matter to the Ministry of Defence."[37] This directive required him to keep the CGS informed on all major issues, re-emphasizing London's ultimate authority. It stated that unless urgent operational considerations made it impossible, he was to obtain guidance from the MOD "on any matters which, in your opinion or that of Her Majesty's representative's in Northern Ireland, *have political implications of concern* to HMG [Her Majesty's Government] or which concern any major redeployment of your forces."[38]

Chichester-Clark continued to press London for many more troops and more robust action, with limited success. In his final request before resigning in March 1971, he played the *après moi le déluge* card. In response the ministerial committee approved the dispatch of some additional troops, "not so much because these reinforcements were essential from a strictly military point of view as *because they might help to ensure the political survival of the Northern Ireland Administration, which it was in our interest to sustain.*"[39] Chichester-Clark received a commitment for more rapid and robust reaction to incidents.[40] But the committee concluded that it was being "played," with pressure being brought to bear through official means and the press, and agreed that it would have to be wary of such manipulation in future.[41]

Nevertheless, the pressure from Stormont was unrelenting. Faulkner's first meeting upon becoming the Northern Ireland prime minister was with the new GOC, Lt. Gen. Sir Harry Tuzo. Faulkner's memoir says they shared some common perspectives on the security problem:- that the escalation of violence had to be stopped and that the army could not just stand by – it had to "seek out and destroy the terrorist" – but that any action it took must be guided by policy. For his part Tuzo advised Faulkner that the "minimum force" approach was not just a policy that could be changed at any time but a legal obligation imposed on soldiers as citizens. He showed the PM the general orders under which the army operated (the new directive issued in February) and then suggested some new measures. Faulkner says that by the end of the discussion he "was convinced that really effective progress could be made."[42] But, as always, the internment option loomed in the background, even if unspoken.

PLANNING INTERNMENT: POLITICS TRUMPS SECURITY

In his otherwise impressive study of internment, *Operation Demetrius*, Martin McCleery gives short shrift to the civil-military decision-making process.[43] Yet, like the initial deployment of troops in 1969, internment had been preceded by months of debate and planning. Under the SPA, Stormont had the authority to introduce it and "in theory" could have done so at any time of its own choosing without the agreement of the British government. However, since the army was already heavily committed to internal security operations in the province and probably would be needed to guard internees, "it was accepted by both governments that internment would not be introduced without such agreement."[44] It also would be politically sensitive. This point was acknowledged when Home Affairs Minister Porter raised the matter at a meeting of the Stormont cabinet in July 1970. He noted that the option was kept under constant review, but also that the view thus far had been that the "adverse repercussions would outweigh any likely benefit."[45]

Chichester-Clark was asked publicly over subsequent months whether Stormont was considering internment, and his standard reply was that if the GOC and the chief constable recommended it he would act immediately, but they had not done so. His position shifted the onus of decision-making responsibility onto the security forces, which left them – and London –dissatisfied. The internment option raised both practical and political issues that the Home Office's Northern Ireland department attempted to address in a brief prepared for a meeting between Chichester-Clark and Heath in mid-February 1971.[46] By that time the internment option also had been raised several times in Parliament.[47]

First and foremost the HO brief addressed the practical matter of accommodating detainees. At the time, the estimate of people likely to be detained was 350–450, and there were no adequate facilities to hold them. In December 1970 Stormont had asked the British government if HMS *Maidstone* (a naval vessel anchored in Belfast Lough, then in use as a base for troops) potentially might be used as holding centre. Neither the home nor the defence secretary viewed this as an attractive proposal; among other things, the optics were not good. If it was to be used, it should be for as short a time as possible.[48]

Then there were the questions of operational effectiveness and political effects. The GOC and the chief constable believed that if all the known activists were picked up others currently unknown would fill the vacancies. Moreover, internment would boost IRA recruitment and would bring an end to ongoing criminal investigations already hindered by the "wall of silence" that surrounded cases involving the nationalists.[49]

What the Home Office proposed was that the British government tell Chichester-Clark that it had authorized a contingency study of (as opposed to a plan for) the practical aspects of internment. While there was some risk that members of his government would use knowledge of this study to push for internment on the first pretext, the paper noted that the Stormont PM was well aware of the domestic and international repercussions of such action.[50]

This last point was borne out in the meeting on 13 February, which came a week after the first British soldier had been killed by an IRA sniper. In response to this attack, and clearly playing to his party's hard-liners, Chichester-Clark had proclaimed that, "Northern Ireland is at war with the Provisional IRA."[51] Still, in the London meeting he was more circumspect. He restated his own opposition to internment as well as that of the police. He said that it would bring the crowds back out into the streets, give new life to the civil rights movement, and increase the risk of political kidnappings. He foresaw three possible situations that might make internment inevitable: if it were introduced in the Irish Republic; if the IRA launched a campaign of political assassination; or if it proved impossible otherwise to break the nationalists' "wall of silence" that shielded IRA suspects from prosecution. That said, and notwithstanding the need to consult with the British government, Chichester-Clark reiterated a basic position: that it was up to Stormont to decide whether to use internment. Heath refused to be drawn on that point. Instead, he reflected more widely on whether the security situation had shifted enough to warrant a change in the security forces' strategy to regain "tactical advantage."[52] The meeting ended inconclusively.

Just prior to Chichester-Clark's next (and final) meeting with the British government, the IRA killed three off-duty soldiers. Historian Thomas Hennessey asserts that this event was "a watershed" for Chichester-Clark; his morale and that of his ministers declined noticeably thereafer. Some 4,000 Belfast shipyard workers marched on his party headquarters to demand internment of IRA leaders.[53] A few days later, on 15 March, GEN 47, Heath's cabinet committee on Northern Ireland, produced a paper on internment. It noted that, while there was no great demand for it at the moment, continuing interest could produce a climate in which Stormont felt compelled to persuade the British government to agree to take that step. However, if faced by "prolonged and intensified terrorism," London itself might itself conclude that internment was "the least damaging way to counter it."[54] The paper then laid out the pros and cons of internment. On the plus side the security forces had reliable information about "a number of dangerous men," and the normal processes of criminal investigation were being obstructed by the "wall of silence."[55] Weighing against it were several important considerations: it would be "politically damaging internally and internationally"; there was no guarantee that all of the "dangerous men" could be identified, and in any case they might be replaced by others unknown to the authorities; it would stimulate recruitment to the IRA; the Catholic minority might rally around the IRA; and experience elsewhere suggested that interning people who could be seen as "political prisoners" was likely to lead to hostage taking.[56] The contingency study authorized earlier had concluded that the only practical location to hold detainees would be a military camp in the province. Two (Ballykinler and Long Kesh) were available, but neither was wholly suitable, and the latter would require some construction.[57]

It is clear that the committee felt that the negatives outweighed the positives. The Northern Ireland PM (unaware of the committee paper's contents) raised the topic of internment in a meeting with the home secretary on 16 March, noting that the head of RUC Special Branch was leaning in favour of it. However, more concerned with a perceived need for immediate resolute tactical action by the security forces, he did not pursue the matter.[58] As noted earlier, the British government's refusal to approve increased tactical action (which did not include internment) prompted his resignation.

The next day MI5 offered its views on internment to the Home Office. Drawing on unspecified experience (but possibly referring to

Operation Anvil in Nairobi, Kenya, in 1954), the security service suggested that it be applied only to the Belfast area, and that it include persons belonging or suspected of belonging to either the IRA or the Ulster Volunteer Force. Limiting the policy to the one urban area would indicate the government's intention to use it sparingly. The service thought it would "drive out a considerable number of troublemakers and terrorists from Belfast."[59] The Irish Republic had used the strategy to similar effect. MI5 thought that the terrorists could not operate with the same degree of confidence outside the Belfast ghettos. But it also conceded that this approach would increase security problems (including more bombings) in the rest of the province and drive some suspects into deeper hiding in Belfast. How the HO responded to the security service brief is not known.[60]

During the course of an intergovernmental meeting on security policy on 1 April, the new Northern Ireland PM, Brian Faulkner, insisted that he would not agree to any proposal to use internment *"unless he was advised by the Army and the police that internment would bring IRA terrorism decisively to an end."*[61] He emphasized that he, the GOC and the chief constable of the RUC were all opposed to it. In the meantime, however, he felt it was prudent to have plans in place, and the meeting then discussed plans for using Long Kesh military camp as an internment site.[62] The HO and the MOD followed up on the latter issue.[63] Faulkner's emphatic statement about internment was certainly consistent with British and Stormont policy at the time but stands out in striking contrast to the way internment later came to be used and justified.

While the period from April to the end of June was relatively quiet, by July 1971 bombings and shootings had each exceeded 300 incidents. Fifty-five people had been killed and over 600 hospitalized. Riots in Derry (Londonderry) had led to two civilian deaths.[64] An editorial in the *Times* in mid-July pointed to "a sustained campaign of violence by terrorists" that was creating "a political atmosphere in which it is hard for moderate men to act with discretion."[65] Faulkner was under a lot of pressure from the Protestant majority and his own party to introduce internment. He, in turn, sought the agreement of London for this step.[66] By July the British government itself was being bombarded with questions in Parliament on Northern Ireland from across the political spectrum, though it was not until 29 July that even strident unionist Ian Paisley asked the home secretary whether internment was under consideration. He received no answer to that question.[67]

In his memoirs Faulkner says that the bombings in Belfast in mid-July "tipped the scales and I took the decision that we must operate internment. No one objected, and we started to discuss the mechanics of the operation."[68] McCleery writes that it was the bombing of the *Daily Mirror* offices – the most costly to date – that led Faulkner to that decision. He worried that the business community was losing confidence.[69] However, the documentary record does not support such a direct cause-and-effect decision-making process. Nor does it support Faulkner's claim that there was no objection. The process was more complex and more controversial than Faulkner suggests.

In a meeting at the HO on 15 July, representatives of the Northern Ireland government, the army, and the MOD reviewed the state of contingency planning for internment. The Stormont officials (from home affairs and the GSU) explained that planning had begun but had not been taken very far, partly to preserve security and partly because the scale of the operation had not yet been determined. The army attendees said that Special Branch had drawn up a list of 325 to 375 names, but only 20–40 per cent of these might be picked up in the initial operation. They expected that the initial sweep would take forty-eight hours. The army and the branch noted that there was likely to be a shortage of interrogators. Much of the meeting was taken up with the question of where to house the detainees, since this would require both space and staffing adjustments. The chair of the meeting, an HO official, urged the group to draft a detailed contingency plan in time for the next meeting on 20 August.[70] In the event, Operation Demetrius began before that date.

The Public Records Office of Northern Ireland contains a "Contingency Plan for Internment," which may be the one requested above.[71] A key relevant point in this document is that it states clearly how the decision to launch the operation would be taken. The Northern Ireland minister of home affairs would make the decision, acting on the "advice tendered to the Joint Security Committee by the General Officer Commanding and the Chief Constable," and "before doing so [he] will consult the Home Secretary and the Northern Ireland Cabinet."[72] It is worth recalling as well Faulkner's commitment in March that he would introduce internment only if the army and the police advised that it would bring IRA terrorism to an end.

This key operating assumption was at odds with the prevailing reality. The GOC, Lt. Gen. Tuzo, supported by his minister, Lord Carrington, opposed internment, arguing that other measures, such as harassing and arresting known IRA members, should be tried first. At the very least London wanted to postpone any drastic action until after the Protestant Apprentice Boys march on 12 August.[73] According to a paper written later by Lt. Col. David Ramsbotham, then military assistant (MA) to the CGS, Gen. Sir Michael Carver, the latter also opposed internment and even Faulkner himself appeared to be against it. Ramsbotham suggests that Faulkner recognized the effect it would have on the Catholic population but also that the British government would insist on a quid pro quo: a ban on marches that inevitably would alienate a large, albeit more extreme, element of his own party. For his part Faulkner claims that he also received many letters from members of the Catholic communities demanding tougher measures to "get these terrorists off our backs,"[74] but he does not say that they were asking for internment.

In a 20 July telegram to the HO, Howard Smith noted the high levels of violence and expressed doubt that the army's new security measures (discussed below) would reduce it to "tolerable levels." He stressed the growing public pressure on Faulkner, "who is in serious difficulties with his cabinet," which was strongly demanding internment; Faulkner himself was now seeing it as "the only answer." Smith argued that using internment might give London the chance to avoid worse outcomes: continuing violence, and the prospect of Stormont's collapse, which would lead to direct rule.[75] That was not idle scare mongering. The nationalist Social Democratic and Labour Party (SDLP) had decided to withdraw its thirteen members from Stormont and was threatening to set up a rival assembly to give non-unionists a voice. It justified this move on the grounds that both London and Stormont were refusing to hold an official inquiry into two fatal army shootings of civilians in Derry, which had led to major rioting there.[76]

In the British cabinet meeting on the 22nd Home Secretary Reginald Maudling said the situation in Northern Ireland gave "serious cause for concern." In his view, Faulkner's firm control had been weakened by the effects that the Londonderry riots and IRA terrorism were having on the right wing of the Ulster Unionist Party. "The boldness and efficiency of IRA operations were creating fresh alarm."[77] Faulkner was asking the British government to take more drastic action.

Maudling reported that the GOC intended shortly to introduce measures "which were likely to demonstrate the government's determination to suppress terrorism."[78] He felt the situation was such that cabinet had to seriously contemplate that Britain might be forced to introduce direct rule. During discussion cabinet agreed that direct rule should be the last resort, and *"before it was adopted it might well be right to agree that the Northern Ireland Government should invoke their powers of internment."*[79] Heath wrapped up discussion by saying that the cabinet committee would meet soon to consider the steps needed to deal with the situation. The cabinet had delegated to the committee the authority to take decisions on the Northern Ireland issue.[80]

In the short term, the security forces tried Tuzo's approach: harassing and arresting known IRA members. After discussing this idea with Carrington on 19 July, Carver sent a request on the 22nd for permission to conduct Operation Linklater, to begin the next day. In the same document the CGS also asked for – and apparently received – blanket permission for further operations "particularly on or about 10 August." Likewise, the MOD approved requests for additional units, ostensibly for the harassment operation and to cover the 12 August march, but obviously in preparation for internment as well.[81]

Maudling announced Operation Linklater publicly on the 23rd, giving it – in Carver's view – more significance than it warranted. The home secretary said that it "marks the beginning of a new phase in the battle against the IRA ... Its significance is that it lays stress on the fact that the function of the security forces is not merely to contain disorder and violence, but to search out the men and the organization responsible. This will serve as further confirmation of the determination ... to maintain the constitutional position of Northern Ireland as enacted in the Government of Ireland Act, 1949, by whatever means necessary."[82] The last sentence was undoubtedly inserted to reassure nervous unionists that Britain was not about to abandon the province and allow unification with the republic.

Operation Linklater consisted of two phases. In the first, starting at dawn on the 23rd, about 2,000 troops carried out raids in Belfast and nine other towns, detaining twenty persons, mostly members of the Official IRA. The second phase consisted of predawn raids on the 27th by some 1,800 troops and police. They entered the homes of suspected IRA sympathizers in seven areas in Belfast and in nine other towns, detaining forty-eight people for questioning. The results were not impressive: a handful of weapons found and twenty men brought to prosecution. The CGS reported to Carrington on 28 July that Tuzo felt Linklater had been "worthwhile," although in a paradoxical way. It had shown two important things: that the Special Branch lists were inaccurate and that the existing legal system could not deal effectively with the IRA. Since the group was not illegal, arrested members had to be released on bail, at which time they took refuge in the Irish Republic, out of reach of British law. Furthermore, it appeared that the IRA had been warned of what was planned and had taken precautions. The CGS also learned that the GOC might not have been fully "in the loop" on Linklater. One morning, when shown a sitrep on search results from the previous night, the GOC indicated that he had not known about that particular search; apparently, the CLF had planned it with a senior army intelligence officer at HQNI without consulting the GOC.[83] The minister of state for defence later said that Linklater caused political trouble out of proportion to the results and even those who supported firm action were critical of the fact that those arrested had to be released immediately.[84]

Faulkner called Maudling on the 28th to say he was pleased with the army's "swoop operation" but emphasized that it would have to be repeated to yield benefits. He said that, if it were seen to be a single operation, "there would be a backlash of the gravest consequences."[85] He probably was warning that, without follow-up, Protestant extremists might see the army effort as ineffectual and thus take matters into their own hands. He went on to say that "every one of his cabinet colleagues" felt that the time had come to use internment, and that he was coming around to that position himself, but he had told them that he would not ask for it until he had received advice from "those professionally concerned with security."[86] Maudling replied that it was right to try other initiatives first, such as Linklater and other swoop operations. Faulkner agreed, "provided that these operations were pursued with the utmost vigour."[87]

That same day Cabinet Secretary Burke Trend asked the cabinet committee on Northern Ireland to consider two questions: how effective internment might be if limited to the North without simultaneous action by the Irish Republic, and how Britain might secure such cooperation from the republic. Heath took the view that if internment was (as it was usually portrayed) the "last stop before direct rule," then it should not be implemented until "we are compelled to."[88] On the issue of effectiveness he noted that cabinet was concerned about the question of timing. It had suggested that internment should precede direct rule, if only to avoid the embarrassment of having to introduce later a measure that had been denied to the government that direct rule had replaced. But this assumed that events would proceed in an orderly fashion, which he conceded might not be the case. The matter of the republic was much more delicate. The PM felt that Britain would have to take into account the views of the Irish PM, Jack Lynch, and that the timing of requesting his cooperation would require some diplomatic finesse to avoid either giving offence or risking a leak about the operation.[89]

The GOC told the committee the following day that the army did not have the full cooperation of the RUC and that, since the police were unwilling to hold IRA members for the full period allowed under the SPA, "the harassing operations would soon begin to lose their effect as a demonstration of the Army's resolution to eradicate terrorism."[90] But the committee deferred any decision on a proposed marching ban until Faulkner's attitude was known and until the British government had learned whether the government of the Irish republic was prepared to launch an internment operation of its own in return for a ban of marches in the North.[91]

While the focus of this study is Northern Ireland, it is important to acknowledge that out of necessity the British government had to deal with many issues simultaneously. At the end of July 1971, the parliamentary order paper was crowded with a wide range of domestic, economic, and foreign policy problems. Northern Ireland was only one of these, and it was not necessarily seen as the most important. A workers' takeover at the Upper Clyde shipyards, brought on by the government's decision not to save the yards from closure, garnered far more attention in Parliament at this time than did Northern Ireland. And while the Ulster situation apparently was not seen as sufficiently serious to keep the PM from commencing his summer holiday, the shipyard crisis was a different matter: Heath quickly returned to London to deal with it.[92] Northern Ireland did not regain centre stage in Parliament until the debate on adjournment on 5 August. The tone of discussion then was testy, possibly heightened by IRA threats to settle the conflict "once and for all."[93] Nationalist MPs blamed Stormont for the rising violence while some unionists called for a new security force to help keep order. Former home secretary James Callaghan, who led off the debate in a civil tone, reflected on the IRA's "declaration of War" and the army's changing role as it was drawn into a counterterrorism campaign. He asked the serving home secretary directly what the army's opinion was regarding internment. Maudling declined to answer.[94]

Despite the threats and the impending showdown with Stormont over security policy, the government did not postpone Parliament's summer recess. This might appear as a cynical ploy to ensure that it could introduce internment without facing acrimonious parliamentary debate. But the opposition parties did not ask for an extension of the sitting, and even at this late stage the government was seeking to avoid taking what is saw as a drastic step.[95] On 2 August Defence Secretary Carrington had met with the minister of state, Gen. Carver, and Arthur Hockaday mainly to discuss internment, which was expected to be the major focus of a forthcoming visit by Faulkner. While there was some suggestion that Maudling was coming around to favour it, Carrington discounted the idea. He asked the CGS to consult the GOC on his position. Carrington emphasized that the military advice on the issue must be objective; the GOC was not to be asked his views in a way that made it appear he was expected to advise in favour. The CGS reported later that Tuzo was still opposed to it.[96] Heath's autobiography claims, however, that the GOC conceded that there were compelling grounds for it, such as IRA intimidation of witnesses.[97]

The official record does not support Heath's recollections. In a brief minute to key MOD officials the same day, Hockaday summarized the gist of Carver's conversation with Lt. Gen. Tuzo. The GOC said that he did not recommend internment on military grounds; he considered it "militarily unnecessary."[98] Nor was Faulkner demanding it (the GOC had spoken to him that morning). But Faulkner had warned that unless something produced "decisive results fairly rapidly" he would be "cut down."[99] The GOC had several other military options available but he did not think that he could "produce sufficiently rapidly the military effect that he believed necessary for political purposes."[100] We can see here a subtle but significant shift in the GOC's perception of the goal of security force efforts: from countering terrorism and enhancing security to propping up Stormont politically. Heath's memoir makes no mention of this shift.

Tuzo went on to say that combining internment with a ban on marches would not change his opinion. He thought it best that the

Apprentice Boys march be allowed to go ahead, since banning it would be seen as a victory for the IRA. Internment could be introduced at a later stage. However, if the two actions were to be combined, it would be best to introduce internment before the marching ban – that is, a few days before 12 August. This document also contained a handwritten note to the defence secretary saying that Howard Smith was "surprised" that Tuzo was as firmly opposed to internment as indicated in the minute.[101] This is itself surprising, since the GOC's views were not newly formed and were well known within the MOD and the cabinet. It suggests a lack of effective communication between Tuzo and Smith and also between the latter and officials in London. It may also be indicative of the views of some officials (expressed later) that Smith, who later became the head of MI5, had a reputation as a "weak man" who was seen as being too close to the Ulster Catholics.[102]

The shift in the rationale for internment was also apparent in the DMO's 3 August debriefing of Maj. Gen. Farrar-Hockley, who had just relinquished his post as CLF at HQNI. According to a Foreign Office (FO) official who attended the debrief, Farrar-Hockley made a compelling case for internment, arguing that Operation Linklater had "rattled" the IRA, that its command structure was poor, and that arresting some leaders (whom he named) would do "substantial damage" to the movement. He also felt that mid-level IRA members would give up a "substantial intelligence dividend."[103] When confronted with Tuzo's view that it was not militarily necessary, Farrar-Hockley agreed, saying that the army would continue "cutting the IRA down" even without internment. However, he asserted that "the question was ultimately political: would the politicians' will to govern not erode faster" if internment were not introduced?[104] The FO official then noted that Carrington was determined to ensure that the Northern Ireland politicians took responsibility for internment and should not be allowed to let the army take the blame for it. This meant that while internment should not be adopted as the result of unionist pressure, arguments about "military" and "political" grounds would have to be spelt out.[105] Thus, however reluctantly, even Carrington seemed to be acknowledging that such an operation might become necessary for political reasons.

That same day the CGS met with the ministerial committee at Number 10. Asked for his opinion on the Apprentice Boys march, he said it should be allowed to go ahead and that there was no need for internment at that time. The committee concluded that if Faulkner asked for internment it would be granted only if the GOC recommended it on military grounds. The GOC was asked to prepare a paper specifying the criteria for such a recommendation. Another paper would cover all aspects of internment.[106]

The latter paper covered familiar ground: first, the pros and cons of internment. Foremost among the pros was that it would show Faulkner's supporters that he was determined to suppress violence. It was also expected to lead to the detention of "a substantial number of known dangerous men" and thus lead to a lessening of tension. Finally, it would break the nationalists' "wall of silence" that protected the gunmen and thus could yield information that would lead to convictions. Against these benefits lay the GOC's opposition; the inability to remove all the "dangerous men," and the likelihood that they would be replaced; the prospect that the Catholics would rally around the IRA, which itself would resort to reprisals; and the political damage at home and abroad arising from supporting internment.[107]

Second, the military annex addressed procedures for deciding whom to detain and to release and included an appreciation of the likely effects. The latter was contradictory, suggesting on the one hand "a longish quiet period" and on the other preplanned counteractions and reprisals by the IRA and an increasing spread of civil disturbances. This inconsistency reflected the uncertainty about the trajectory of the conflict, which had not evolved in a predictable way. The paper also raised the vexing question of how to present internment publicly. Referring to the security situation would be unavoidable, but the government also would have to acknowledge that the GOC had not recommended the operation on military grounds.[108] In a note to Sir Philip Allen, Hockaday added his own comments on the military aspects, noting that the "package" (internment plus a ban on marches) involved trading a means relevant to only one day for one whose consequences would be of "indefinite duration." He also asked, "if we play the internment card unnecessarily or prematurely, what other cards do we hold short of direct rule?"[109]

The intelligence annex predicted a "substantial intelligence dividend" but noted that those benefits could not be separated from MOD's assessment of the operation's military effectiveness. It anticipated that the operation would pick up IRA members from the senior to the junior levels; the middle and senior ranks would have the most value for intelligence, but the senior "hard cases" might be able to resist sustained interrogation. The annex also suggested that internment might encourage some Catholics to come forward with information, since the operation would reduce the threat of reprisal.[110] But Lt. Col. Clive Brennan, then general staff officer (Grade 1) intelligence at HQNI, recalls that Brigadier Frank Kitson, commander of 39 Brigade, was "really, really upset" by the internment decision because he was certain that all the suspected IRA members his troops had been watching would immediately go underground.[111] In the event, he was proven right.

Maudling sent Faulkner a blunt message on the 4th. While conceding that the decision to enact internment was Faulkner's, Maudling reminded him that it was subject to agreement by London and that Faulkner had committed himself to being guided by the recommendations of the security authorities. London would have no objections if those authorities made the case that internment would help the campaign against the IRA. But for now, the home secretary said, the GOC was not recommending internment on military grounds.[112]

That should have settled the matter. But Maudling then muddied the waters by saying that, having received military advice, the two governments then would have to take into account "the political considerations which are numerous and complex."[113] The MOD concurred on this important point.[114] Maudling went on to acknowledge that Faulkner was under considerable pressure to introduce internment and that it might become necessary. He then discussed when it should be imposed; from London's perspective (based on the GOC's view), that would be after the Apprentice Boys march on 12 August. He invited Faulkner's comments and extended an invitation to discuss it in person, but then dissuaded him by indicating that the publicity surrounding such a visit "would inevitably create a very difficult situation."[115]

Robert Armstrong, Heath's private secretary, understood immediately the implications of Maudling's concerns about a visit by Faulkner. He warned the Heath that "this is beginning to look unpleasantly like Major Chichester-Clark's last visit. The timing is about as bad as it could be in relation to the debate in the House of Commons. Mr. Faulkner will be expected to have brought something back home with him ... Otherwise his own position becomes very weak. If ministers are not prepared to agree to internment, and there is nothing else [to offer him], he had better not come, despite the Home Secretary's agreement that he should."[116] Armstrong went on to add that he felt that Carrington's argument – that internment is a "last fling" – was very persuasive. It should be done only "when you visibly have to, and not before: not as part of a deal for banning marches."[117] He closed by suggesting that Sir Philip Allen be sent to Ulster as a substitute for a visit to London by Faulkner.

Whatever the merits of Armstrong's advice, it soon was overtaken. On 5 August Tuzo called Carver to say that Faulkner had done an about face: he was now prepared to ban the marches and in return to ask for approval for an internment operation. The GOC said that Faulkner had been swayed by a request from several moderate Protestants who had asked that the 12 August march be banned because of the likelihood of trouble. Tuzo himself had not changed his mind about the lack of military necessity for internment but felt that politically Britain had no alternative but to support the request.[118]

Possibly simultaneous to this, Howard Smith sent a detailed telegram to Maudling, making the case for supporting internment. He emphasized the mounting pressure on Faulkner, noting that some cabinet members feared that militant unionists Paisley or Craig would benefit from the fear permeating their constituencies. The two men were saying that internment was not enough and that the RUC had to be rearmed and the B-Specials resurrected. Even some moderate unionists were feeling that eventually "they will have to take matters into their own hands."[119] The IRA's widely publicized threat to settle the conflict by force "once and for all" may have helped inflame such thinking.

Smith went on to note that Stormont believed internment would satisfy these calls for action. Faulkner and his colleagues were concerned about the effects of continued bombings on the business community. In Smith's view Faulkner had come to see the pressures as irresistible, that internment was not only inevitable but "urgently necessary" and that it would "do the trick." If Faulkner did not get internment, Smith said, he will "lose heart ... [He will] cling to office as long as he can but his conversion to reform (which was largely a political calculation) may wear thin." He could suffer defections from the cabinet, making his position "untenable."[120]

Smith's telegram seems to have arrived in time to exert some influence. The GEN 47 committee had received Faulkner's request and took it up at their meeting on the morning of 5 August. The ground was already shifting in favour of internment, largely because of the fear that if the London government failed to support Faulkner on this issue, his position would become, as Smith noted, "untenable." If his government fell, Britain would have to impose direct rule, something Westminster wished to avoid if possible. GEN 47 was coming to see the use of internment as a way to postpone that eventuality. Heath summed up the discussion, noting that whatever the impact of Britain's refusal might have on Faulkner's fate, it would be the British government that would bear responsibility for approving internment. Therefore, the full implications of such a move had to be laid out to Faulkner before a decision was taken.[121]

Faulkner flew to London on the 5th with Tuzo, Sir Graham Shillington (head of the RUC), and their security advisers. Heath, along with Maudling and Carrington, Foreign Secretary Douglas-Home, Sir Philip Allen, and the CGS, met with Faulkner's team later that day. Even the carefully worded formal record can barely disguise the fact that the meeting was tense and confrontational. Heath initially insisted that the price of the British government agreeing to internment would be an indefinite ban on marches, which Faulkner rejected as impractical. Faulkner also said it was unrealistic to expect that the Apprentice Boys march could be banned. Heath countered that without such a ban London would not agree to enact internment. He reminded Faulkner that the GOC had stated that there was no military necessity for internment. "It must therefore be regarded as a political act, which would be thought to be directed against one faction and must … be matched by some political action, in the form of a ban on marches, which would represent its counterpart in relation to the other faction."[122]

Faulkner still balked at a universal ban on marches, pointing out that many small ones passed off without difficulty. He said that Protestants "would regard internment as no more than a merited punishment for the violence of the IRA and their Roman Catholic supporters."[123] They would not see the need for a quid pro quo on their part. Since Stormont needed their support for any reconciliation efforts, it would be foolish to alienate them with an indiscriminate ban.

On his need for Protestant support Faulkner's position was unassailable, and in this respect he had the British government over a barrel. After further discussion the British ministers conceded some ground to Faulkner. They agreed to a ban "until further notice" – initially for a period of six months. Discussion then turned to public presentation of the operation. The British insisted that it would have to be made clear that it was Stormont's decision (after consultation with London) and, since the GOC remained opposed, the decision would have to be justified on the basis of having been made after "all relevant considerations" were weighed. To deal with the "why now" question, it was thought that referring to the recent increase in bombings would be sufficient.[124] This, of course, flew in the face of the GOC's view that the security situation could not justify the move. In summing up, Heath emphasized the need for information security regarding the operation and stressed that Faulkner would have to make it "wholly clear" to his cabinet that British support was contingent upon the ban. Faulkner agreed to "proceed accordingly" and to send a draft of the announcement to the home secretary before its release.[125]

With the conclusion of this meeting, the capitulation of the British government over internment was complete. In effect, London had allowed itself to be blackmailed by Stormont. To postpone one unpalatable political initiative (direct rule), it had agreed to an equally unwelcome one that could not be justified on security grounds and was bound to impact the security situation and to embroil London even deeper in the conflict. Indeed, in a private (and possibly unrecorded) meeting with Faulkner earlier in the day, the British delegates had warned him that if internment failed there were no more intermediate steps. "The next step, and the only remaining step, would be direct rule."[126]

In his paper on internment, Lt. Col. Ramsbotham, who recorded the day's events for the CGS, described the meeting's three hours – and the rest of the day – as "some of the most unreal I have ever spent."[127] The GOC had called Carver's office only that morning to let him know that Faulkner was coming to London to ask for internment. The CGS, who was en route to an official duty in Wales, was contacted and brought back to London. The PM and his advisers first met separately with Faulkner's team, then with the GOC and the CGS, the sequence then being repeated. During their first appearance, Tuzo gave an appreciation of the security situation while Carver repeated his view that the Apprentice Boys march should be allowed to go ahead, subject to changes to the route and with that route guarded. The two generals left, returning to Carver's office while the Stormont delegation was recalled for a second session with Heath's team. "After time for a whisky and soda," Carver and Tuzo were "summoned for the last time to be told that the 12 August march was to be banned and that internment had been authorised for Tuesday 10 August – the GOC must now make the detailed plans."[128]

HQNI drafted the operational instruction for Operation Demetrius on 6 August in cooperation with RUC HQ and the GSU. It followed the standard army planning format, laying out the "situation: enemy and friendly," the mission, the plan for execution of the operation, the tasks for each brigade, coordinating instructions, cover plan, code words, forces allocated, and legal aspects. The implementation of the plan entailed five phases: arrests, transfer of those arrested to regional holding centres (RHCs), Special Branch interviews of each person held at RHCs to determine who would be detained, transfer of detainees to the detention centres, and selection of some for in-depth interrogation.[129]

Tuzo called Carver about 11:00 that morning to say that, in light of speculation by the press (which had seen the GOC and Faulkner arrive at Aldergrove airport the previous evening) and the likelihood of a leak from the RUC, the operation should be moved ahead one day, to the 9th. The GOC had earlier expressed his concern that the planning for internment was not good and that the RUC was less well prepared than he wished. He had wanted to have seventy-two hours to ensure that proper briefings and orders were done at all levels and liaison conducted between the RUC and the army.[130] Moving the operation to the 9th compressed the planning process to the minimum limit. Battalion commanders were to be briefed on the evening of the 6th, their intelligence officers the next day, and company commanders on the 8th, with troops being issued their orders that evening. Despite the tight timelines, the CGS agreed and then went on three weeks leave, delegating the plans to the new CLF, Maj. Gen. Robert Ford, under whose direction "last minute detailed planning took place in a feverish atmosphere."[131] One measure of the haste is that the criteria for deciding which persons to keep in detention and which to release were not drawn up until well after the operation had been completed.[132] This was the Northern Ireland government's responsibility and one of its signal failures.

The failure to establish detainee criteria in advance of the operation redirects our attention to a question raised by recurring references to the arrest lists: how good was the security forces' intelligence on the IRA? Sources already cited suggest that it was insufficient. Ford's testimony to the Bloody Sunday Inquiry lends weight to this view. He had called a meeting at HQNI, attended by his brigade commanders, representatives from the RUC and Special Branch, and the director of military intelligence. He recalled that the list of suspects to be detained "was extremely questionable." There was a lot of argument over who should or should not be on the list. "My Brigade Commanders and I fully realized that the list was doubtful but we also knew we had nothing better to work on."[133]

McCleery examines this issue at some length in his book but leaves the reader with an inconclusive answer. On the one hand, based on his analysis of the numbers of those detained plus the known PIRA who evaded capture (178 did so), he concludes that the arrest lists were less indiscriminate than the conventional wisdom suggests. But he then goes on to say that "the inconsistency of the intelligence was further reflected by the British analysis of the arrests."[134] McCleery reinforces this point by citing an HO document that stated that "a disturbing picture emerges from our own inquiries. Among those detained there is ... a 'hard core', perhaps 80 strong of IRA activists. This includes some very dangerous men. But the total appears to include many cases ... whose republican connections amount to no more than inactive sympathy."[135]

Although the Home Office had not been involved in the selection of detainees because it had no authority over Stormont's use of the internment power, it nonetheless was critical of the vague details and absence of evidence presented in the internment orders to justify the arrests.[136] Towards the end of his chapter on the introduction of internment, McCleery concludes that it "had been introduced with limited intelligence, and, as a consequence, the initial arrest lists were augmented with names of people who were political opponents of Stormont."[137] In short, his book supports the accepted narrative about the inadequate quality of intelligence.

What is striking is that, although Operation Linklater had demonstrated the weaknesses in RUC Special Branch intelligence on the IRA, this did not serve as a brake on planning. If anything, the pace increased; political expediency seemed to give Operation Demetrius a kind of momentum of inevitability that proved unstoppable. In fact, when Faulkner and Heath met again on 19 August to review the situation, the British PM pressed Faulkner to approve a "second lift" of terrorist suspects as soon as possible.[138] The politicians seemed oblivious to the political and security consequences of their actions.

To his credit, however, Faulkner kept his word to the British government. On the morning of the operation he told the press that the decision to impose internment was his, albeit "after weighing all relevant considerations, including the views of the security authorities, and after consultation with Her Majesty's Government."[139] Nonetheless, while emphasizing the "unacceptable" level of violence, his statement did not mention that the GOC had disputed the need for internment on security grounds. Nor, of course, did he concede that it was done to save his government.

AFTERMATH

In his memoirs Reginald Maudling says that "no one could be certain what would be the consequences" of internment.[140] Given the several warnings from the GOC and others before the decision was taken, this assertion does not stand up to scrutiny. In fact, Maudling later contradicts himself by saying that "the effect on the Catholic community, with all its memories, would be bound to be severe."[141] The facts speak for themselves. General Tuzo's worst fears were realized in the aftermath of the internment operation. Riots, shootings, bombings, and arson broke out on an unprecedented scale in the nationalist areas.[142] In spite of Tuzo's efforts to moderate the situation by lowering the profile of the army in those areas, and in stark contrast to Heath's expectation that internment would reduce violence, it escalated rapidly. PIRA leader Sean MacStiofan says that after 9 August the group shifted its strategy from a selective to a widespread bombing campaign and attacks against members of the locally recruited Ulster Defence Regiment (UDR).[143] And internment drove more angry young Catholics into the ranks of the IRA.[144] McCleery says that "it is universally agreed that the introduction of internment resulted in an upsurge in IRA activity," despite Faulkner's denial of this fact.[145]

The other driver of violent opposition was the claim that some of the detainees had been subjected to brutality at the hands of soldiers and police. The press followed up these reports and exposed a more systematic interrogation regime, forcing the British government to appoint an official (Compton) inquiry into the allegations. It transpired that in September and October the security forces had subjected fourteen detainees to "deep interrogation" – five coercive physical and psychological techniques that were meant to persuade the subjects to reveal information. Tony Geraghty states in his book *The Irish War* that these had been used to train British servicemen to resist interrogation in the event of being captured in war and were similar to methods used in previous counter-insurgency campaigns. He says that the army and air force intelligence services provided the interrogators.[146]

The official record at the time clarifies the story. According to Hennessey, who used original official sources, on 17 March 1971 Lt. Col. Brennan handled a query from the RUC Special Branch about interrogation training. The D/INT supported the request for training assistance, and a week later it was discussed at the MOD with representatives from MI5. Discussion focused on the creation of an interrogation centre, but the security service was not prepared to commit to that, so it was agreed that the Joint Services Interrogation Wing (JSIW) at the School of Service Intelligence, Ashford, Kent, would provide the training assistance.[147]

McCleery says that twelve RUC SB inspectors attended the course in April. Records of the GEN 47 meeting on 18 October 1971 confirmed this. Carrington acknowledged that the RUC interrogators (there were twenty in all) were reluctant to use the methods in Northern Ireland, but were induced – either by argument or by (unspecified) pressure by the military personnel present during the interrogations (twelve members of the JSIW) – to do so. They were also reassured that if they followed the instructions "they would not be held responsible if their methods came under criticism."[148]

There was some confusion among senior British officials over the question of who had approved the military's role either in training or supervising the interrogations, and thus the degree of London's complicity and responsibility. Under the SPA the Stormont minister of home affairs had the authority to move detainees between facilities, this apparently constituting "a political endorsement of a need for interrogation (no special *legal* authority is required for the deep interrogation of a person already detained under the Special Powers Acts)."[149] Gen. Carver, the CGS, who was on leave when internment was launched, had not recommended deep interrogation to the SSD. Instead, it was approved by the director general of intelligence in the MOD, who was not in the chain of command reporting to the CGS. Apparently, even Tuzo was unaware of the methods.[150] But Carrington and Maudling had discussed the issue on 10 August and "had acquiesced" in allowing the army to provide "advisory services" for the interrogations that the minister of home affairs was expected to authorize.[151] MOD ministerial approval was required for the provision of army support for each individual interrogation. It was Lord Balneil, the minister of state for defence, who had to give such approvals, and it is clear that he was not happy about it. In a memo to Carrington he wrote, "I have not been involved in the discussions which have led to the arrangements governing the procedures for deep interrogation ... I am not completely satisfied with certain aspects of these arrangements. We seem to be in some danger of losing all control over the use of interrogation by Stormont which, despite the niceties of the political and legal position, would fall to HMG to defend."[152]

He expressed concern that the authority of the Stormont minister of home affairs to move detainees was not "clear and unequivocal" authority to approve interrogation. Balneil also wanted to retain the practice of approving each request for army support, and he sought clarification that such approval was limited to support only and did not constitute approval of the interrogation itself.[153] Carrington later told GEN 47 that he had been advised of the "principles" guiding the process, including medical supervision and assurances that the methods would be applied "humanely" – without "brutal or degrading treatment." It was on this basis that he and Maudling had agreed to the interrogations. But he could not say whether the interrogators had complied with those principles.[154]

In the end, Balneil was proven correct. While the interrogations yielded an intelligence bonanza that impressed even Tuzo, this was overshadowed by the political fallout.[155] The British government bore the brunt of criticism for the use of interrogation methods that, while falling short of "torture" in the strictest sense, amounted to – in the words of a 1978 European Court of Human Rights ruling – "inhuman and degrading treatment."[156] The criticism was fair and deserved to a considerable degree: the army had trained the RUC interrogators and persuaded them to use the methods, and its representatives were present when they did. But the documentary record makes it clear that no one in London, in or out of uniform, wanted to accept responsibility for having done so. In a very real sense there was an abdication of responsibility at all levels.

As a result of the Compton Committee report and two subsequent reports that addressed whether deep interrogation methods were appropriate or should be changed, Heath announced in March 1972

that Britain would no longer use those techniques to extract information from terrorism suspects.[157] However, the political damage already
had been done. In late September Carrington told the cabinet that "it
was too early to say that Internment had failed," but he was forced to
concede that it had helped the IRA, "and the task of the troops was
becoming increasingly difficult."[158] Throughout the autumn shootings, bombings, attacks on the security forces, and casualties increased
steadily. Except for occasional arrest operations, the Catholic ghettos
became no-go areas for the security forces, and the IRA was able to
operate there with impunity.[159] That situation was not reversed until
Operation Motorman in August 1972.

SUMMATION

Internment was a *political* decision and a *political* operation from
start to finish. While it had a significant security dimension, the driving force behind it was politics. Faulkner was desperately trying to
fend off his critics within his own party; internment was the option
most likely to satisfy them and keep his government in office. Heath
and his ministers were equally determined to avoid imposing direct
rule, which would have followed if Faulkner's government fell. Thus
they felt they had no option but to support him on internment.
Consequently, both governments overrode the advice of the senior
army commanders, all of whom rejected the military necessity for
internment. On no other security issue during the 1968–74 period
were the politicians and the military so clearly at odds. This disagreement could have caused a crisis in civil-military relations. Yet,
it did not. The GOC and the CGS had been asked for their advice; it
was proffered but in the end not followed. Neither officer resigned
on a matter of principle. Nor did they or any other soldier refuse to
carry out the internment operational order. Internment may not
have been sound security policy, but the army had no legal or constitutional grounds to refuse to implement the decision, and did not
do so. Internment clearly overlapped into both the political and military spheres of responsibility. But both parties respected each
other's roles and responsibilities in their respective spheres. Ultimately, the civil authority prevailed, as it must in a democracy. But it
was the army that had to deal with the consequences, and it paid the
higher price.

5

Bloody Sunday, 1972

On 30 January 1972 British troops from Support Company, 1st Battalion, the Parachute Regiment (1 PARA) shot and killed thirteen people during an arrest operation conducted at the end of a civil rights march in Londonderry (Derry). The soldiers claimed that they had been fired upon by the IRA and were returning fire against armed persons. In its final report issued in June 2010 the Saville Inquiry, convened to examine the events that led to those deaths, concluded that while paramilitary groups had engaged in some violence during that day, none of those killed by the army had been armed. Instead, the army shootings resulted from a "serious and widespread loss of fire discipline among the soldiers of Support Company."[1] It faulted 1 PARA's commander, Lt. Col. Derek Wilford, for deploying his troops in a manner that brought about the tragedy.[2]

Two days after the shootings, an irate mob burned down the British embassy in Dublin. In the months after Bloody Sunday – as the event came to be known – the political situation in the North deteriorated further. The IRA escalated its bombing campaign along with attacks on the army; fifty-six soldiers were killed in the period between Bloody Sunday and the imposition of direct rule in late March.[3] Equally if not more menacing was the formation of the militant loyalist Ulster Vanguard Movement (UVM) by former Stormont cabinet minister William Craig. Oblivious to either the political consequences or the optics of a crackdown on the IRA in the aftermath of Bloody Sunday, Craig and his followers were frustrated by the British government's unwillingness to countenance a tougher line against the republican extremists. The UVM held public paramilitary meetings to demonstrate its commitment to retaining the union with Britain. In a February speech Craig said, "God help those who get in our way."[4]

Given the dramatic and tragic nature of the events of Bloody Sunday and the violence and political controversies that followed, it would not have been surprising had they led to a crisis in political-military relations. After all, the actions of the army had plunged the British government into a political disaster that had ramifications well beyond the province. The prime minister and cabinet could have been justifiably angry with the army. Yet a crisis in civil-military relations was averted. This chapter explains why by examining security policy and operational planning in the pre–Bloody Sunday period and the government's handling of the aftermath. It will show that no crisis emerged because the government did not insert itself into the tactical level of planning and conduct of operations, and it made a conscious effort to distance itself from the inquiry that followed while taking steps to ensure that the inquiry did not undermine the army's morale.

THE POLITICAL CONTEXT

The reaction in Catholic/nationalist communities to the August 1971 internment operation was so hostile that, later that year, those areas, especially in Londonderry, had become (in intelligence parlance) "denied areas" for the British.[5] The number of violent incidents and casualties escalated dramatically during the remainder of the year. In the seven months prior to internment, 34 people had been killed; after internment, there were 200 bombings, 180 nail bombs, many shooting incidents, and 118 fatalities by year's end.[6]

By introducing internment the British government had dodged the bullet of direct rule. But, it remained an option, however distasteful, for London while it sought a political solution through tripartite talks held in September between the prime ministers of Britain, Northern Ireland, and the Irish republic. To no one's surprise, in the tense post-internment atmosphere the meeting produced no momentum on any significant political issue.[7] Northern Ireland prime minister Brian Faulkner and British prime minister Edward Heath met again in October, when Heath pressed for political reform while Faulkner pushed security as the essential precondition for change.[8] In the absence of political agreement, Faulkner's view prevailed.

SECURITY POLICY, JULY 1971 TO JANUARY 1972

In his study of the historical background to Bloody Sunday, written for the Saville Inquiry, Paul Arthur says that the events of that day compounded a "sense of uncertainty as to who was ultimately in control" of the security forces.[9] That concern was not new at that point; it had been growing since the first deployment of troops in August 1969. Bloody Sunday was, in many respects, the last straw. Less than two months later the British government suspended Stormont and introduced direct rule, in large measure to ensure national command and control over the use of the army in Ulster. But Arthur's study makes the odd assertion that, while most of the British Army's postwar operations took place in conflicts similar to Northern Ireland's, "it was not properly trained to handle a policy of civilian control."[10] It is not clear what he meant by this. As Hew Strachan's work shows, civilian control of the army has rarely been in doubt in the modern era. And throughout the series of campaigns from Palestine to Aden, the army always had been under the control of civilian authorities.[11] The real question, which plagued the Northern Ireland campaign until 1972 and that probably was unique to it, was: which civilians?

Paul Bew wrote that, even before internment, the general officer commanding was "very circumspect in his approach to the Derry situation."[12] The army in Londonderry was operating under the terms of Operational Directive 3/71, which had been issued 2 July 1971. It had stated that there was to be a gradual increase in Royal Ulster Constabulary presence in the city and a concurrent scaling back of army operations there. But the army was to position forces in reserve at selected locations to deal with outbreaks of violence and rioting if the RUC were unable to handle them. Riot control was to be conducted using minimum force, but units were to arrest as many rioters as possible, relying on "imaginative planning ... considerable guile and cunning."[13] Finally, the city commander was to build up contact with the community and local leaders in order to isolate "minority extremists and hooligan elements."[14] No other military activity was to take place in the city without the "specific authority" of the commander of 8 Brigade. The routine unit operations included patrolling and snap roadblocks/vehicle checks, but house searches were prohibited unless approved by the brigade HQ. Troops were to use their firearms only under the rules stated in the Yellow Card – a printed copy of the rules of engagement issued to each soldier on internal security operations. The directive also specified the circumstances under which CS gas could be used, and enough such circumstances were listed to give a unit commander fairly wide latitude in deciding when to use it. However, the directive stated that it was 8 Brigade policy not to use CS in Derry "unless absolutely necessary."[15]

On 20 August the GOC, Lt. Gen. Sir Harry Tuzo, had decided to lower the army's profile in the city, in the hope that moderate opinion might gain some traction. At the end of the month he attempted to strike a deal with moderate nationalists in the city: he offered to stop military operations for a month if they could deliver peace. He told a sceptical Northern Ireland cabinet that, while the effort might fail, he thought it was worth trying "to break out of the circle of violence."[16] But subsequent events on the streets dashed these hopes.[17] By the time Heath met with Faulkner in early October, the British prime minister had already come around to the view "that the first priority should be the defeat of the gunmen by military means and that in achieving this we should have to accept whatever political penalties are inevitable."[18] The driving force behind this stance seems to have been the British government's fear of direct rule, although Paul Bew suggests that some senior British officials accepted that it likely would happen eventually. Since political initiatives were stalled and continuing the status quo would lead to direct rule,[19] a change in security policy towards a more proactive counterterrorism program was the only option left on the table.

Prior to meeting Faulkner, Heath had asked the CGS, Gen. Sir Michael Carver, to produce a military appreciation of the situation, including proposals for what the army would do "if they were instructed that the primary objective was to bring terrorism in Northern Ireland to an end at the earliest possible moment, without regard to the inconveniences caused to the civilian population."[20] The note also asked what troops would be required to achieve this end. Carver sent his appreciation a few days later, having compiled it in haste with little input from the GOC and none from the chiefs of staff. He pointed out that the problem was both political and military and that those factors "cannot be disentangled." The history of previous counterterrorism campaigns, few of which had been wholly successful, suggested that "a purely military solution is most unlikely to succeed." Yet, however it was achieved, "the isolation of the terrorist from the population is a sine qua non of success."[21] He described the current military policy in the province as one of "maximum vigour in the elimination and apprehension of identifiable terrorists, tempered by a scrupulous care to avoid actions which are, or may be represented as being, indiscriminate as between the terrorists and the ... minority community, or deliberately discriminate between Protestants and Roman Catholics."[22]

He went on to add that security operations were tempered in order not to hamper political initiatives intended "to bring representatives of the minority community into fuller participation in political life," to persuade the Catholics that they were not "second class citizens," and ultimately to erode the support that a substantial portion of Catholics gave to the IRA.[23] In Carver's view, therefore, security force operations ultimately served a political purpose and had to be conducted accordingly. However, he also pointed out that while military operations were limited by political policy, as the level of violence had risen so had the degree of minimum force used to deal with it.[24] This change supports David French's argument that minimum force was a flexible threshold: it was up to the soldiers to decide "what level of force was appropriate in a given situation."[25] Moreover, it was also a matter of perception: what the army regarded as minimum often seemed excessive to civilians experiencing it.[26]

Carver implied that about two-thirds of the troops were providing basic security, leaving about one-third free to pursue the IRA through patrols, roadblocks, searches and "hot pursuit." But as increased IRA activity forced the army to commit more forces to static security tasks, fewer were available to operate against the terrorists. He felt that the IRA had the initiative and could sustain it. Its goal, he believed, was to use a terrorist campaign to force direct rule and then to persuade the British public to abandon the province. Carver then identified three key problem areas – Andersonstown (Belfast), the Bogside and Creggan (Derry), and the border with the republic – and outlined the force levels and duration to deal with each. To deal simultaneously with all of them would require more forces than currently deployed, for an indeterminate period and with no certainty of success. An intensified effort would harden attitudes, rally support for the IRA, and strengthen the group itself – in short, exactly the opposite of the desired effect.[27]

Tougher measures could include fewer limits on the use of lethal force, movement restrictions on the population, more covert operations, and closing certain border areas. The CGS identified three operational choices with respect to Londonderry. The first would continue current policy, which was to control the rest of the city and to conduct raids into the "hard" areas to search for gunmen when intelligence allowed. The second course would have the army entering those areas and patrolling at will. Such a course would not include the removal of barricades or the restoration of law and order, but it could be done with current force levels. The final option was to occupy and dominate the no-go areas. He described that as "a practical military operation," though it would stir up Catholic opposition and would lead to casualties. It also would require more troops. Choosing this course "must be a political and not a military decision."[28] The CGS was careful to point out that a tougher approach could have second-order effects: further policy implications, such as rearming the RUC, imposing restrictions on news media, the need for martial law courts if the security situation deteriorated further, and a complete closure of the border. He expressed some doubt about the likely effectiveness of many of the restrictions on the population, because the machinery to implement them in Northern Ireland did not exist.[29]

The force requirements to tackle all three trouble spots simultaneously were nearly as high as anticipated for direct rule and were manageable only if the government was prepared to forego continuous surveillance of the border (which would require more troops than could be sustained). Given, these practical considerations, there were three courses of action. The first would continue operations at "low intensity" in the hope of assisting political progress. The CGS felt this would cost less in military terms and was less likely to alienate the Catholics, but it would not appease extreme unionists. Thus, it might lead Protestants to form their own "third force" and in turn force the government to impose direct rule. The second option was to abandon any hope of political progress and to adopt most of the tough measures noted above. This could yield some military success against the terrorists and would reduce unionist pressure, thereby forestalling the prospect of direct rule, but at the cost of a Pyrrhic victory. The CGS favoured option three: continuing current policy but lifting the restrictions imposed on the GOC by the desire not to disturb current political initiatives. This would permit intensified border operations and an operation in Derry.[30]

Heath's request to Carver and the CGS's response demonstrate the civil-military relationship at work. The government was asking for the

CGS's professional advice on security policy. He gave it, making clear which decisions lay in the political domain and which were military, while also offering his judgment on the political implications of the several courses of military action proposed. Both actors were operating within the purview of their constitutional responsibilities. There is nothing in this exchange to suggest a clash or a problem.

When Heath met Faulkner on 7 October he described the situation as "grave socially, economically and politically" and warned that the British public was "losing patience." For his part, Faulkner cited a Northern Ireland civil service review that warned "that a breakdown in government might occur in a matter of weeks."[31] Given this grim scenario they agreed (with the support of the home, foreign, and defence secretaries) to a three-part security program. Its objectives, in order of priority were: "to intensify security operations in Belfast, making full use of the intelligence which has been gained as the result of internment"; to control the border more effectively; and to deal with the "unsatisfactory situation in certain parts of Londonderry."[32]

This new program was reflected in a new security policy, drafted by the staff of CLF Maj. Gen. Robert Ford. Issued 26 October 1971 and titled *Commander Land Forces Directive for Future Internal Security Operations* it defined the army's mission in familiar, bland terms: "to restore and maintain law and order" by working with the police in aid of the civil power.[33] This much, at least, was not new; it is what the troops had been doing since August 1969. But the document title and the mission statement were somewhat misleading. Upon closer reading the new shape of the army's role becomes clearer. The directive started with the assumption that the security forces were engaged in a "campaign against the IRA"[34] – a strategic political construct that emerged from both the intent of the internment operation and the outcome of the Heath/Faulkner meeting. It claimed that this campaign was "making real progress" against the IRA but had "only just begun to undermine the belief that the IRA is capable of winning."[35] The army's new role was "to demonstrate by military successes the certainty of defeat of the IRA."[36] It was to be conducted "on three simultaneous and inter-related fronts: the intelligence front, the operational front, the public information front."[37] This was much more than an effort to restore and maintain law and order; it was a comprehensive counterterrorism campaign plan.

The directive set two priorities: first, "defeat of the IRA's campaign of violence" and, second, "to overcome threats to law and order from all other directions, including in particular inter-sectarian strife."[38] The first priority involved five tasks: defeating IRA armed attacks with "resolute armed action within the terms of the current rules of engagement" (ROE); responding to all other forms of violent IRA activity with "vigorous follow-up action"; with Special Branch support, arresting all IRA suspects as quickly as the interrogation system would allow; protecting important targets from IRA attack; and fast and accurate reporting to ensure that information staff were able to report "the truth about security force actions quickly and convincingly."[39] Notwithstanding the fact that a campaign against the IRA was bound to bring the security forces into conflict with the Catholic community, the forces were to try to maintain impartiality, since getting that community to reject IRA violence was "an essential ingredient of our ultimate success."[40] The last goal was unrealistic: Catholic communities would never see the army as impartial.

The directive spelled out for 8 Brigade a specific action program for Londonderry: to "progressively impose the rule of law on the Creggan and Bogside" by countering hooligan activity, mounting arrest operations, and carrying out patrols through IRA-dominated areas. Furthermore, the brigade should be ready to "occupy and dominate the Creggan and Bogside" as soon as sufficient troops were ready.[41]

This policy represented a sharp break with Lt. Gen. Tuzo's low-key approach to the city. At the end of October Brigadier Pat MacLellan took command of 8 Brigade, and on 10 November he issued Operational Directive 4/71 (OD 4/71), which explained how the brigade would implement the CLF's policy. His directive noted that neither the RUC nor the army controlled the Bogside or Creggan, where "the mob rule of the gun prevails."[42] His mission statement was identical to the CLF's, as was his general statement on execution of the mission. OD 4/71 then went into detail on the brigade's tasks for the three fronts. On the intelligence front the directive called for full exchange of ideas and information and the development of a close working relationship between the army and the RUC; making full use of MILOs and strengthening links between soldiers and Special Branch; making use of the Special Anti-Terrorist Team, which, though under command of the city battalion, operated in support of Special Branch; and ensuring that all ranks were alert for information at all times and that they would immediately report anything unusual.[43]

On operations, MacLellan called for "positive, quick, and effective" reactions to any rioting or terrorism. He echoed the CLF's call for "resolute armed action" against the IRA within the ROE. Troops would return fire when events demanded it and the law permitted. They should keep the terrorists in "a permanent state of anxiety" about what they would do next; all the troops' actions should surprise them with their unpredictability. There would be "hot pursuit" to arrest gunmen. The brigade was to use "imaginative tactics" to disperse and arrest "young hooligans" (those who habitually engaged in rioting). But at the same time MacLellan insisted that soldiers maintain high standards of conduct, courtesy, and especially fire discipline.[44]

Finally, he stressed the importance of the "information war." The information effect of operations had to be kept in mind at all times. The troops' behaviour always must be "impeccable." If they defeated the IRA but lost on the "information front" they would have achieved a "Pyrrhic victory."[45] MacLellan called for a "never-ending series of small arrest operations" to be sustained at the "highest possible intensity." Units were to conduct frequent irregular patrolling, day and night. Patrols in strength in the Creggan and the Bogside would start as soon as brigade force levels allowed (early December), with the aim of re-establishing law and order in those areas. But, except in "hot pursuit" situations, troops would not search homes without permission from brigade headquarters. Finally, every effort would be made to improve relations between the army and the community through contact with local leaders.[46]

The effects of the CLF's and Brigadier MacLellan's directives were immediately apparent on the streets. By mid-December the army had carried out a series of battalion-strength searches in the Bogside and Creggan. These and other operations exploiting intelligence (which it said had come in at "a gratifying rate") had resulted in the capture of two significant arms caches and the arrest of some 100 wanted men. As expected, the army's initiative had been met by IRA violence (shootings and bombings) that continued well into January. In spite of a mood of cautious optimism the CGS reminded cabinet of "the virtual impossibility of halting the IRA's activities by security measures alone."[47]

The CLF visited Londonderry in early December, following which he wrote a paper entitled *Future Military Policy for Londonderry: An*

Appreciation of the Situation by CLF. The paper reviewed the evolving situation in the city from July (the increase in violence, the perceived failure of the low-profile policy), then offered and assessed several security policy options, and made some recommendations. The three options he saw were: first, to revert to the previous policy (containing Creggan and the Bogside from the periphery), but to adopt a "much more offensive attitude"; second, to continue the current policy (major operations, but no permanent presence, in those areas); or finally, to establish a full-scale permanent presence in the troubled areas.[48] After considering the pros and cons of each course (none of which was perfect), including both the security and political implications and force level requirements, he recommended a return to course one: a policy of "containment," modified, as suggested, to permit selective offensive operations into Creggan and the Bogside when intelligence made them feasible.[49] This was not the ideal solution; it was simply the least bad option. And it was the policy in place at the time of Bloody Sunday.

PLANNING FOR THE CIVIL RIGHTS MARCH

Army planning for an anticipated civil rights march began in early January because initial indications were that the march was to be held on the 16th of that month. But the organizers postponed the march, which gave both them and the security forces more time to prepare for it.[50] Organizers' planning continued in spite of the fact that HQNI issued an instruction on 19 January stating that the ban on marches would be enforced.[51] There seems to be almost no disagreement that the army was told to stop the march.[52] But there seems to be some confusion as to who had the authority to issue the order and how specific was their guidance. Maj. Gen. Ford told the Saville Inquiry that he had issued the order that the march was to be stopped, "on the grounds that it was an illegal march and orders had been issued saying that it was, like all the other marches."[53] Furthermore, in the view of the inquiry "he gave that order because he had to do so; the decisions made by politicians gave him no real choice."[54]

Anthony Stephens, then head of DS10 at the MOD, told the inquiry that the shared view of the GOC, the UK government representative at Stormont, the MOD, and the Home Office was that the aim of the security forces was "to prevent the march from achieving its intended object and to bring its organizers to book. The march will be halted and prevented from continuing; it is ... a matter of judgment of the security forces to decide at what point to halt it."[55]

During a 25 January phone call Ford told Brigadier MacLellan that, "while the decision whether or not to stop the march was one for the JSC, the Brigadier should assume for planning purposes that he would be ordered to stop the march."[56] The CLF then ordered MacLellan to submit to him the next day a plan to deal with the march. At a meeting at the MOD on 26 January, Stephens seemed to confirm what Ford had told MacLellan: "It is primarily up to the Joint Security Committee in Northern Ireland to decide on the tactics which the security forces should adopt for dealing with this march."[57] Yet, that same day it was the Director of Operations (D/Ops) Committee that decided to stop the march from *"leaving the Bogside/Creggan area."*[58] GEN 47 "rubber stamped" the containment plan the following day.[59]

Two things stand out here: one is that there seems to have been a discrepancy between a decision to stop the march from leaving the Bogside/Creggan areas and one to stop it altogether. The discrepancy becomes all the more apparent in the 8 Brigade plan; it did not include putting barriers inside the Bogside (to stop the march there) but would allow the march to proceed along William Street to a point close to the Guildhall. In fact, the army announced at 10:15 a.m. that it would stop the march at a time of its choosing.[60] The second point concerns the decision makers. Ford and Stephens had emphasized that it was up to the JSC (which included members of the Stormont government) to decide whether the march would be allowed and how the army was to handle it. But as noted earlier, in spite of the original intentions the JSC had been excluded from considering operational matters almost from the outset. By this time the D/Ops Committee seems to have assumed that role, even though its purpose was to decide on the respective tasks of the army and the RUC. "It was not the role of this committee to determine matters of operational detail."[61] But it did. Equally significant, the D/Ops Committee did not include any Stormont representatives. It consisted solely of military and police officers: the GOC, CLF, chief of staff, the D/INT, the chief and deputy chief constables of the RUC, and the head of Special Branch.[62] So, if Ford's hands were tied, it was not, as he alleged, by local politicians.

It was during the planning period that the CLF decided to add 1 PARA to the forces available to Brigadier MacLellan.[63] The battalion had received considerable criticism – from both inside and outside the army – for its "rough" handling of a demonstration at the Magilligan internment camp in early January.[64] Nevertheless, the decision to use the unit was not changed, because it was "the only experienced uncommitted battalion."[65] Moreover, in spite of the tragedy that transpired on the day of the march, there is no evidence in the records to suggest that such a deadly clash was inevitable. The Special Branch estimate on the march stated: "no trouble anticipated."[66] Indeed, the evidence suggests that the army went to great lengths to tone down its posture for the event. The confirmatory notes for battalion orders groups (O GROUPS – meetings at which unit commanders issue orders prior to operations) emphasized a "low key" – not a confrontational – approach by the army, reminded the commanders that the media would be "out in force and looking for contentious material," and warned them that the "outcome of this weekend could have very long term effects on the campaign."[67] The security forces were not to take any action against the marchers unless they attempted to breach the army barricades and/or "violence against security forces takes place."[68] This directive seems to have been common to all battalions, including 1 PARA. This is not to suggest that the army expected the march to pass off without incident. The 8 Brigade operational order issued 27 January stated that it expected rioting from the "hooligan element" that would accompany the march and "almost certainly snipers." It went on to say that the threat during the march included "IRA terrorist activity ... to conduct shooting attacks against the Security Forces."[69]

Intelligence gathered from clandestine human intelligence sources before the march suggested that sniping attacks were possible on that day. But as discussed below, it is not clear that this intelligence reached the army units concerned, and the Saville Inquiry concluded that it did not influence the troops' behaviour on the day. Rather, it appears that they prepared for the threat of snipers as simply standard operating procedure (SOP).[70]

The HQNI operational summary for the week of 28 January stated that "intelligence reports indicate that the IRA are determined to produce a major confrontation by one means or another during the march."[71] It did not say what form that might take. The weekly intelligence report on Northern Ireland compiled by Brigadier Lewis of the MOD defence intelligence staff said simply "gunmen may be present."[72] The source of this information is not identified.

The confirmatory notes mentioned earlier stated that the "threat from hooligans, gunmen, bombers and arsonists remains unchanged."[73] This was a general threat assessment; the notes did not mention specifically a potential threat from snipers in the Rossville Flats. However, both Lt. Col. Derek Wilford and Major Edward Loden, commander of I PARA Support Company, told the 1972 Widgery Inquiry that the possibility of coming under fire had been mentioned during the battalion O group. Loden specifically referred to the Rossville Flats as a possible site for sniper fire. A I PARA captain told the Saville Inquiry that "we were to expect IRA ambushes and were to prepare for IRA gunmen."[74] On the face of it this seems to suggest that specific intelligence reached I PARA and influenced its preparations for the operation. However, as the battalion adjutant pointed out, it was normal to expect snipers: "We could never rule out the fact that we might be shot at – any time, any place. The IRA were good at ambushes ... and it would be foolhardy in the extreme to assume that you would not be shot at ... It was a fundamental principle that we had to be prepared to be attacked at any time."[75]

The regimental sergeant major of I PARA explained that the battalion intelligence officer briefed the battalion O group on the IRA. "He did not say that we would come under fire but as with any high rise flats, the Rossville Flats were seen as potential sniper positions. There was always the possibility of sniper fire wherever we were in Northern Ireland."[76] Company and platoon O GROUPS took a similar approach; troops were warned about the potential for shooting from high buildings, including the Rossville Flats. But troops were given "no special orders about opening fire"; they were to follow the Yellow Card.[77] In short, the preparations for sniper attacks seem to have been simply SOP, not a response to specific intelligence. And the Saville Inquiry concluded that the shootings did not result from deliberate prompting to pre-emptively engage snipers.

Former prime minister Heath told the inquiry that "the tenor of the discussion" at the GEN 47 meeting on 27 January was that the march was expected to be peaceful, although attempts by "hooligans" and the IRA to "exploit the march for their own purposes" were anticipated, since that was common to such marches in the province. Heath said he wasn't aware "of any specific proposal to mount an arrest operation during the march."[78] But in any case cabinet did not normally involve itself in tactical details. He did recall that "the possibility of

using live firearms was not discussed, and no specific political authority was sought or given for the use of firearms. It would have been
understood that firearms should be used only if those in command
on the ground considered their use to be absolutely necessary, and
only as permitted by the Yellow Card."[79]

AFTERMATH AND INQUIRY

According to Heath, when the first reports of shootings reached him
they were "totally unexpected."[80] The news only got worse. The army
had killed thirteen civilians, all of whom apparently were unarmed.[81]
While the details surrounding the shootings were at the time confus-
ing and contradictory, which the *Times* observed was normal in such
an event, there was no escaping the fact that a tragedy of major pro-
portions had occurred.[82]

According to Lt. Col. Ramsbotham the CGS had anticipated trouble
and had arranged that Col. Dalzell-Payne (head of MO 4, which was
staffed through that day) should call him if there were any significant
incidents. Carver (who did not have a television) was notified by telephone soon after the shootings. Dalzell-Payne called him twice more
during the evening with further information, and the CGS also may
have received a call from the defence secretary. The next morning he
read the sitrep, then briefed Defence Secretary Lord Carrington using
a marked map.[83] This account suggests that the higher command and
reporting system was working as it should.

Bloody Sunday presented the British government with two crises
simultaneously: first, one over the political fate of the province and,
second, a public crisis of confidence in the army's handling of the situation in the province. The army was castigated in the press for the
shootings and for the inconsistencies in its account of the events. Various eyewitness accounts described the troops firing "indiscriminately" into the crowd of peaceful, unarmed marchers. Lt. Col. Wilford,
and other army spokesmen, insisted that his troops had come under
fire and had returned it, but not indiscriminately. Nevertheless, the
most vocal observers and critics described the incident as a "massacre"
or "mass murder."[84] John Hume, the leader of the Social Democratic
and Labour Party, drew parallels to apartheid South Africa, calling the
incident "another Sharpeville," referring to the incident in which
South African police had fired on peaceful protestors, killing dozens.[85]

Seven priests collectively accused Wilford of "willful murder" and
called the paratroopers "trained criminals" who "differ from terrorists
only in the air of respectability that a uniform gives them."[86] Even
allowing for the understandable anger of a community that already
felt itself under siege before the shootings, sentiments such as this
could not be dismissed out of hand or ignored. Moreover, the anger
spilled over into a rancorous emergency debate in Parliament, during
which MP Bernadette Devlin crossed the floor and assaulted Home
Secretary Maudling.[87] So, this situation easily could have become a
crisis in political-military relations as well.

The following chapters will show that the British government dealt
with the political crisis by imposing direct rule then later launching
a political power-sharing plan. It moved even more quickly to head
off a crisis over the army's role in the conflict by convening a judicial
inquiry. This was itself a political tightrope for both the army and the
government. As discussed at the outset of this study, institutional
autonomy – freedom from politicization – is one of the hallmarks of
a professional army in a democracy. Driven as they are by political
imperatives – primarily to take pressure off a government – inquiries
by their very nature are political instruments. In the aftermath of the
internment operation, Prime Minister Heath had noted that all of his
ministers felt that the "Army's resistance to special inquiries or official
tribunals" was "well-founded."[88] Nevertheless, Heath told the Saville
Inquiry that it was clear that there would be "great and widespread
political sensitivity and concern" about the events of Bloody Sunday,
not just in the UK, but in the Irish republic and the United States.
"Much of that concern would focus on the role of the security forces and the nature and extent of their responsibility for what had
occurred."[89] Consequently, he felt that it was "imperative ... to allay
public concern and buttress the morale of the security forces" by
establishing the facts and getting them "put on the public record as
soon as possible."[90]

The importance attached to such concerns was not a matter of misplaced priorities. With the RUC still unable to police on its own significant areas within the province, the army was the *only* remaining
security force. Maintaining its ability and will to operate effectively
was essential. Thus, Heath was determined to establish the facts and
get them on the public record as soon as possible. At a meeting on
31 January he and his cabinet colleagues quickly concluded that the

correct way to do this was to appoint an independent inquiry that had the power to call for evidence.[91] That same day the government asked Lord Chief Justice Widgery to conduct the inquiry. His appointment was announced in Parliament the next day. While heated debate continued, and former PM Harold Wilson and Liberal leader Jeremy Thorpe questioned the wisdom of a one-man inquiry, Heath was unmoved.[92]

That the three goals of the inquiry – to establish facts, allay public concern, and buttress security force morale – were not necessarily compatible or complementary does not seem to have occurred to Heath and the cabinet. If conducted objectively, an inquiry could yield facts that would neither reassure the public nor exonerate the army and buttress its morale. So, Lord Widgery faced a delicate task: balancing demands for transparent accountability to the public with the necessity of sustaining army morale while the forces were still engaged in difficult, sensitive operations, and with the need to avoid any appearance of conflict of interest or government interference in the investigation.

Heath told the Saville Inquiry that he did not try to "steer" Justice Widgery towards any outcome, although he did warn him that the inquiry would be caught in the middle of the "propaganda war" that prevailed at the time. Historian Thomas Hennessey observes that, despite protestations to the contrary, Heath's comments could be seen as a blatant attempt to influence the chief justice, but he does not draw a definitive conclusion on that issue. It is possible that the propaganda factor persuaded both cabinet and Lord Widgery himself that the inquiry should be concluded as quickly as possible. With this in mind he limited the scope of his inquiry to the events of the day "and in particular the period of the shooting."[93] In Heath's view a narrow and time-sensitive inquiry would soon allow the troops involved to carry on with their duties with the inquiry behind them.

What he did not say was that it also would preclude scrutiny of any larger issues surrounding security force policy in the province. That would prevent awkward questions in Parliament, a possible breakdown of the bipartisan consensus over Northern Ireland, or any public dispute between the government and the military over the handling of the conflict. The Widgery Inquiry was, in fact, a skilful political manoeuvre that effectively and formally enabled the government to avoid playing a direct role in investigating the events of

Bloody Sunday. In this respect it solved two problems simultaneous-ly. First, it pre-empted any potential partisan charges that the govern-ment was engaged in a cover-up. Such charges might have arisen had it conducted the investigation itself. Second, it forestalled a potential showdown with the military chain of command that could have developed from just such an internal politically driven inquiry.

The inquiry heard testimony from 117 witnesses, including priests and civilians from Derry, press and TV reporters and their assistants, soldiers (including the key officers), the RUC, doctors and other med-ical experts, and counsel for the families of those killed.[94] Ramsboth-am notes that the CGS "did not go into print about Bloody Sunday at all,"[95] so as his military assistant he offered his own reflections on the general's reactions. The CGS visited 1 PARA officers in the immediate aftermath of the incident and told them bluntly:

> no-one must keep anything back when giving their evidence
> before those who were preparing ... the preliminary investigation,
> which of course would be used by lawyers at the subsequent legal
> inquiry. Provided everyone told the whole truth, and thus could
> be shown to have acted in good faith, then no-one need have any
> fear that the judicial machine would not stand by them. But if
> anyone held anything back, which then came out at the legal
> inquiry, which Army Defence counsel had not known about, then
> there would be trouble. He ... could not support any hiding of
> facts, nor would he.[96]

While there is no evidence to suggest that the outcome of the inquiry was "fixed" politically in advance, the government (and pre-sumably the army) got what it wanted – not much more than a slap on the wrist. Widgery's conclusions largely vindicated the army. While conceding that the behaviour of some troops "bordered on the reck-less," the report concluded that there had been "no general breakdown of discipline."[97] Instead, it shifted the blame to the organizers of the march who went ahead with it in spite of the ban. Relying on foren-sic evidence (which has since been discredited) it supported the claim that the troops had been fired on first, although it stated that the event would have passed off without serious incident had the army not launched its operation to arrest the "hooligans." Not surprisingly, critics and especially the nationalist community in the province regarded the inquiry report as "a whitewash."[98] It simply reinforced their sense that in all respects the odds were stacked against them. Even Carver himself was privately dismayed. Ramsbotham says that the CGS was "an absolute stickler for the truth, the whole truth and nothing but the truth – even on tiny matters. Thus when new evidence was presented in front of Widgery he felt that his personal directions had been flaunted."[99] His first reaction to the Widgery Report was "that he would not have been very proud of his battalion had he been CO of 1 PARA."[100]

By the time the report appeared in April 1972 the political situation in Northern Ireland had changed dramatically. Violence was escalating rapidly; with it, casualties and damage increased at a rate not previously seen in the province. Stormont had been prorogued and Westminster had assumed direct rule over Ulster. But the questions arising from the events of Bloody Sunday, and imperfectly answered by the Widgery Inquiry, were not laid to rest until the Saville Inquiry issued its report in June 2010.

SUMMATION

In his study for the Saville Inquiry, Paul Arthur says that Bloody Sunday compounded "a sense of uncertainty" about which civilian authorities were in control of the security forces. But the evidence presented in the Saville Inquiry does not sustain a case for uncertainty. While it was Faulkner who insisted that security take precedence over political reform, Stormont appears to have played almost no role in developing security policy during the autumn of 1971 or in preparing the army's plans to deal with the march.[101] Rather, it was Heath who requested the security assessment from the CGS, and General Carver sent it to the British PM only, not to Faulkner. And in the aftermath of Bloody Sunday, it was the British government that set in motion the Widgery Inquiry, and – as will be shown in the next chapter – made the decision to prorogue Stormont and take over the governance of the province. It seems clear that, during the period after internment, Stormont was gradually being marginalized.

Yet, because Bloody Sunday looms so large in light of its consequences, it still raises an important question: was London sufficiently engaged in the security policy process, or did it leave too much in the hands of the army alone? To answer this, it is necessary to disentangle the shift in security policy from the preparations for the march; the one did not necessarily lead to the other.

In the immediate aftermath of the internment operation, there was a conscious effort on the parts of the GOC and the CGS to align security actions with political goals: to lower the tempo of operations in order to gain space for political initiatives by moderate nationalists. Tuzo and Carver did not have to be told to do this; they had enough operational experience to know that it was required. In fact, they had to persuade the politicians in London and Stormont of its value. But when Tuzo's approach did not yield the desired political results, it was Heath, Faulkner, and Heath's senior ministers who set the broad goals and parameters of a new security policy in October 1971. Having done so, the politicians left the operational details to the army. This demonstrates first the direct engagement of the civil power in this process, although it was the last time before direct rule that Faulkner played any major role in developing security policy. Second, it highlights the clear delineation of responsibilities between the civilian and military authorities. From this point on the security forces alone – not the civil-military JSC – seemed to take the lead on turning policy into operational plans.

The political leaders had urged the army to pursue a more "aggressive" posture against the IRA and to sort out the "unsatisfactory situation" in the nationalist areas of Londonderry. What the army produced was a more comprehensive, proactive counterterrorism campaign plan. The results of that approach were manifest in a new pattern of operations in Derry in December 1971. That said, both the CLF and Brigadier MacLellan, whose brigade was responsible for the Londonderry sector, acknowledged that when it came to turning security policy into operational plans the army's options had to be tempered by the potential political impacts and the need for the its behaviour to be "impeccable." The perceptions of the local population notwithstanding, the army's "new" approach in Derry probably fell short of what Faulkner would have preferred: it was a variation on an existing theme, not a whole new way of conducting operations.

Moreover, it is clear that, in spite of the decision to deploy 1 PARA for the civil rights march and the subsequent behaviour of that battalion, the army's plans and preparations for the event do not appear to have been shaped or driven by this new counterterrorism policy. Indeed, the whole tenor of pre-march planning was to emphasize a low-key approach to handling the march, not a confrontational one. Although the march was banned under the policy agreed upon in August, it was expected to be peaceful and the decision was made to allow it to proceed rather than to prevent it. The army expected to have to deal with a "hooligan element" and the possibility of snipers, but these were treated as routine problems, not as an elevated threat that put soldiers on edge. While the planning for the march was solely in the hands of the security forces, there is nothing in the evidence to suggest that those plans were out of step with London's aims.

Finally, in the aftermath, the political leadership in London, specifically Prime Minister Heath, took the lead in creating an inquiry that would attempt to "square the circle" of transparency, public reassurance, maintaining troop morale, and preserving the army's professional institutional autonomy. That the Widgery Inquiry could not achieve all of these goals and satisfy critics of the army's behaviour is understandable but is not central to my argument. What is important for this study is that Bloody Sunday cannot be explained as a product of confusion over or of a breakdown of high-level civil-military command and control.

6

The Army and Direct Rule, 1972

Bloody Sunday had brought into sharp focus the fact that, since August 1969, the British government had been caught between a rock and a hard place in its dealings with Northern Ireland. Constitutionally, it held ultimate responsibility for political affairs in the province, yet it exerted little control over them because power had been devolved onto Stormont. And while Stormont was responsible for law and order, Westminster had provided the troops used to maintain order since the outbreak of the Troubles.[1] Thus, it was London that was held to account when things went wrong, as was the case on Bloody Sunday. In the wake of that tragedy it was clear that the status quo was no longer acceptable. Less than two months later London suspended Stormont and imposed direct rule on Northern Ireland.

Direct rule never was the preferred option. Even once Britain became intimately involved in the conflict in 1969 it always was seen as the position of last resort. As former prime minister Edward Heath told the Saville Inquiry, "we wished to avoid that [direct rule] if possible."[2] Nevertheless, as noted in chapter 2, contingency planning for that eventuality had begun at the end of January 1969. And from the outset the command and control issue was at the forefront of political and military discussions related to those plans.

PLANNING FOR DIRECT RULE

Discussion about direct rule revolved around two closely related questions: how would Britain govern the province, and how would the chosen process affect direction of the security forces? In September

1969, with troops deployed on the streets on Northern Ireland, the British cabinet requested a review of the contingency plan, which by that time included a draft bill (to suspend Stormont and impose direct rule), a checklist of departmental actions required, papers on matters "ancillary to the Bill," and papers outlining "various hypotheses on which intervention might be needed."[3] A Home Office memorandum focused on the question of whether the draft bill was "right in principle." It drew particular attention to the possibility of retaining some kind of assembly in the province while it was under direct rule. The Home Office concluded that neither a legislative assembly nor a deliberative assembly would be workable in the situation.[4] Consequently, Britain would have to govern the province itself. In fact, when the matter came before the cabinet committee on Northern Ireland in May 1970, the memorandum under discussion then raised the possibility that Stormont might never resume its role even once the emergency was over.[5] As to who would be in charge, the majority of the committee favoured rule through the governor rather than a "minister resident," in part because the GOC would find it easier to deal with a governor.[6]

On 9 March 1971 Home Secretary Maudling told cabinet that the political cohesion within the Northern Ireland government "appeared to be slowly disintegrating."[7] If the government of the prime minister at that time, James Chichester-Clark, were overthrown, the situation would be very serious. There was a need, he said, to revise contingency plans for this eventuality. During a meeting of the ministerial committee the following day, it was suggested (by whom is not recorded) that, if Britain were forced to impose direct rule, "a more radical approach, and more far reaching measures to stamp out terrorism, similar to those … adopted in Malaya in the 1950s, might have to be considered."[8] The committee asked Maudling to circulate a paper on the state of direct rule contingency planning, and Defence Secretary Lord Carrington to prepare one on the military requirements of such a decision.[9]

In fact, military planning for this eventuality was already well advanced. In February the Chiefs of Staff Committee had approved a report on the status of direct rule planning that also was to recommend where further action was required.[10] At the same time the COSC agreed to ask the GOC to plan to provide a military cell in the Northern Ireland security secretariat (proposed in the report and discussed below); to review the initial force requirements; and to prepare his own detailed contingency plan "embracing all the decisions and actions necessary in the event of the imposition of direct rule."[11] The committee also decided to instruct the director of defence operations and plans (D/DOP) to keep contingency planning for the province under review and to coordinate with the Ministry of Defence the preparation of the GOC's plan.

After providing an assessment of the conditions that might lead to direct rule, the COSC report included a Joint Intelligence Committee assessment of the possible security situation under it. The worst case scenario anticipated a breakdown of law and order plus guerrilla warfare, in which the security forces would have to defend themselves as well as trying to keep the two sides apart. They might also be required to run some services. Therefore, greater military resources would be required. But the report acknowledged that it was possible that the security situation might not be much worse than at present.[12]

The constitutional and political framework anticipated in this report did not resemble what eventually transpired. But, since command and control of the security forces as discussed below rested on the proposed structure, it must be summarized briefly. A bill for Parliament drafted by the Home Office and already approved by ministers would suspend Stormont, replacing it with a governor and appointees. The governor would be responsible to the home secretary, while ministers at Westminster provided policy direction. Security matters would be considered by cabinet (or a cabinet subcommittee), where the secretary of state for defence (SSD) would represent the military view. In Northern Ireland itself, "the GOC and the Chief Constable would present their views on security matters to the governor in the Joint Security Committee; he in turn would as necessary report to, or seek guidance from Westminster on any major policy issues in this field. The GOC would remain directly responsible to the Secretary of State for Defence through CGS, on behalf of the Chiefs of Staff."[13]

The report examined three possible models for command and control of security forces and their operations: a continuation of the existing system whereby the GOC coordinated activities of the army and security activities of the Royal Ulster Constabulary; an arrangement similar to the temporary set-up in August 1969; and a structure in which the governor also would be commander-in-chief (similar to the "Supremo" role exercised by Gen. Gerald Templer in Malaya). But the report said that "it is not considered acceptable, either politically or militarily, to delegate functions in the defence field to the governor,"[14] so that option was not pursued further. The second model was preferred in the event of a worsening security situation, as the coordination of the police and military would be more straightforward than under the existing arrangement.

The governor would preside over the Joint Security Committee, served by staff of the Northern Ireland Cabinet Office. To ensure that the JSC and executive committee had ready liaison with security forces commanders, there was to be a military cell at Stormont, staffed by military personnel and a liaison officer from the RUC. This cell, together with Northern Ireland Cabinet Office staff, would constitute the security secretariat mentioned above. It was recommended that HQNI contingency planning include the formation of the military cell, drawing up its terms of reference, and making recommendations to fill posts. Assuming that the D/OPS would still have command of the RUC for security operations, his instructions for joint military and police matters would be issued by HQNI. Detailed instructions, when required, would be issued under authority of the CLF, the chief constable, and other service commanders in the usual manner.[15]

The report touched briefly on intelligence, noting that the need for a restructured organization had recently been identified and that the JIC had produced a report on what was required. It stated that there was the need for a director of intelligence, to be based at RUC HQ, who would be responsible to the governor for coordinating all sources of intelligence deployed in the province. Setting up an intelligence subcommittee of the JSC was already under consideration.[16]

In the closing summary, the report claimed that most aspects of contingency planning for direct rule were in hand. However, further reviews would be needed, and the D/DOP was best placed to do them, preferably through a working group on which the Home Office was represented. The working group would report on its progress to the Official Committee on Northern Ireland, which would be invited to comment "on those aspects for which progress appears to be limited by political considerations."[17]

The COSC report demonstrates several significant points. First, military planning was already several steps ahead of that of the civilian (political) authorities. Second, even if the situations were not entirely analogous, the military was drawing upon experience from and structures applied in recent colonial emergencies. Third, while the report correctly anticipated the need for an integrated approach to security operations, the command relationships between the military and the police remained unresolved. Finally, military planners could not discuss military and political issues separately.

However, the home secretary was rethinking the political dimension. He told the ministerial committee on 17 March that an alternative bill had been drafted that would vest executive power in a cabinet member of the British government. In discussion the committee took the view that Parliament was unlikely to accept an arrangement whereby executive authority would be exercised, in a part of the UK that was represented in Parliament, by a governor who was not answerable to it. Therefore, authority should be vested in a cabinet minister.[18]

Sir Philip Allen then prepared a paper that explored the question of which minister should be responsible for the province under direct rule. He presented only two options: leaving the home secretary in charge with support from other ministries, or appointing a secretary of state for Northern Ireland (SSNI). Allen's paper clearly favoured the latter course because it would give Northern Ireland its own spokesman in the cabinet and in Parliament on a par with Scotland and Wales, and the minister would have full authority to work on a long-term solution to governance issues. However, the paper also noted that the position posed some administrative problems: how to balance the need for the minister to be present in both Belfast and London; the need for offices and staffs in both locations; and how to meet the ongoing need for close cooperation with the Home Office on security matters, such as authorizing telephone and mail intercept warrants.[19] This paper, then, did not anticipate giving a Northern Ireland secretary sole executive authority over all security matters in the province; responsibility would remain divided.

By late July 1971 Maudling told the British cabinet that "the situation was such that we had to seriously contemplate that we might be forced to introduce direct rule."[20] But the government was unwilling to take that step at that time. As discussed in chapter 4, it approved the internment operation instead, in order to keep Faulkner's government in power. Two months later the defence secretary reported to cabinet that the security situation was as discouraging as the political one. "It was too early to say that internment had failed," he said. "But … recruitment to the Irish Republican Army (IRA) in the Republic of

Ireland was rising; and the task of the troops was ... increasingly difficult."[21] In discussion the consensus emerged that, if the three-way
talks between Heath, Stormont prime minister Brian Faulkner, and
Jack Lynch, the prime of the Irish republic, failed to achieve any
improvement in the situation, and law and order was more seriously threatened, "we might rapidly be driven to impose direct rule on
the Province."[22]

On 26 October the vice-chief of the defence staff (then Air Chief
Marshal Sir John Barraclough) told the COSC that the Defence Operations Executive had reviewed the state of contingency planning for
direct rule. The DOE had reported that military aspects were well advanced but that certain matters that were the responsibility of the
Home Office "continued to give cause for concern."[23] Barraclough also
reported that a subcommittee of the Official Committee on Northern
Ireland had been set up to keep contingency planning under review,
and the DOE had agreed to put problems requiring further study to
this subcommittee. The VCDS also said the JIC had been asked to
update its report on intelligence arrangements for direct rule and to
do a comprehensive study of the situation that might occur if it was
imposed. Although it had not yet agreed to start this work, the JIC secretary was at that time raising the matter with the cabinet secretary.
The DOE had suggested that the MOD should continue to press for the
preparation of up-to-date assessments.[24]

Cabinet Secretary Burke Trend had directed that the subcommittee
be established to ensure that the various departmental plans were
consistent and as comprehensive as possible.[25] A new division of the
Home Office also had been created specifically to plan for direct rule
and to conduct a study of possible political initiatives by the British
government. That study was expected by mid-November. In the meantime the subcommittee agreed that the MOD's contingency planning
required the best possible intelligence, so the first order of business
was to ask the JIC to draft a new assessment that incorporated a range
of scenarios for imposing direct rule and the consequences of doing
so. It tasked the departments to examine points raised by the MOD and
would also examine the public relations aspect of direct rule, since
the government's view of its relative success would be influenced by
media reporting.[26]

At the next meeting the Home Office confirmed that imposing
direct rule would not change the command relationships in the

province. The GOC would report to the defence secretary through the normal military chain of command and would act under the direction of the new minister just as he did currently with the Stormont PM. However, the HO and the MOD would have to jointly examine the proposed direct rule legislation to ensure that the security forces would have all the powers they might need. It was suggested that a proposal that the new minister would exercise Stormont's powers by order-in-council might not be sufficient to cover the powers of the security forces.[27] By the time the subcommittee met in early December, the HO and the MOD were drafting instructions for legislation to provide the security forces with additional powers to be exercised under direct rule.[28]

The advanced state of the military's planning was apparent in a 24 November memorandum to the subcommittee. The document listed twenty-two appendices to the MOD contingency plan, which had been drafted by the staff of the ACDS (Operations). These addressed such significant issues as legislation (defining the army's powers to preserve peace and to maintain order and essential services, and detailing an Act of Indemnity); the GOC's requirements, including force levels, legislation, intelligence, public relations, and internment; a plan for secure satellite communications; composition of the DOE for discussion of Northern Ireland issues; border security; provision of a military cell to work within the British machinery of government at Stormont; and a directive for the GOC.[29] That the military planning was so comprehensive can be attributed to the fact that operational planning was a well-rehearsed routine activity for the armed forces, which (unlike many government ministries) had large staffs dedicated to just that task. Furthermore, it also had the greatest incentive to be well prepared: its soldiers were already engaged in a deadly conflict, which direct rule might make worse. How much worse the situation might become was the subject of a JIC assessment delivered to the subcommittee on 18 January 1972. The report, which the JIC admitted was "highly speculative," predicted that direct rule would provide only a brief "breathing space," since both sides would see it as a step towards merging Ulster with the Irish Republic. So, more violence was possible.[30]

The available records (which are incomplete) suggest that further planning proceeded at a less than urgent pace within bureaucratic channels until Bloody Sunday forced the government's hand. Then, in the space of a few weeks in March 1972, the cabinet decided to impose direct rule, and all the command and control issues surrounding it had to be resolved rapidly.

FROM PLANNING TO IMPLEMENTATION

On 3 March 1972 the home secretary fired the opening salvo in the debate about how best to address issues related to direct rule. He began his memorandum to cabinet with an ominous warning: "All possible courses of action or inaction are fraught with danger."[31] He added that "the time had come when we must choose between the dangers of action and the dangers of inaction."[32]

Maudling then made several points. First, he noted that the army had made considerable progress, especially in Belfast, but that the situation outside Belfast and Londonderry was "very serious." Second, the price of success had been very high; half of the British Army was deployed in Northern Ireland, and Britain was now responsible for a growing number of detainees. Third, the army could not entirely eliminate shootings and bombings, and any lull caused by army action against the IRA would not last long. He concluded that the time had come to transfer responsibility for law and order to Westminster. His main reasons were two-fold. First, since he thought it likely that the army would be responsible for law and order in the province "for years to come," and since the army was answerable to Westminster, it did not make sense to leave the responsibility for law and order to Stormont, "*who have no control over the main instrument maintaining it.*"[33] Second, he believed there was no chance of persuading the Catholic minority that Stormont administered law and order impartially. Therefore, the power to legislate on matters relating to law and order should be transferred to London, and the army should control the RUC's security role. At the same time, Stormont's governance powers should be transferred temporarily to a secretary of state.[34]

This was a momentous proposal – to take a step that the cabinet had long tried to avoid. Consequently, cabinet did not warm to it immediately. Ministers were concerned mostly about the reaction of the Protestant community, who might see it as a step towards unification of Ireland. There was doubt that the RUC and the civil service would cooperate with an imposed system of direct rule. By the end of their discussions on 7 March, cabinet had not reached a decision.[35] But a consensus had emerged to the effect that "*it was inherently unsatisfacto-*

ry that, although the Army was constitutionally under the control of the United Kingdom Government, Ministers at Westminster had no responsibility for law and order in the Province, which the Army played the principal part in maintaining. Moreover, they [cabinet ministers] had publicly to defend the policy of internment while having neither the power to influence the detention orders which were made ... nor proper access to the information upon which these decisions were made."[36]

When cabinet reconvened on the 9th, discussion yielded considerable agreement that the Heath government should seize the political initiative with four actions: a referendum on the border; the transfer of responsibility for law and order to Westminster; some modification of internment policy; and the appointment of a secretary of state for Northern Ireland (SSNI).[37] At this point, these actions were not seen as constituting direct rule in itself, but as steps preceding it. Resolving the question of responsibility for law and order seemed to be the first priority.

Still, cabinet ministers were concerned about Faulkner's possible reaction to these ideas. If he refused to lead a government once London had taken responsibility for law and order, then that might result in the imposition of direct rule, "whether the UK government wanted it or not." The wisest course might be to hand responsibility for internment to Westminster, leaving remaining law and order matters to Stormont. On the other hand, "it would be intolerable to permit the situation ... to deteriorate further without some new and radical action on the part of the Government."[38] And, in practice, internment could not be separated from other aspects of law and order.

At this stage it was the role of the proposed SSNI that dominated military discussion about direct rule, because the original contingency plan had not anticipated such a position. Consequently, both the GOC and the CGS felt moved to raise their concerns about the need for a clear chain of command. Lt. Col. Ramsbotham wrote later that contingency planning was "closely monitored by the CGS, who was particularly keen to ensure that the GOC's Directive was quite clear."[39] Given the likely hiatus while a Northern Ireland Office was set up, "he was most anxious to ensure that ... the chain down which political advice would be given to the GOC ... should be quite clearly laid down."[40]

The CGS raised the matter at a meeting in the MOD on 7 March. He pointed out that, under the revised directive for direct rule drawn up by the COSC in 1971, the GOC-D/OPS would assume operational command of the RUC for security operations. But in fact he did not have the legal power to do so. And if he were given this power, it would call into question the independence of the police from ministerial control. The CGS felt that the GOC should revert to the existing directive on this question, which did not make the assumption that the RUC would be under command of the GOC. The CGS said he would write to Lt. Gen. Tuzo to tell him of this change. The permanent undersecretary agreed that the GOC should retain control of security operations but not command the RUC. The same applied to the D/INT – he would coordinate the work of the RUC Special Branch and military intelligence but would not command the branch. Finally, security committees would be set up by the new SSNI, not by the GOC.[41]

The GOC responded quickly to the proposal to rely on the existing directive. In a 9 March note, Gen. Carver reported that Tuzo had *"raised an important point, that of political guidance."*[42] The GOC suggested that the directive should be amended to read: "You will obtain political guidance from the Secretary of State for Northern Ireland."[43] In addition the GOC would seek guidance from MOD on any major redeployment of forces. Tuzo went on to say that it would be up to the Northern Ireland Secretary of State *"to decide on any political implications of any military course, seeking endorsement from the cabinet as necessary."*[44] The CGS responded by saying

> *This is a most important point, and I am not entirely happy that he has got it correct.* As I see it, [the GOC] will receive political guidance *as far as local political implications in Northern Ireland are concerned* from the Secretary of State for Northern Ireland or his local representative ... in the same way as the GOC now receives political guidance from the UK Rep. However, I feel that general political guidance relating to political implications in respect of the general responsibilities of HMG, and of implications affecting the Army as a whole, must come to him from the Secretary of State for Defence, *through me.*[45]

Nevertheless, the CGS said he was glad that the GOC had brought the matter to their attention, since it raised the question of the respective responsibilities of the secretaries of state for Northern Ireland and defence. He closed his case by saying that *"it is of greatest importance to the GOC that ... [this question] should be clarified at the earliest opportunity."*[46]

It had been expected that direct rule would resolve the problem of divided political control of the armed forces in Northern Ireland. But it is clear that neither the GOC nor the CGS thought that it would. The GOC could still be left receiving guidance from two civilian masters, albeit now from within the same government.

For the moment this debate remained confined to the halls of the MOD.[47] It did not engage the cabinet, which was still focused on the larger issue of what to do about Northern Ireland governance as a whole. The PM told cabinet on 14 March that it had to decide whether or not to launch a political initiative. Clearly, Heath thought that it must. He feared that failure to do so immediately would result in a situation in which terrorism could never fully be eradicated, large areas of Londonderry would be outside the control of the security forces, and terrorists based in the republic would be able to operate in the rural areas of the North with relative impunity. Heath also believed that relaxation of internment was perhaps the most important element of a political initiative. But since internment was controlled by the Northern Ireland government, the British government would have to assume control of law and order as it affected public security in order to make any change in that policy. After some discussion, the cabinet agreed that enlarging the British government's role by taking over law and order would make it desirable to have a secretary of state for Northern Ireland.[48]

That same day Lord Balneil, the minister of state for defence, sent a minute to Carrington, reinforcing the CGS's position on the source of political guidance: "It is clearly unacceptable to make this the Secretary of State for Northern Ireland."[49] However, since this new minister would be a cabinet member, Balneil thought that the MOD should take into account the following points. First, he noted "that any arrangement must recognize that you as the Secretary of State for Defence are solely responsible to the Prime Minister for the Armed Forces and cannot pass the responsibility to another Secretary of State, notwithstanding the special circumstances of Northern Ireland."[50] Second, he thought it would be "entirely reasonable" for the GOC to consult the Northern Ireland secretary on routine matters and others "which fall within his discretion" as was done with Stormont through the JSC. "But in the event of any difference of opinion he should seek guidance from the Ministry of Defence."[51] Likewise, the GOC should obtain guidance from the MOD on any other matters that might have "significant or general political implications" or which involve the major deployment of his forces.

Balneil's intervention did nothing to end the debate; if anything, it may have prolonged it. The deputy undersecretary for defence waded in, pointing out that Balneil's suggestion that the GOC seek guidance from the MOD in the event of a difference of opinion with the Northern Ireland secretary "contravenes the doctrine of collective responsibility ... Moreover, as it stands the wording implies an appeal to officials against the advice of a minister!"[52] The remedy would be for the GOC normally to consult the permanent secretary to the SSNI. Therefore, the wording might be "to consult with the SSNI's *Department* in day to day matters."[53]

Derek Stephen (AUS/GS) reinforced this argument by pointing out that it was preferable for the GOC to look to one minister, not two. He added "that the Secretary of State for Defence is bound to answer in Parliament for things done or not done by the Army and is therefore entitled to be in control," and that, "because of the doctrine of collective Ministerial responsibility, it would be for the Secretary of State for Defence to give guidance to CGS and the GOC, with the authority of his colleagues after they have evolved policies and resolved any differences of opinion among ministers."[54]

Stephen then followed up with a note and diagram laying out a possible division of responsibilities. His operating assumption was that the GOC would remain directly responsible to the CGS "but would *consult* fully with the *local* representative of the S of S for N. Ireland; and that either the S of S for N. Ireland would preside over the Joint Security Committee or his junior minister would represent him."[55] The alternative, noted Stephen, was to leave things as they were, with coordination between the civil and military carried out at the ministerial level or by contact with the officials of the Northern Ireland secretary's department. To him, either arrangement seemed workable.[56] He felt that the problem in his organization diagram was that it left the defence secretary "not answerable to Parliament for the major field of the Army's current activities."[57] But, as serious as that was, it was not the only problem; the chart left the GOC off altogether. Perhaps, having specified in his note that the GOC would report directly to the CGS, Stephen did not feel it necessary to put him in the diagram. But it left the GOC's working relationship with the Northern Ireland secretary in limbo, at least in so far as the diagram was concerned.

At the request of Defence Secretary Carrington, and after a discussion in the secretary's office, his PUS added his views on 15 March. Based on the assumption that the SSNI would be responsible for law and order, he told Carrington that, "I feel bound to agree with Lord Balneil that, as Secretary of State for Defence, you would have to remain responsible for the behaviour of the Army in Northern Ireland."[58] By this he meant that it would be fine for the new Northern Ireland secretary, as the minister responsible for law and order there, to deal directly with the GOC (and with the CGS if necessary) on everything connected with current operations. However, "if ... an Army unit ran amuck in carrying out an operation approved by a Secretary of State for Northern Ireland this would be a matter ... affecting the behaviour of the Army ... and it would remain one with which you would have to deal."[59] He acknowledged that this division of duties might appear "a little untidy," with the CGS reporting to two ministers, but he believed it would be workable. Balneil, however, took exception to this line of argument. In a minute to the defence secretary he wrote, "I am afraid I cannot see how, as PUS suggests in his minute of 15th March 1972 you can be expected to be responsible for the 'behaviour' of the Army but not in control of it. My view is still that the responsibility for the Armed Forces must firmly rest with you."[60] He conceded that the SSNI would and should have a greater say than Faulkner did over the use of the army, calling for a close working relationship with the GOC and the MOD. But he felt this could be achieved through consultation, "without the Secretary of State for Northern Ireland exercising control over the Army's activities."[61]

As the discussion proceeded without resolution, Stephen was asked to seek guidance from historical experience. On 17 March he produced a brief that explored command and control arrangements in Cyprus, Aden, and Hong Kong, the first two having experienced prolonged insurgencies. In the Cyprus case, the governor was responsible for the employment of the security forces, but command was vested in the director of operations, who was responsible to the governor "for operational control of all security forces, military and civil, in their task of maintaining law and order."[62] Thus, a single person – the D/OPS – coordinated security activity of the administration, the police, and the military. Stephen could not find the directives issued to the GOCs in Cyprus or Aden, and so relied on memory and his experience at the MOD in 1967 to recall that the GOC in Aden was accountable to the

MOD for the conduct of all military operations there and that, in turn, the secretary of state for defence was answerable to Parliament for such matters.[63]

In Hong Kong the existing directive showed that for planning and conduct of operations the commander British forces (CBF) was responsible to the CDS in London. The governor, subject to direction from the British government, was responsible for security policy decisions. The CBF was to advise him on all security matters affecting the colony and was "to take no military action without his agreement."[64] Stephen cited the Hong Kong example to buttress his argument that the GOC "should remain directly responsible to CGS and CDS for planning and conduct of military operations" but should act "in agreement" with the secretary of state for Northern Ireland or his representative.[65] Given this, and since the GOC in Northern Ireland did not (and would not) have the same degree of control as, or the single reporting chain of, the D/OPS in Cyprus, there did not seem to be any way around having two sources of authority in Northern Ireland.

In a lengthy minute to the CGS on 20 March, Carrington's PUS acknowledged at the outset that command and control was "a difficult issue about which a great deal of theoretical stuff could be written," and summed up by saying, "all this is pretty delicate stuff."[66] Indeed, as the foregoing debates show, it was a constitutional minefield that taxed the minds of soldiers and civil servants alike. Not surprisingly, even the political leadership recognized the tangled nature of the problem. The PUS wrote that, "I detected at the S of S's meeting that he [the home secretary] really wanted to hand over as much as possible in the way of responsibilities for operations in Northern Ireland to the new minister."[67]

He noted that since the Home Office envisaged three new ministers for the province (a secretary of state and two ministers of state), there always would be a resident British minister, who presumably would chair the JSC. In that case it seemed "undesirable" that all of its decisions with regard to the use of the army should be referred to ministers in the MOD. If army operations "were undertaken with the approval of a new Minister of State for Northern Ireland it seems to me that he and his Secretary of State should answer in Parliament for those decisions."[68] That said, he felt it was important to establish the principle that the GOC could appeal to the MOD if "he objected on military grounds to anything the Minister of State ... asked him to do."[69] In the case of major operations the PM and the SSD should be consulted, "if not the Cabinet as a whole."[70] The PUS noted with interest Stephen's point that the governor in Cyprus had been responsible for "the employment of the security forces," but he did not pursue that analogy further. Ultimately, he concurred with Stephen's earlier (handwritten) note to the effect that the CGS would be responsible to the defence secretary for the general behaviour of the army and for such questions as further reinforcements. But the CGS would deal with the SSNI on matters regarding current operations if the secretary needed his military advice.[71] These points were repeated in a draft letter to the cabinet secretary.[72]

All of this, of course, remained hypothetical until the government reached a decision on direct rule. That was not long in coming. On 22–23 March the PM and the home and defence secretaries met with Faulkner and explained to him the four actions that the cabinet had approved on 9 March. Faulkner refused to accept the government's plan. In fact, William Whitelaw, soon to be the first SSNI, recalled that Faulkner felt the plans were insulting and completely unacceptable. Apparently, he believed Heath was bluffing, and he countered the British plan with proposals for several measures short of direct rule: a selective release of internees; joint London/Stormont chairmanship of the JSC; new emergency legislation to replace the SPA; a bill of rights to be enacted at Westminster; and periodic referenda on Ulster's status within the UK.[73] The two PMs agreed to consult their respective cabinets further. Heath summed up by noting that if, after discussing matters with his cabinet, Faulkner could not go beyond his limited counterproposals, then the UK government would have to take over responsibility for law and order. Then, if Faulkner indicated that he could not remain in office in those circumstances, the British government would have no choice but to introduce direct rule. The Stormont parliament would be prorogued and a secretary of state for Northern Ireland would assume its powers.[74]

In the event, that is what happened. The two cabinets met separately on the 23rd, and their positions remained unchanged. Faulkner drafted a letter of resignation before flying to London to meet with Heath, but agreed to stay on until Westminster had passed enabling legislation for direct rule. The next day Heath announced that London was suspending Stormont, imposing direct rule, and appointing a new secretary of state to run the province.[75]

COMMAND AND CONTROL UNDER DIRECT RULE

Direct rule was intended *inter alia* to simplify the command and control of the security forces in Northern Ireland by eliminating the dual system of responsibility that prevailed while Stormont functioned as an autonomous government. It achieved that aim to a considerable degree. Taking Stormont out of the equation allowed London to assume full responsibility for law and order and for the actions of the security forces.[76]

The CGS had attended the meetings on 22 and 23 March. His main contribution was to insist that the GOC give Whitelaw a short briefing to emphasize that there were certain decisions he would be required to take. The MOD would present a separate full briefing, chaired by the CGS himself.[77] On 23 March the MOD issued a new directive to Tuzo, effective the next day, outlining his responsibilities as GOC and D/OPS, and defining his command and control relationships under the new political structure. The directive affirmed his overall responsibility for security *operations*, including operational command of all land, air, and sea forces in the province, and his authority to *coordinate the tasking* of the RUC for security operations.[78] His relations with superior military and civil authorities were defined clearly. As GOC he would be responsible to the CGS acting on behalf of the CDS, and through him to the defence secretary, "for the conduct of operations by the Armed Forces in Northern Ireland."[79] The SSNI was to be responsible for maintaining law and order in the province. In his capacity as D/OPS the GOC would advise the SSNI (or his representative) on the military aspects of his responsibilities for law and order; consult him on all policy matters concerning the operations of the armed forces in the province "and act in agreement with him on such matters"; and be a member of the JSC.[80] In the event of a disagreement with the SSNI or his representative *on military grounds*, the GOC was to refer the matter to the CGS, who would take it up with the CDS and the defence secretary "before a final decision is taken."[81]

This directive ensured the integrity of the military chain of command while providing a consultative process for managing policy relating to law and order and security. While this arrangement fell short of full unity of command, within the constitutional framework of British governance in the domestic sphere it probably was the most that could be done. From London's perspective direct rule was a mixed blessing. It now had full, uncontested responsibility for political and security affairs in the province. But responsibility did not translate into *control* of events there. Britain faced a rising insurgency by the IRA and an emerging threat from loyalist militants who resented the replacement of Stormont and who viewed direct rule as a step towards reunification of Northern Ireland with the Irish republic. The most extreme among them, including William Craig, were openly discussing an independent Ulster.[82] There was no political solution in sight that would satisfy both sides. So as the security situation continued to deteriorate, whatever measures it took to regain control would be London's responsibility alone to bear.

7

Operation Motorman, 1972

THE OPERATION

At 4:00 a.m. on 31 July 1972, some 30,000 troops moved into the
so-called no-go areas – those neighbourhoods barricaded by the IRA
or Ulster Defence Association (UDA) in Belfast and Londonderry
(Derry).[1] Although prepared to fight if necessary, the security forces
encountered little resistance, and by the end of the day the previously "hard areas" were firmly under army control.[2] Rather than mount
a fight it was bound to lose, the IRA withdrew or went into hiding.
Over the next few months the increased British presence and intelligence took its toll on the IRA as hundreds of members were arrested.[3]

Although British operations in Ulster in 1972 have been criticized
for a heavy reliance on repression that failed to defeat the IRA, the
results of Operation Motorman call these judgments into question.[4]
After an initial flurry of IRA retaliatory attacks, the levels of violence
in the province dropped dramatically and never returned even close
to the pre-Motorman levels.[5]

Motorman is important for this study in two ways. First, the planning and preparations for it illustrate the new command and control
relationship at work. Second, it highlights the interaction of political
and military factors that influenced planning and decision making.
This chapter will discuss first the political and security context that
gave rise to the decision to launch the operation. It will then examine
the command and control relationships in the wake of direct rule.
Next, I discuss the implications of the low-profile operational policy
and then the contingency planning that initially anticipated a much

more drastic operation than what was undertaken. Finally, I will explain the decision-making process that culminated in the launching of Operation Motorman.

THE POLITICAL AND SECURITY CONTEXT

It is clear that in the wake of Bloody Sunday the government understood the urgent need to break the political deadlock between unionists and nationalists, something only it might have the power to do. With direct rule placing control of the security forces firmly in its hands, London could ensure that security policy and political policy were pursued in a mutually supportive way. As William Whitelaw, the first secretary of state for Northern Ireland (SSNI), explained, the decision to impose direct rule involved "a deliberate choice of a policy combining political and military measures."[6] This included releasing some of the internees.[7] Historian Huw Bennett sees Whitelaw's approach as an effort, wholly in keeping with Clausewitzian strategic theory, to bring London's political objectives and the military means at its disposal into closer harmony.[8]

To achieve this effect, army operations in nationalist no-go areas were scaled back to what was described as "low-profile," to give political initiatives time and space to develop. In Whitelaw's words, this entailed restraining military measures to "well short of anything that could be represented as repression."[9] The army conducted significantly fewer patrols and other operations in those areas.

In the short term the no-go areas gave the IRA virtually "liberated territory," with a predictable outcome: terrorism increased. According to Whitelaw, 5,500 shooting incidents occurred in the four months leading up to Operation Motorman. Journalist Ed Moloney claims that, despite a brief respite in early May, the IRA it carried out 1,200 incidents in May alone and more the following month.[10] But GEN 79 (the cabinet committee on Northern Ireland, which by then included the SSNI) concluded that given the government's policy there was little alternative to a low profile.[11] Even as the security situation worsened, the government was reluctant to change security policy. The chief of general staff reported to GEN 79 on 25 May that the situation in Andersonstown (Belfast) was deteriorating; "Gunmen were now so numerous that troops could only patrol at night and in vehicles."[12]

However, this low profile did have the intended effect of lowering political tensions with the nationalists to some degree, and this did provide a political opening, albeit not one that played out as the government might have hoped.[13] The replacement of Stormont (a long-standing republican goal),[14] Britain's tolerance of the no-go areas, and its adoption of the low-profile security policy may have convinced the Provisional IRA (PIRA) that it was on the verge of victory.[15] On 20 June with Whitelaw's blessing P.J. Woodfield of the new Northern Ireland Office (NIO) and Frank Steele of MI6 met secretly with PIRA members David O'Connell and (future Sinn Féin leader) Gerry Adams. They confirmed that the IRA was prepared to call an indefinite ceasefire provided certain conditions were met. While Whitelaw's delegates rejected most of their conditions and other proposals, they agreed to face-to-face talks between the IRA and the SSNI as long as a ceasefire held for ten days. Woodfield came away from the meeting convinced (incorrectly) "that there is no doubt whatever that these two at least genuinely want a cease fire and a permanent end to violence."[16]

The IRA ceasefire began on 26 June 1972. Whitelaw says he immediately faced a lot of pressure to meet with its representatives. If he did not it would leave the political initiative in the PIRA's hands. He concluded that "no solution seemed possible unless their point of view were represented."[17] So, after the ceasefire held for the ten-day minimum that had been agreed to at the first meeting, the face-to-face discussions went ahead.

On 7 July the government flew an IRA delegation to London. In spite of the positive mood that had prevailed on 20 June, neither side had high expectations. Adams, who attended these talks as well, was highly sceptical of their likely value and of the ceasefire itself, which he thought the British would try to prolong to undercut the IRA.[18] Nevertheless, buoyed by their apparent success in getting this far – and perhaps as well by the knowledge that they had just received a major shipment of weapons – the IRA representatives presented Whitelaw and his advisers with a set of demands that amounted to an ultimatum of surrender. Senior PIRA leader Martin McGuinness said that "the only purpose of the meeting with Whitelaw was to demand a British declaration of intent to withdraw."[19] This clearly reflected a lack of political preparation on the part of the PIRA. Because the armed struggle – the "physical force tradition" – was dominant in PIRA ideology, the gunmen were driving the agenda. Sinn Féin was always seen as the political wing of the IRA, as subservient to the armed militants, not as the body that provided strategic guidance to the insurgency. Consequently, the PIRA delegation had no political negotiating strategy, only a "take it or leave it" proposition. Not surprisingly, the British declined to take it.[20]

After this the hard-liners in the PIRA prevailed. They seized on a bungled government decision as a pretext to end the ceasefire. Without consulting local Protestants, the Northern Ireland housing executive had announced that Catholics would be allowed to move into houses in the Lenadoon area of Belfast that had been abandoned by Protestants. Following Protestant objections, it reversed its decision. The reversal led to a clash between Catholics and the army, giving the PIRA a reason to end its ceasefire on 9 July.[21] Twenty people died in clashes over the next three days. The PIRA then raised the stakes in tragic fashion. On 21 July, in what became known as Bloody Friday, it set off twenty-one bombs in Belfast in less than an hour, killing nine people, injuring 130, and causing widespread destruction and outrage. This premeditated display of PIRA power backfired on it politically,[22] playing into the hands of the government. It already was developing plans for a major offensive against the IRA. Now it had the pretext, which the CGS later "freely admitted was deliberately exploited to justify Motorman."[23]

THE COMMAND AND CONTROL RELATIONSHIP

Direct rule had simplified the command and control relationship to a significant degree but, as suggested earlier, it did not wholly eliminate friction between the civil and military authorities. In a memo drafted for the defence secretary at the end of May 1972, the CGS, Gen. Sir Michael Carver, opined that it was difficult to define the army's role in Northern Ireland at that point and that this was causing "confusion, doubt and difficulty."[24] This memo followed by less than a week a visit by the CGS to the province and seems to have been prompted by two things. The first was Secretary Whitelaw's observation that "the IRA would have to be lived with because they could not be eliminated. The aim must be to reduce terrorism to a level where it does not interfere with political progress."[25] The policy mandating low-profile operations was intended to achieve this end. The CGS understood the reason for the policy, although he was concerned about its impact on security and on the army itself. Lt. Col. Ramsbotham's paper on direct rule and Operation Motorman (written later) makes clear the second issue. In his memoirs, Carver spoke highly of his admiration for Whitelaw.[26] But privately the CGS apparently held the view that the Ministry of Defence (and by inference, the army itself) was being marginalized by Whitelaw's agenda and even more so by his Northern Ireland Office. He noted that the SSNI was relying on NIO officials for security advice "and some of this was nonsense."[27] There was also, Ramsbotham wrote, "Ministerial [defence secretary] displeasure at being kept out of the picture."[28] In particular, a decision to lift the ban on marches without input from the MOD was "bitterly resented."[29] Former NIO official Sir Frank Cooper later attributed this failure to consult to lack of experience: "Initially the Northern Ireland Office didn't have anyone who knew anything about the military."[30] In light of such perceived marginalization, the CGS saw a need to reassert the army's prerogative in the field of its professional responsibility. In retrospect, it appears that the IRA's blunder on Bloody Friday provided the army with the opportunity to do so.

SECURITY POLICY: LOW PROFILE

In his 2013 article on Operation Motorman and British counterinsurgency strategy in Northern Ireland, Andrew Sanders argues that direct rule "provided those in London with a little more autonomy to pursue a more aggressive counterinsurgency agenda."[31] The evidence, however, does not support this assertion. As noted above, SSNI Whitelaw insisted that security policy be synchronized with his attempt to reach out politically to the nationalist community. The resulting low-profile army operations were far from being "more aggressive."

After some initial confusion on the part of the army about the security policy implications of direct rule, its commanders accepted the political need for this approach.[32] In fact, Huw Bennett argues that the army made good use of the "breathing space" provided by the low profile to improve the standards of its operations. It ran theatre-specific training courses, particularly for non-infantry units assigned to the infantry role. Several hundred officers, non-commissioned officers, and other ranks attended intelligence courses specifically oriented to the Northern Ireland situation. Efforts were made to improve army public relations and information policy.[33]

Some commanders resented the limits on their operations and the increased casualties to their troops. The CGS himself was concerned about the impact of the low-profile approach on morale.[34] The other negative aspects of this approach were two-fold. First, the quality and quantity of intelligence from the nationalist communities declined dramatically as the army lost contact with the population generally and with its regular information sources.[35] The second problem was directly related to the intelligence issue but concerned the larger question of the purpose of low-profile army operations. It was clear what military and political effects the SSNI wished to *avoid*; what was less obvious was what effects on the IRA these operations were actually meant to *achieve*.

In his 30 May memo to the secretary of state for defence, General Carver pointed out that the army's role had been clear during previous phases of the conflict. Up to the time of internment, it had been to prevent sectarian strife and to protect the Catholic population; from internment until direct rule, it had been to defeat IRA terrorism. Under direct rule, the aim was to "maintain our position" (what that position was he did not specify) and to do "everything we can, positively and negatively, to encourage non-violent methods of pressure and persuasion to bring violence to an end."[36] This was proving to be "a slow and uncertain process."[37] What concerned Carver was that the IRA was gaining strength in the situation, while the army was losing contact with the IRA and losing the initiative. If the army were to renew battle with the IRA later, it would do so from a position less favourable than at the time of the internment operation, thereby requiring more troops and possibly more force. He held out little hope that Whitelaw's goals would be achieved in the present climate and saw no evidence that the PIRA was weakening.[38] However, he felt the best approach for the army in June was "to keep the profile as low as we can without losing ground."[39] In spite of his differences with Whitelaw, Carver's final statement was consistent with the secretary's policy and wishes.

Presciently, as it turned out, Carver was concerned that the PIRA could announce a truce at any time and that this would present a problem for the British. What conditions would Britain accept during a truce? Would it cede control of the Catholic areas to the IRA? (He was asking if the current temporary no-go areas would become permanent.) He anticipated correctly that the IRA factions would demand "participation in political discussions," that Whitelaw would be forced to oblige, and that the IRA would accept nothing less than unification of Ireland. But the CGS also felt that if the PIRA saw no prospect of achieving these goals, it "would have strong reasons to renew their terrorism."[40] Events proved him right on every point.

In the medium term, Carver wondered what the army's role was to be. Whitelaw had made it clear that there was to be no return to the approach taken between internment and direct rule – that is, trying to "arrest or eliminate" every suspected IRA member. Indeed, Whitelaw felt they could not be eliminated, so they would remain in the Catholic areas, where, from Carver's perspective, they would be "inviolate, a threat to the Army, the RUC, the Protestants, the Government and any moderates."[41] Yet the army could not simply return to barracks or hang around as a target. Carver's solution was an amnesty that would allow both sides (republican and loyalist) to hand in their arms without penalty. If that was achieved, then the army could be pulled off the streets and a reorganized RUC could take its place.[42] Carver asked Carrington to discuss these issues with the SSNI, and concluded by stating that the army needed a clarification of its aims before the summer marching season got underway.

In the event, decisions and actions in Northern Ireland forced the government's hand and ultimately went some way to address Carver's concerns. In a conversation on 15 June the GOC, Lt. Gen. Sir Harry Tuzo, told Carver that he thought the PIRA was in "disarray" and, like Carver, correctly anticipated that it would soon seek talks with Secretary Whitelaw. In reference to the no-go areas, Tuzo felt that "no politician can continue to live with the Derry situation as it exists."[43] He also remained at odds with the political leadership on internment. He favoured releasing all IRA detainees if the group made an unequivocal commitment to end violence. But Whitelaw felt that was "too grave a step to be taken at present."[44] A week later, when Whitelaw told cabinet that the IRA was expected to announce a ceasefire, he said that if the statement was issued "*the Armed Forces of the Crown would obviously reciprocate.*"[45] This was a political commitment wholly within the purview of the SSNI, but it is not clear whether he had the army's or the MOD's support for it. However, the aftermath of the failed talks played into the army's hands. Ramsbotham felt that the housing executive's botched handling of the Lenadoon decision, which led to a clash with the army that gave the IRA a plausible excuse to resume its attacks, had discredited the NIO officials as "security experts." This allowed the army to make its voice heard once again.[46] And when it spoke it did so with the confidence and authority of a force that had the full support of the government and was prepared for the worst.

PLANNING FOR THE WORST: OPERATION FOLKLORE

On 13 July Prime Minister Heath told cabinet that he felt Britain *"should continue to pursue a policy of political and military restraint, tempered by a firm military response to flagrant provocation."*[47] This approach, he hoped, might lead to an end to violence and a chance to restart political discussions. But, he added, if the breakdown of the ceasefire was irrevocable, the cabinet might need to consider other courses of action: *"In consultation with the appropriate ministers [the prime minister] had begun examining a number of contingencies."*[48]

Bennett places the start of the operational planning process at 24 July, but official records show a much earlier genesis of the plan that ultimately became Operation Motorman.[49] Moreover, it was not a simple linear process from a single plan to the operation itself. There were three separate planning efforts, working on different timelines. HQNI was supposed to develop its own plans between 15 and 17 July. But the commander land forces at HQNI was drafting the one that eventually became Motorman as early as 7 July – the very day that Whitelaw met with the IRA. HQNI sent the plan to the SSNI on the 9th. In the ensuing days, the machinery of government in London inserted itself into operational planning in a major way. Former MOD official Arthur Hockaday (by then of the Cabinet Office) first drafted a set of possible scenarios to frame options and then set up a working party in the cabinet secretariat to develop a separate plan. It included members from the Ministry of Defence, the Northern Ireland Office, the Home Office, and the Foreign and Commonwealth Office (FCO). The group first convened on 17 July, drafted and circulated a plan, and discussed it with HQNI. At the same time, the MOD set up its own working party, led by the D/DOP, to coordinate input from all services into drafting another plan. The two London efforts were to be merged into a single plan by 21 July.[50]

Hockaday presented his group with a drastic scenario: an irrevocable collapse of the ceasefire, rising IRA terrorism and UDA reprisals, and a decision by the government to take "ruthless but non-discriminatory action to put an end to intersectarian violence and to administer a violent shock in the hope of bringing both factions ... to realise the imperative necessity of an agreed political solution."[51] Such action would entail imposing a temporary state of emergency on Northern Ireland and placing the rest of the UK "on a warlike footing to the extent necessary for the conduct of the operation."[52] Troops would move in force into Belfast and Derry, search all premises for arms and explosives, and occupy the no-go areas. In addition, they would impose curfews and would be authorized to use deadly force to enforce them. All leave would be cancelled; the army would draft in every soldier who could be spared from the UK Land Forces and the British Army of the Rhine, and would requisition ferries to move the troops to Ulster.[53]

In his cover letter to Kenneth Jones at the HO, Hockaday conceded that some of what he was proposing "may look like science fiction," but he emphasized that the working party had been tasked with producing a paper that would tell ministers how the group would plan "in practical terms" to implement just such a drastic policy option. "We shall not be thanked," he added, "if we tell them that it is all too difficult or too horrible; they will want to know how the difficulties can be surmounted and what horrors might have to be accepted in doing so."[54]

Taking Hockaday's worst case scenario as a starting point, the MOD working party drafted a plan code-named Operation Folklore. It was almost identical to the 1971 plan drafted by the COSC to prepare for the expected opposition to direct rule.[55] Annex 10 stated explicitly that the intention of the working party's effort, with MO 4 doing most of the work, was "to produce a ... paper very like DOP 511/71 which covered Direct Rule. In fact, many of the appendices in 511/71 are still relevant and can be easily revised."[56] In his brief to the CGS and the VCGS, the director of military operations (Maj. Gen. Ronald Coaker) posed a series of discussion points and questions to be raised with Lt. Gen. Tuzo during a planned visit on 14 July. These included the system of government by decree, the mechanics of declaring a state of emergency, the concept of operations, revising the directive to the GOC, powers, intelligence, force levels, and logistics. The MOD team would visit HQNI on 17 July to hear and discuss the GOC's recommendations on each question.[57]

In tone and shape Folklore certainly was consistent with Hocka-day's planning assumptions. It also fit the army's desire to reassert its place in defining security policy. If sectarian violence forced the army to take on both sides at once, the plan entailed "swamping of the province by every available soldier."[58] During what amounted to a month-long "occupation" of the province, the military would have to help run public services. The operation would be presented as a response to a "dramatic grave emergency."[59] To implement the Folk-lore plan, HQNI proposed a force level of forty-seven units (twenty-seven above levels in the province at that time) and the complete dis-armament of the population, to be achieved by house-to-house searches throughout the province.[60] Other measures might include curfews, expanded powers of search and arrest for the security forces, detention or internment, special courts with new rules of evidence, and free-fire areas.[61]

Although unprecedented on British home territory since the Irish rebellion of 1916–21, operations of this sort had been used in counter-insurgency campaigns in former colonies during the withdrawal from empire. Following the Irgun's July 1946 bombing of the British civil and military HQ in the King David Hotel in Palestine, the army had cordoned and searched the entire city of Tel Aviv. Of a population of 170,000 people, the army screened some 102,000, and one in ten of those were detained for more thorough questioning by the police. In the end, 787 were sent into long-term detention, but the perpetrators of the bombing were not caught. Then, as terrorism increased the fol-lowing winter, Britain imposed martial law on Tel Aviv and part of Jerusalem, and in Nathanya in 1947.[62] Likewise, during the Mau Mau revolt in Kenya in 1954, the army conducted Operation Anvil: a large cordon and search and mass detention operation in Nairobi.[63] More than 50,000 people were screened and nearly half were detained with-out trial. These operations had yielded mixed results, but there was no denying their shock value.

What emerges from the documentary record is that, even before Bloody Friday occurred, the government and the army were contem-plating similar treatment for Northern Ireland. Ministers and officials were preparing a package of "really draconian security measures throughout the province, backed by a really high force level."[64] The intention was that the extra troops and powers would allow the secu-rity forces to reclaim the no-go areas. The intense security measures would "drastically affect the everyday lives of all the inhabitants, guilty and innocent alike."[65] The planners hoped this would prompt the moderates to turn on the extremists, forcing them to stop the violence so that normal life could be restored.[66] But the CLF himself said that disarming the population was "impossible," suggesting that an amnesty might work better. And Coaker anticipated that the GOC might question whether the operation could be reconciled "with the aim which is to stabilise the situation for a resumption of HMG's political initiative."[67]

DECISION MAKING

As intended, on 22 July the Cabinet Office and MOD plans were consolidated into a single report, which Burke Trend submitted to Heath the following day. The report laid out the worst case scenario and assumptions, the draconian plan for restoring order (including the CLF's suggestion of an arms amnesty instead of an indiscriminate search), the implications, and the political initiative meant to bring about long-term stability. The report did not pull its punches. It anticipated loss of life, polarization of attitudes and alienation of the two communities in Ulster, the need to re-introduce internment, and the likelihood that the legislation needed to implement the state of emergency would not command bipartisan support in Parliament. It suggested that the atmosphere created by the military operation would not be conducive to the success of any possible peace conference. The operation also could alienate the international community, leading to pressure on the economy and on sterling. The report concluded that, unless the military operation were accompanied by a political initiative, it might achieve only modest, localized, temporary success. But the prospects for a political initiative following such an operation were not promising.[68] Four annexes addressed military plans, civil administration, legislation, and political initiatives.[69]

After discussing the report with the CGS and the permanent secretaries, Burke Trend on 23 July sent the prime minister a memo that summarized what he saw as the key points Heath had to consider, such as the need for legislation, for massive reinforcements, and for the reintroduction of internment. The memo also emphasized that the drastic action proposed in the report presupposed that violence had reached the point at which "any kind of tolerable existence in

Northern Ireland is on the verge of becoming impossible."[70] Trend
said further that, "we have not yet reached that point; and the general opinion of my meeting was that even the IRA violence of Friday
does not really provide us with adequate grounds for moving to
the course of action envisaged by the report."[71] With that pronounce-
ment, Operation Folklore was effectively discarded. On 27 July, as GEN
79 met to approve Operation Motorman, it instructed officials to keep
the Folklore plan under review, and they did so at least up to November 1973.[72]

In the meantime, Trend's 23 July memo to Heath, undoubtedly
influenced by Bloody Friday and the reaction to it in the media,[73] also
argued that "the present policy of maximum conciliation tempered
by a firm but selective response to provocation may no longer suf-
fice."[74] This being the case, the government might wish "to consider
an alternative course of all-out military action directed specifically
against the IRA."[75] Such a plan was already in hand. That same day the
DMO circulated a draft plan for Operation Motorman, a scaled-down
version of Folklore with more limited objectives (the occupation of
all no-go areas) and requiring fewer troops.[76]

The selection of this plan was not immediately a foregone conclusion. In the GEN 79 meeting on 24 July, Whitelaw suggested "that Ministers should form a view on the general policy to govern security
operations *in the coming weeks*."[77] In light of Bloody Friday and the
rapid generation of plans for a major counterterrorism operation, his
remarks seemed to fall short of a clarion call to immediate action.
Apparently ignoring the Motorman plan at that point, he went on to
identify the three courses of action he saw available to the government: to continue the existing policy of selective responses to events;
to conduct an operation to restore security forces' presence in the no-
go areas; or to launch a "comprehensive operation" to saturate the
urban areas with troops and disarm the population (that is, the Folklore plan). He felt that the report by officials (discussed above) ruled
out the third option because of the likely political repercussions. At
the same time, he wasn't entirely convinced the second option would
succeed; leading IRA men were likely to disappear before they could
be arrested, the Catholic population would be alienated, and the IRA's
ability to sustain its campaign "would be only partially impaired."[78]

Nevertheless, the SSNI recognized that it was necessary to intensify
operations in order to put more pressure on the IRA and "*to conciliate*

Unionist opinion.[79] With the latter point in mind, he noted that the Bogside and Creggan areas of Derry had symbolic value, and that launching an operation against them would not require the massive influx of additional troops required for Folklore. Moreover, it could be launched on relatively short notice – within a week of ministerial approval. This seems to have been the genesis of a variation of the Motorman plan that was later code-named Car Can. Whitelaw acknowledged that, should this option be accepted, a wide range of issues remained, many of which had been identified in the Folklore report: command and control of the RUC and Special Branch; the use of (and issues arising from) internment and interrogation; and the legal issues regarding soldiers' use of force and powers of arrest.[80]

The summation of the discussion says the committee agreed that, if the situation warranted, more intensive military action restoring "a military presence in the Bogside and Creggan areas ... should be a prime objective."[81] It also suggested that the defence secretary authorize the CGS to discuss the military aspects with the GOC. The ministers wanted to discuss the matter further, based on a report on its military scope and feasibility, and on the views of the SSNI on its political implications.[82] So, three days on from Bloody Friday, the government had not reached a decision on how to respond.

On the face of it, this slowness to respond seems odd, given that a military plan to re-occupy *all* of the no-go areas (Operation Motorman) already had been drafted and circulated. But there appears to have been an element of political expediency at work. First, the plan suggested in GEN 79 represented a not too subtle shift – that is, to an operation that would be limited to the no-go areas of Derry only. This change would require further consultation among senior military leaders. Second, just as in the case of the internment operation one year earlier, the British government hoped that such an action would deter action by loyalist militants. Third, the delay in decision making required to consider the Car Can option probably would play to the government's advantage in the domestic political arena. Because of the weekend break, the SSNI had yet to brief Parliament about how the government intended to respond to Bloody Friday. Allowing debate in the House would maintain the "tradition," however superficial, of consulting Parliament before acting. Trend himself had suggested this – "any parliamentary action in the meantime, e.g. a debate on Monday, being presumably of a 'holding' nature."[83] So, with a plan to re-occupy the no-go areas now in his back pocket (though not yet approved) Secretary Whitelaw described with rhetorical flourish in the House on 24 July the effects of the Bloody Friday bombings, then appealed for parliamentary support for as yet unspecified action against the IRA: "No one can deny ... that Her Majesty's Government have now an absolutely unchallengeable right to ask the House, the country and, indeed, the whole world for their support in an absolute determination to destroy the capacity of the Provisional IRA for further acts of inhumanity."[84] He then went on to outline the government's two-part strategy: "Our first objective must be to destroy the capacity of the Provisional IRA to terrorise the community ... Our second objective is to pursue urgently our aim of finding a new basis for the administration of Northern Ireland in which the minority will have a true part to play and in which we can work towards measures that benefit Northern Ireland as a whole rather than favouring one community or another."[85]

Speaking for the Labour opposition Merlyn Rees, who would become SSNI two years later, endorsed stronger security measures but also posed some prescient questions for Whitelaw: "Is it clear to the Army what its role is? Is the Secretary of State for Defence to play a greater political role? Has there been a change in the Government's policy towards the no-go areas?"[86] He also wondered aloud if the government had considered what might happen if the proposed conference failed to reach an agreement.[87] Other members of the House were less measured in their criticisms of the government. They variously blamed it for allowing the IRA to grow in strength, and criticized it for negotiating with the IRA and for a supposed failure to search for arms more thoroughly. Some demanded martial law, while others suggested revising the border, demanded special court procedures for terrorist offences, or claimed that Britain did not understand that the Irish problem was the British presence itself.[88]

The SSNI left it to his minister of state, Paul Channon, to respond to the many points raised. But Channon wisely refused to be drawn on the important questions put by Rees, since a decision on the no-go areas had not been taken at that point, and in any case he probably did not know the details.[89] He was not present at meetings of the GEN 79 committee and was not on the circulation list of the plans for Operation Motorman.

Even as debate raged in the House, that plan and some alternatives were under active consideration. As proposed by GEN 79, and after meeting with Carrington and the attorney general, the chief of the general staff flew to HQNI to discuss with the GOC the possibility of an operation against only Creggan and the Bogside. Carver told Tuzo that the target date for the operation was 31 July, although "no firm decision could be expected before the GEN 79 meeting on Thursday July 27th."[90] He also said he was "under contract" for that meeting to set out "the courses of action open to the security forces."[91] The CGS asked HQNI to prepare a paper for him to use in his meeting with Whitelaw the next day, "which set out the advantages and dis-advantages of MOTORMAN, CAR CAN or any other course."[92] The CLF explained that he and the GOC preferred simultaneous action in Derry and Belfast because it was impossible to predict how the IRA would react. If it were faced with overwhelming force, the IRA might "go to ground" and hide its weapons. But some members might stand and fight, and an operation against the Derry no-go areas alone might generate massive civil disobedience, "which could disrupt anything other than a sudden and quick assault."[93]

Further discussion raised the point that a simultaneous operation in Belfast and Londonderry would make it clear that the security forces were taking action against the whole of the IRA, while an operation in Derry alone would appear vindictive. It would cause violence in Belfast that would require additional troops. Deploying extra troops to the province was a challenge. Operations against one city or the other could be done more quickly, with troops deployed from UKLF. But to act in both cities at once would require troops from BAOR, which would not be available until a week after their deployment was authorized.[94] This raised the problem of timing; the group pondered how long the operations in response to Bloody Friday could be delayed while still allowing the security forces "to cash in on the present mood of the people."[95] Carver wrapped up his meeting with the GOC by asking if it might be a good idea to suggest to Whitelaw that he be given a military liaison officer. The intention of this proposal was to avoid a repeat of past occasions in which no records of meetings had been kept, resulting in some misunderstandings about what had been agreed. Tuzo concurred, and the CGS agreed to discuss it with the SSNI the following day.[96]

After a morning of briefings from brigade commanders, Carver and Tuzo met with Secretary Whitelaw, the permanent undersecretary of the NIO, and the assistant undersecretary for Northern Ireland. Whitelaw opened the discussion by saying that all of his political advisers agreed that it was time to take action, particularly against the Bogside and Creggan, which they considered to be more important than Belfast. He urged that the two areas in Derry should be dealt with first; Belfast could wait. He said the operation should be mounted "as soon as possible," before the mood that would support action faded. Cabinet could not approve the operation before its meeting on the 27th, but he wanted the operation launched on the 29th, to precede both any pronouncements by the UDA regarding their intentions towards the Derry no-go areas and a demonstration planned by the Northern Ireland Civil Rights Association for the 30th to commemorate the six-month anniversary of Bloody Sunday.[97]

The CGS disagreed on both format and date. He pointed out the risk of uproar that might prevent a follow-on operation in Belfast if Derry was tackled first on its own, then explained that, by postponing the larger operation to the 31st, more troops would be available from the NATO force in Germany. Whitelaw was unmoved; he felt that the political disadvantages of the larger operation outweighed the military advantages. Tuzo weighed in by pointing out that there would be an inevitable reaction in Belfast to an operation in Derry and that it would be better to have troops already in place in those areas where trouble was likely to break out: Andersonstown and Ballymurphy. Whitelaw's deputy, the PUS, undercut his political master by siding with the CGS and the GOC, saying that "the writ of the Crown ought to be reasserted in all areas."[98] Under pressure from all quarters, Whitelaw began to give way. He acknowledged the wisdom of the later date. He questioned the need for armored vehicles Royal Engineers (AVRE) to clear barricades, but Tuzo pointed out that the barricades were symbolic and would be protected by covering gunfire. Without the AVREs, soldiers would be shot trying to remove them.[99]

The one point on which Whitelaw would not be moved was his refusal to endorse the reintroduction of internment. He was convinced that doing so would turn the Labour Party against the operation, a bipartisan approach to the problem, and the army itself. He was not prepared to risk losing public support, thus and jeopardizing any political initiative. Carver pressed him on what to do about known gunmen who might be picked up but against whom there was insufficient evidence for trial. Carver resorted to "doomsday" language, saying bluntly that, "unless there was some way of removing them from the streets the IRA could not be beaten."[100] Put on the spot by the prospect that the operation might yield no tangible results, Whitelaw relented slightly. He was prepared to approve twenty-eight-day detention orders, but no long-term internment. While the GOC argued that the threat of internment provided valuable leverage for gaining information without resorting to interrogation, the discussion effectively ended there.[101] Carver approved the deployment of three additional battalions, pending approval by Whitelaw. He then returned to London to brief Carrington.[102] The careful bureaucratic language in the report compiled by Carver's military assistant barely disguises what was clearly an acrimonious discussion. Neither the army nor Secretary Whitelaw had come away with all that they had wanted.

While the CGS was concluding his discussions in Northern Ireland, Car Can was beginning to take concrete form as a variation on or an alternative to the Motorman plan. Although GEN 79 had not specifically requested it, the CGS had come away from that meeting with the impression that the ministers needed a paper laying out the pros and cons of Car Can versus Motorman. A.W. Stephens, the head of DS10 at the MOD, started to draft the paper in the CGS's absence, only to discover that HQNI had prepared its own study at the request of the CGS. This illustrates how easily the military and civil structures could find themselves duplicating each other's efforts as a result of confusion.

Stephens incorporated HQNI's key points into his 25 July paper. While the details of Car Can are sketchy in the sources consulted, it promised several advantages over Motorman. It required fewer reinforcements (three battalions rather than seven) and could be mounted two or three days sooner, which, Stephens wrote, "is important if public recollection of Bloody Friday is beginning to fade."[103] He then added that it would address "the main strand of Protestant (and government back-bench) criticism of no-go areas and thus remove pressure from those quarters."[104] But it had the same disadvantages that applied to Motorman: it would be seen as a one-sided blow against Catholics and would be exploited as such in IRA propaganda. Moreover, Stephens pointed out, it would be "difficult to justify, to the

Catholics and to the world at large, singling out the Bogside and Creggan for specially intensive 'invasion' and occupation – when the worst ... recent Provisional violence has been in Belfast."[105]

Brigadier M.S. Bayley of the defence intelligence staff criticized the Car Can plan on the grounds that it would provoke "an immediate and violent reaction" in the Catholic areas of Belfast, for which the security forces would not be as well prepared as they would under the Motorman plan.[106] In the meantime, HQNI devised a compromise: a two-phase operation code-named Motor Car. It would open with the assault on the Bogside and Creggan, and finish with the rest of Motorman (i.e., removing the barricades in Belfast). But this offered only the advantage of starting sooner; the extra reinforcements would still be needed to deal with Belfast and would have to be in place in advance to deal with any unrest there arising out of phase one.[107] Car Can and Motor Car, therefore, did not offer viable alternatives, narrowing the government's options considerably.

As a number of officials had suggested, time was an important consideration. On 26 July Carver drafted and sent to the defence secretary a paper to be presented to the GEN 79 meeting the following day. It made the case for action before memories of the Bloody Friday bombings faded:

> It is important to exploit quickly a situation in which firm and effective action by the Army against the IRA appears acceptable to a wide range of opinion, including a significant proportion of Catholics. If this opportunity is not taken, it may be very difficult to pursue any operational policy which holds out any hope of making significant in-roads into IRA strength and their hold on the Catholic community. The Army's feeling of frustration and the dangers of a violent Protestant reaction would be resurrected.[108]

There was an implicit element of fear mongering, if not blackmail, in this message; the CGS was not above manipulating the fears of the politicians that things could get worse. Yet there was a strong element of practicality to it as well. In his view, there was a brief window of opportunity, occasioned by a temporary shift in Catholic attitudes, that would allow the British forces to enter and take control of the

Bogside and Creggan without much local opposition. But it would have to be done soon to avoid a prolonged fight. That said, the CGS and the SSNI were politically astute enough to recognize that it would cause less trouble if the operation were postponed until after the NICRA march on the 30th. So, 31 July – ten days after Bloody Friday – appeared to be the earliest practical date to launch it. The CGS's paper then asked the committee to approve reinforcements (four battalions from UKLF and three from BAOR) and to decide whether to act against the Bogside and Creggan first or to conduct simultaneous operations in Derry and Belfast.[109]

Without waiting for GEN 79 to deliberate, the cabinet met on the morning of 27 July and approved Operation Motorman, a launch date of 31 July, the deployment of the reinforcements requested by the army (including the AVREs), and the idea that a statement should be issued, warning residents of the areas of the impending operation. It would ask them to remove the barricades themselves or to request help from the army.

The cabinet left it to GEN 79 to recommend the content and timing of the warning.[110] The cabinet's decisions were influenced by several changes: Secretary Whitelaw had come around to the idea of a simultaneous operation in Belfast and Derry, and the CLF had reported that the operation could be mounted in full on 31 July, even if all the reinforcements had not arrived from BAOR. The DMO, therefore, recommended to the CGS that he press for the simultaneous operation.[111] GEN 79 met on the evening of the 27th and with relatively little discussion agreed that any warning message should be framed within the context of the government's political objectives – that is, "of removing terrorists from the heart of their communities, and thus preventing further atrocities; of restoring to all sections of the community the protection of the security forces; and of creating conditions in which the search for a political solution acceptable to all sections of the … community might proceed."[112]

Any warning, of course, eliminated the element of surprise, and would give time for IRA members to hide their weapons and disappear, if they had not already done so during the hiatus between Bloody Friday and the operation, which they must have anticipated. But the committee felt that every opportunity should be taken to minimize casualties.[113] While it violated a fundamental principle of military operations at the tactical level, issuing the warning made strategic and political sense in a counter-insurgency context.

In a telegram to Tuzo on 27 July, Coaker explained that cabinet had approved the use of AVREs to remove barricades, subject to a number of conditions: that they be referred to in public as "armoured bulldozers"; that their approach to the start line be concealed as much as possible; that they be used against the initial barricades only and not be sent into the "heart of Creggan and Bogside" unless needed to save lives; and that their turrets be traversed to the rear to reduce their warlike image.[114] In this case political considerations clearly and directly shaped tactical operations, with cabinet dictating how a certain piece of equipment should be used. This is not to suggest that the cabinet's concern about the optics of using tanks was misplaced; they were acutely aware of the political ramifications of the operation as a whole and of how the use of tanks might be perceived by the Catholic population and the media. That said, like the advance warning, this directive was another example of political direction shaping the tactics of a high-profile and high-risk strategic operation.

In fact, political considerations permeated the whole approach to Operation Motorman. The CLF's directive for the operation emphasized that it was consistent with the government's political objective: "to secure peace in Northern Ireland by reconciliation tempered by firm action against the terrorists. Our operations will therefore ... be conducted against the IRA only and not against the Catholic population."[115] The intent of the operation was to neutralize the IRA's "ability to influence events until a political settlement is achieved."[116] The message to be sent by Motorman was that it was not punitive, but rather meant to be "liberating," designed to recreate peaceful conditions in the Catholic areas so political progress could be achieved.[117] Of course, the Catholic population would not have seen the operation in such benign terms.

While the first priority was to neutralize the IRA, preventing any further deterioration in public order was to be achieved "in a completely impartial manner and without needlessly antagonizing any section of the community."[118] The CLF said it was vital to regain and retain the support of both Catholic and Protestant communities. So, the security forces would have to control the "interfaces" between the two, to ensure that all troops understood the need to maintain the goals of the political initiative launched with direct rule, and to secure the cooperation of the Protestants in removing their barricades "because of the need to appear impartial."[119] Stating clearly that the final resolution of the Northern Ireland problem must be a political one, the CLF went on to remind all concerned that "there is a general understanding, even amongst the Catholics, that military action is justified at this time. We must not throw away the advantage this gives us by unnecessary or stupid actions."[120] The CGS made similar points to the GOC in a letter the next day. He reiterated the need to avoid antagonizing those who were not directly supporting the IRA. He also stressed that troops must adhere to the "overriding principle" that only minimum force be used. Commanders had to bear in mind the importance of keeping the risk of casualties and damage to homes to a minimum.[121]

His letter was quickly followed up by a telegram from the DMO saying that the CGS's letter contained ministerial decisions reached only that day, reflecting a more impartial approach to the operation. He added that the PUS had "strongly advised" that, from a political and legal standpoint, it was in the army's interest that the CLF's directive be amended to bring the two documents into harmony.[122] The difference was largely over public relations: the CGS wanted it made clear that there was to be no "fraternization" with the UDA and that the Protestant barricades must come down no later than 8:00 a.m. on the 31st. He also stressed that, in spite of the objections by the GOC, the SSNI would issue a statement at 10:00 the evening before the operation, warning that the security forces would be removing the barricades and that civilians should stay indoors during their removal. Attorney General Sir Peter Rawlinson had pressed for this, pointing out that issuing a warning would leave the army in a much stronger public relations position should casualties occur.[123] While the GOC was tactically correct and well within his professional duty and competence to raise objections to the warning, it was entirely appropriate for the political leadership to impose its decision on the operation. The matter was closed, and the operation went ahead following the warning.

SUMMATION

By the time Operation Motorman occurred, the political and security situation in Northern Ireland had deteriorated to the point where the government had lost control of some portions – albeit relatively lim-

ited portions – of British territory. It had ceased to exercise its authority in what had become no-go areas in Belfast and Londonderry
where the IRA exercised authority and control. The IRA had, in effect,
created "liberated territory" – one of the hallmarks of successful insurgency. Protestant militants, inherently suspicious of London's intentions, were barricading some of their own strongholds. This was not a
situation that any government could tolerate for long and still be considered the legitimate authority. Operation Motorman represented a
classic counter-insurgency effort to regain the initiative simultaneously on two fronts: the strategic political battle for legitimacy (the right
to rule) and the tactical security battle for control (the ability to
rule).[124] It achieved the latter with relative ease: as the security forces
restored their presence with bases and patrols, the no-go areas ceased
to be such. Intelligence began to flow from the population, and a
wave of arrests disrupted the IRA. Most important, the levels of violence dropped dramatically. Restoring the legitimacy of British rule in
the eyes of the Catholic nationalist population, however, was not
achieved. It would take another quarter century of security and political efforts to persuade the IRA and its supporters that remaining
within the United Kingdom was politically acceptable.

The planning and decision making surrounding Operation Motorman makes one thing abundantly clear: While direct rule streamlined
the command and control process by taking Stormont out of the
equation, it did not eliminate political-military friction. One possible
source was the new Northern Ireland Office, which, if Frank Cooper
is correct, comprised civil servants with little experience dealing with
the military and security issues. But the SSNI himself may have been
the real source. William Whitelaw was no shrinking violet; he was
assertive and self-confident and had all but a blank cheque from
Heath to run Northern Ireland. He was a stark contrast to former
home secretary Reginald Maudling, who, in any case, had exercised
less influence over provincial affairs while Stormont still functioned.
Whitelaw listened to the army's concerns and advice, but he did not
feel obliged to follow their lead blindly. Nor should he have. But even
Carrington hinted that he felt that the SSNI had not consulted him to
a sufficient degree.

Moreover, early in his tenure Whitelaw seemed inclined to put so
much emphasis on political considerations that security policy suffered. The low-profile security policy was a case in point; as an effort

to reduce political tensions it made sense, and went some way to achieving that goal. But in terms of maintaining security in the province it was counter productive. The escalation of IRA violence in spring of 1972 could in part be attributed to the fact that, as a result of the low-profile approach, the army had lost contact with its sources of information and with the IRA itself, and thus its operations against the paramilitary group were less effective. Indeed, the army leadership felt that it was unclear what its operations were intended to achieve. Furthermore, the IRA seems to have perceived this posture as an indication of British weakness or weariness. Sensing possible imminent victory, it seized this opportunity to initiate a ceasefire, to enter into talks with the government, and to deliver an ultimatum that it thought would lead to a British withdrawal. When its hopes were dashed, it lashed out with even greater ferocity on what became known as Bloody Friday. So, the low-profile policy neither advanced the process of political reconciliation nor enhanced security; in all respects it was a failure.

In stark contrast to the debate over internment exactly one year earlier, there was, after Bloody Friday, no fundamental disagreement between the civil and military authorities over the need for a major operation to restore British control and authority in the no-go areas. The planning and decision-making process was prolonged mainly by debate over means, format, scale, location, and timing. In a sense, Operation Motorman was a compromise. Once the more drastic option (Folklore) and the more selective one (Car Can) had been discarded on political grounds, it was all that remained. And it was a plan on which the politicians and the army found sufficient common ground to reach agreement. Even so, differences had to be resolved. During this process the CGS resorted to fear mongering, but with no discernable effect.

Although Secretary Whitelaw refused to countenance a return to internment, he approved the use of temporary detention orders to hold those suspected of terrorism but against whom there was insufficient evidence to proceed to prosecution. The army was able to convince him of the wisdom of conducting simultaneous operations in Derry and Belfast rather than in Derry alone. It made a persuasive case that the former course would yield greater security dividends while the latter would prove more problematic. On the question of issuing a warning before the operation commenced, the army had to yield to the political benefits at the cost of a loss of tactical surprise. That warning and the ten-day lag between Bloody Friday and the start of the operation undoubtedly allowed the IRA to go to ground before Motorman began. Yet, given the time needed for the civil and military structures to develop and discuss complex plans, to alert and deploy troops from Britain and Germany, to allow some debate in Parliament, and to allow the NICRA march to proceed on the 30th, it is difficult to see how it could have been launched much sooner.

In short, the civil-military command and control system worked as it had evolved to do. The political leaders defined the political objectives to be achieved, and the army leaders devised methods and operations that were intended to fulfil those political goals. Throughout this process the army operated in its traditional role as both a professional instrument of policy and a political actor. It could hardly do otherwise; to serve its political masters effectively it had to engage in and influence the operational policymaking process by providing its professional advice. It then executed the operations that its advice had helped to create. Likewise, the political leaders and their senior civilian advisers sought to impose their vision, preferences, and limits on the army's operations. Although they strayed into the army's professional domain, it was necessary and unavoidable to achieve an agreed policy. But this two-way interaction blurred the lines between the professional and political roles of the army – and of the political leaders.

That is not to say that the political goals and the military methods and operations dovetailed perfectly; they did not. What the politicians hoped to achieve – either with the low-profile policy or through Operation Motorman – was not wholly attainable through the military means applied. Yet, by exploiting the IRA's missteps, Motorman achieved what low-profile did not: a significant reduction in the level of violence, which in turn created conditions in which political solutions could be explored in a bipartisan context. That process commenced in 1973 but collapsed in 1974 due to the militant loyalist insurrection discussed in the following chapter.

The Army and the Ulster Workers' Council Strike, 1974

STRIKE, INSURRECTION, OR COUP?

From 15 to 28 May 1974, a militant Protestant group calling itself the Ulster Workers' Council (UWC) conducted a general strike in Northern Ireland. Its aim was to bring down the province's new power-sharing executive and the Council of Ireland that had been negotiated in 1973 and installed in early 1974 to replace direct rule.[1] The action, which was more like a political insurrection or coup d'état than a strike, led and enforced by Protestant paramilitaries, was a complete success;[2] it brought commerce and public services to a halt across the province and toppled the disputed institutions.[3] As a result Britain reinstated direct rule.[4]

The UWC launched its strike by announcing on 14 May a reduction of electricity supply to Belfast, which began the following day.[5] That was just the opening salvo. The real power behind the UWC was the Ulster Army Council, a shadowy coalition of paramilitary groups formed in January, whose rhetoric left little to the imagination. In its 14 May statement the council said: "If Westminster is not prepared to restore democracy, i.e. the will of the people made clear in an election, the only other way it can be restored is by *coup d'état*."[6] Although the strike had been carefully planned, it seems to have caught the population by surprise. There were many work stoppages on the first morning but there was little mass support for the strike.[7] So the strike leaders turned to the paramilitary Ulster Defence Association to enforce it. UDA spokesman Glen Barr and commander Andy Tyrie later admitted that they had resorted to blatant intimidation and that it had succeeded. They also conceded that if they had not done so the strike would have failed.[8] So, from the outset it *was* a coup, not a popular uprising.

Over the next fourteen days conditions in the province deteriorated rapidly. The power supply was gradually reduced, forcing factories to shut down and plunging homes and businesses into darkness. That and blatant intimidation kept most businesses closed, disrupting the supply of food and other basic essentials. The paramilitaries then took control of food distribution, ensuring the public's dependence on them. They erected barricades across many roads, thereby disrupting both private and public transportation, which was already hampered by shortages of petrol due to the strike. It was a measure of the unpopularity of the power-sharing experiment that most Protestants supported the strike, however grudgingly, and that in the end the province's executive was forced to resign.[9]

ARMY OPERATIONS DURING THE STRIKE

During and after the strike, what stood out in the minds of many observers was the British Army's apparent lack of action to break it. A 1974 Northern Ireland Department of Commerce review noted that "there is no doubt that security forces were inactive or ineffective in dealing directly with what undoubtedly was a politically motivated rebellion."[10] In his memoirs Brian Faulkner, who had chaired the provincial executive, said that "we always found the Army making excuses for doing nothing and very slow to respond to any suggestions put to them."[11] This inaction clearly rankled the man whose political career was ended by the strike. After all, there were some 15,000 regular army troops in Ulster, on the face of it more than enough to put down a strike led by a handful of rabble-rousers. Writing then and later, journalists, scholars, and politicians alike have speculated that the army's inaction was due to a crisis in civil-military command relations, pitting the generals against the politicians in a major dispute over how to handle the strike.

Before we can examine the allegations of a dispute in any detail, it is essential to review briefly what the army actually did during the strike. Its official analysis of Operation Banner, the code name for the whole Northern Ireland campaign, makes only the briefest mention of the army's role during the strike: the distribution of fuel, which the report says was done *against military advice*.[12] That phrase alone suggests that there *was* some disagreement between the army and the politicians. But the army was involved to a much greater degree than that one activity would suggest.

Desmond Hamill, writing in the mid-1980s, says that, "for the first three days the Army left everything to the police because reports suggested that it was not too serious and more important, because no 'cries for help' came from the police."[13] Nor did any such cries come immediately from the politicians. At its meeting on 17 May, the executive devoted little time to the strike.[14] Under the terms of the power-sharing agreement, the British government retained responsibility for law and order, though the executive was free to bring its views on security issues to London's attention. But two days into the strike, the executive did not see it as serious enough to warrant much discussion, let alone to issue a request for army intervention. That same day Merlyn Rees, the new secretary of state for Northern Ireland, briefed Prime Minister Harold Wilson on the "deteriorating" situation and on plans to bring staff from the UK to run the power stations if middle management could not.[15] But the cabinet took no decision at that time.

Likewise, Parliament did not play a significant role in handling the strike. It was not in session when the strike began, and did not sit until 20 May, when Minister of State for Northern Ireland Stanley Orme gave a statement about the strike in the House. It adjourned on 24 May and did not sit until 3 June, by which time the strike was over.[16]

While the politicians delayed taking any decisions, the army had not sat idle. Early in the strike it conducted some reconnaissance and pre-planning to take over the power stations. This included assembling several hundred military technical specialists from across the armed forces to run the stations if asked to do so. However, for both technical and political reasons (discussed below), such action turned out to be impractical.[17]

On the 19th, in response to a request from the GOC, Defence Secretary Roy Mason authorized the move of the first Spearhead Battalion (1st Battalion, the Light Infantry) to the province. They began deploying on the 20th.[18] With the GOC's agreement, Rees directed the army to use some 1,500 troops to clear barricades that night.[19] The reinforcements from the Spearhead Battalion provided enough troops to remove roadblocks in some hard-line Protestant areas and to keep main roads open, but minor roads were still being blocked in many places. Moreover, keeping roads open once the barricades had been removed proved frustrating, as many roadblocks were replaced almost as soon as they had been cleared and the troops had moved on. While troops were engaged in this activity, the reserve Ulster Defence Regiment (UDR) was called out to relieve the regular army of some duties.[20]

On the 22nd the second Spearhead Battalion (1st Battalion, the Queen's Regiment) deployed to Ulster, with the advance party departing that evening.[21] The arrival of fresh troops provided the army with sufficient strength to carry out a brief "offensive" against the muscle behind the strike – the Protestant paramilitary groups. On the 25th the 1st Light Infantry and the 42 Commando Royal Marines arrested twenty-two leading paramilitary members, including three high-ranking leaders of the UDA and the Ulster Volunteer Force (UVF), and picked up almost all of the leaders of the Red Hand Commando, another militant Protestant group.[22]

Finally on the 27th the army took on the task of distributing petrol. Landing troops by helicopter, it secured control of the Belfast refinery, drove and escorted tankers that carried petrol to twenty-one service stations across the province, and ran the stations until the strike ended the next day.[23]

Together, the foregoing shows that, contrary to the assertions cited above, the army was not completely inactive during the strike. But it also shows that troops were used with real effect only in the later stages, when it was late to change the outcome.

It is important to recognize that the army's role was not limited to its overt activities on the ground. By far, its more important and influential role was played out not on the streets of Belfast but in the corridors of Whitehall. The chief of the defence staff, the chief of the general staff, and the GOC Northern Ireland were intimately involved in the decision-making process, as will be discussed below. As such they were fulfilling their professional obligations, but their role was unavoidably political as well.

THE ARMY AND THE STRIKE:
A CIVIL-MILITARY CRISIS?

Notwithstanding the army's actions described above, the conventional wisdom has been that it failed – or even refused – to break the strike, and that this was due to a major disagreement between the politicians and the generals. In his 1975 book *The Point of No Return*, journalist Robert Fisk wrote that, "to the public ... it looked as though Army and police were simply refusing to clear the streets and some SDLP ministers ... took the same view. They suggested privately to reporters that a kind of miniature Curragh mutiny was going on at Lisburn [HQ Northern Ireland]; that like their predecessors stationed in Ireland in 1912, some Army officers were unwilling to take on Northern Loyalists."[24]

For the sake of clarity, it should be emphasized that the Curragh Incident was *not* a mutiny.[25] The Third Home Rule Bill for Ireland, passed in May 1914, had been opposed by the unionist paramilitary Ulster Volunteers (UV). The unionist position had considerable support within the army, and some officers in Ireland feared that they would be "coerced" into acting against the UV.[26] The army commander in Ireland, Lt. Gen. Sir Arthur Paget, warned those officers who disagreed with home rule that, if they were not prepared to carry out their orders, they were to say so and would be dismissed from the army immediately. Gen. Hubert Gough, however, told the officers in his brigade that they could resign their commissions rather than confront the UV; fifty-seven, based at Curragh Camp, chose that option. Because they did so before any orders were issued, there was no mutiny per se, and they were reinstated later.[27] But this event caused a political crisis at the time and further polarized the Irish unionist and nationalist communities. Furthermore, the facts notwithstanding, the Curragh Incident took on the mythical mantle of a mutiny, one that has cast a long shadow over the British Army's role in Ireland.[28]

Regarding the 1974 crisis, Northern Ireland scholars Paul Bew and Henry Patterson wrote in *The British State and the Ulster Crisis* (1985) that "the army command in the north had no intention of using troops against strikers to defend a regime [the power-sharing executive] which they were convinced would collapse."[29] In his 1994 book *Fourteen May Days*, journalist Don Anderson says that many former members of the executive felt that the army's reluctance to act arose from the belief shared by the GOC and other senior officers that removing all the barricades the strikers had thrown up would require a massive military operation that would provoke a strong military reaction from Protestant paramilitaries. The army did not want to get into a conflict with them while also trying to contain the IRA. But Anderson cites one executive member who claimed to recall that, every time the issue of increased army action was raised, Rees expressed concern about armed reaction by the Protestants.[30] This raises the questions of whether it was the London politicians who were stalling or whether they were being unduly influenced in that regard by their military advisers. Michael Kerr offers a blunt answer: "it was not that the British [government] ... had lost control of the army: they [the government] simply chose not to act."[31]

British defence scholar Caroline Kennedy-Pipe, relying on the work of journalist Martin Dillon, says in *The Origins of the Present Troubles in Northern Ireland* that Prime Minister Wilson raised with Gen. Sir Peter Hunt, the CGS, the possibility of using troops to break the strike. She goes on to say that in a message sent to the prime minister via the MOD, the GOC, Lt. Gen. Sir Frank King, said he was not prepared to do so, "and in particular he was not prepared to take on the Unionists."[32] Her account, coming from a scholar known for her expertise on British military affairs, carries some intellectual authority. David McKittrick and David McVea make the same case as Bew and Patterson in their book *Making Sense of the Troubles*, citing King as their authoritative source.[33]

But is this conventional wisdom correct? The evidence marshalled in this chapter suggests that it was not, for two reasons. First, it overstated what actually transpired, turning what was normal give and take between politicians and generals about the best course of action into a civil-military leadership "crisis." Second, it tended to blame the inaction mostly on the army, when in fact it was the politicians who were most reluctant to take action. Once the army was given clear direction, it acted effectively and without hesitation. At no time did it refuse to follow political direction.

This raises an intriguing question: if there was no "crisis," no refusal to follow orders, then how did these notions become the accepted version of history? In order to answer this question, this chapter will first set the events in context by explaining the political background to the strike. Second, it will explore the government's decision-making process. Finally, it will attempt to trace the origins and development of the dual "myths" of army inaction and civil-military command relations in crisis. It will suggest that the answer lies in a mix of players and motives: media eager for a story angle and willing to speculate, and disillusioned Northern Ireland politicians frustrated by London's failure to support them.

BACKGROUND TO THE STRIKE

Almost a year to the day after suspending Stormont, the British government issued a White Paper intended to start the process of restoring self-government to the province. Under the plan the British government would retain control of law and order as well as finance. There would a new assembly, to be elected on the basis of proportional representation, and a power-sharing executive on which all parties would be represented. Finally, it proposed a Council of Ireland, made up of parliamentarians from the North and South, which would play a "consultative" role. The Northern Ireland Assembly bill was passed by the House of Commons in May 1973. In an election in June, all of the mainstream political parties in the North (the Ulster Unionist Party, the Social Democratic and Labour Party, and the Alliance Party) won seats in the assembly. However, there remained substantial opposition to the White Paper plan within the UUP, especially since IRA terrorism continued to plague the province. In November, after much debate, the three parties reached agreement on the creation of the executive. Brian Faulkner returned to the lead the province as chief executive, and the other party leaders (Gerry Fitt and John Hume from the nationalist SDLP and Oliver Napier from the Alliance) became cabinet ministers.[34]

Then, in December 1973, the three parties, the British government, and the Irish Republic reached an agreement (known as Sunningdale, where it was negotiated and signed) to create the Council of Ireland. This was to be a bicameral body: the Council of Ministers, with members from the Northern Ireland executive and the government of the Irish republic, would have "executive and harmonizing functions and a consultative role; while the Consultative Assembly, with members from the Northern Ireland Assembly and the republic's Dáil Éireann (the Irish House of Representatives) would have only advisory and review powers. Although the Government of Ireland Act, 1920 provided for such a council, and, under Sunningdale, its mandate was limited to tourism, conservation, and animal health, Ulster unionists feared that it was a step towards forced reunification. The day after Sunningdale was signed, Protestant paramilitary groups formed the Ulster Army Council to oppose it.

In January 1974 Britain handed power back to the Northern Ireland executive and assembly.[35] That same month the UUP voted against continuing to participate in the assembly. Faulkner resigned as party leader, though he remained head of the executive, albeit in a greatly weakened position of power, lacking as he did the support of his own party. Things then went from bad to worse. Sunningdale had not been ratified when Britain held a general election at the end of February. The Conservatives were defeated, and Labour came to power as a minority government. Wilson was prime minister again, Merlyn Rees became the SSNI, and Roy Mason defence secretary. The power-sharing executive remained in place, but its legitimacy and authority had been effectively nullified by the Conservative defeat and that fact that, in the province, anti-Sunningdale unionists won every seat but one. The unionists were now determined to bring down the executive once and for all.[36] With their electoral mandate and with the backing of the Protestant paramilitary groups, they were in a position to do so.

THE EMERGING CRISIS, APRIL–MAY 1974

At a cabinet meeting on 10 April, Rees told his colleagues that the security situation was "cause for great concern" and that the political situation, "already bad, could deteriorate dangerously."[37] It was noted in discussion that while the IRA was trying to give the impression that violence was increasing, the actual figures showed a decline. Still, Rees pointed out that suppressing terrorism required more effective policing, which in turn depended on the cooperation of the Catholic community. Such cooperation was unlikely to occur until the Sunningdale Agreement was ratified, yet pushing it through risked toppling the executive. Rees concluded by saying that he felt "bound to warn his colleagues that the political situation was extremely fragile and there was a danger of political collapse."[38]

The day after the meeting Cabinet Secretary Sir John Hunt sent a note to the Prime Minister Wilson, reminding him that cabinet had agreed to create a small working group to draft a contingency plan to deal with the potential collapse of the executive. This group would include all the current members of the cabinet committee minus the PM himself and the lord president of the council. The defence secretary would be a member, but the CGS would not be invited, at least at the outset. A smaller group of deputy secretaries would do the preparatory work.[39]

Notwithstanding the mandate of the working group created in April, London seems to have been surprised by the outbreak of the strike and was unprepared to deal with the crisis that would bring about the collapse of the executive. It allowed the House to adjourn in the midst of the strike and then was forced to recall it early to deal with the resignation of the executive and the political vacuum that ensued.[40]

COMMAND AND CONTROL DECISION MAKING

The Executive and the Strike

Since the Northern Ireland executive had no authority over security matters, it is not surprising that it did not focus immediately on the army's possible role in dealing with the strike. By 20 May, however, it was sufficiently concerned about its effects that it requested a meeting with Rees. He assured them of London's full support and said that more troops were being sent to the province.[41] But it was not until the 21st that the executive began to discuss possible action by the security forces. There was a consensus that "neither political action nor military action alone would be effective," and that the executive's decision to issue a statement about implementing the Sunningdale Agreement would "depend upon clear evidence of action by the security forces to restore law and order."[42] During further discussion members of the executive agreed that they would release their statement only after Rees had taken "action" on the security front. Furthermore, they agreed to ask him to set up a ministerial committee (on which the executive also would be represented) "to co-ordinate the civil and security aspects of the emergency."[43]

The following day Faulkner reported that Rees had agreed immediately to the idea of an emergency committee, which would meet on the 23rd at Stormont. John Hume, the executive's minister of commerce, then reported on a contingency plan for distributing oil and petrol (adapted from one drawn up in 1972). It would entail taking control of the main source of supply, providing bulk delivery to essential services, and distribution to others through twenty-one service stations. He told his colleagues that the army believed the plan was feasible, provided that there were sufficient troops, and that the legal implications and the possibility of sabotage had been considered. But during discussion, ministers expressed concern that if the army had to divide its attention between maintaining vital services and conducting its security duties, it "could not adequately carry out either."[44] On the 23rd Faulkner told the executive he had asked Rees for a decision by Westminster on its attitude towards using troops to maintain essential services.

As noted above, the army did indeed implement the contingency plan (or something very like it). On the 28th Faulkner reported to his ministers that the army was running a "minimal" petrol and oil distribution system. However, by that point the power stations were in the process of shutting down. In his view the executive faced two options: break the strike, either by waiting it out or through a gradual takeover of essential services by the army; or conduct negotiations with the UWC. Faulkner favoured the latter course. During discussion one minister suggested that the army needed to take "a more active role" while another pointed out that the army "had made it clear" that using it to break the strike was not feasible.[45] But no one seems to have asked whether it was even appropriate for it to do so.

Faulkner and the unionist members of the executive resigned later that day. What is notable in these deliberations is that, while some members wished the army could have done more, there was a general recognition of the limits under which the army operated – it could not be used to break the strike. So, in spite of frustration with the situation, there was no suggestion *in the official record of the executive* indicating that members thought the army had refused to do its duty. However, as will be shown later, individual members had some reservations about the army's role and made their views known to the press. But since London retained authority for security forces operations and control of the army itself, it is essential now to turn to London's response to the strike.

The British Government, the Army, and the Strike

In a statement to the Commons on 1 April 1974, Prime Minister Wilson had tried to assure members that there was no political interference in or constraints on army operations in Northern Ireland. "There is no question whatsoever of the security forces being prevented by political directives from taking any necessary action against terrorists." However, he went on to add that "the forces have always to bear in mind the consequences of their actions on the commercial and social life of the community which they are protecting."[46]

In short, he was saying that there were no formal political constraints or directives, only those of common-sense behaviour in a counter-insurgency context. But Wilson's statement was somewhat misleading, as both Labour and Conservative governments had been trying – with varying degrees of success – to influence or shape army operations since 1969 by providing what they regarded as appropriate political guidance. For its part, the army had tried to provide its political masters with sound military advice to assist their decision making while protecting its professional prerogatives in its field of competence – the conduct of military operations. It was a delicate balancing act on both sides, a complex relationship that would be tested during the UWC strike.

On 15 May, Northern Ireland Secretary Rees advised the PM that he had "put on immediate notice" troops capable of running power stations, while those able to run sewage plants had been placed on short notice. He had also put other troops on standby. Wilson authorized Rees to bring in the troops on standby if necessary without further reference to the PM.[47] The following day Nigel Nicholls at the MOD provided to Lord Bridges (the PM's private secretary) details on the units that the defence secretary had approved for notice to move.[48]

There seems to be an anomaly in this presentation of the decision-making process. The SSNI said that *he* had put troops on notice, while the secretary of defence had approved certain units to be put on notice. Rees may have been referring only to units already in Northern Ireland, and Mason to those units in the UK that might be required to move there. Even so, the SSNI may have unintentionally misrepresented what he actually did. Ordering troops to be placed on notice would have exceeded his authority, since he was not in the military/MOD chain of command. In the absence of evidence to the contrary, it seems fair to conclude that he *asked* the army to place those troops on notice.

In discussions held 17 May at the Northern Ireland Office on military aid for essential services, it was agreed that "no formal machinery would be required in London to deal with any requests which might be made from Belfast."[49] The same day the PM was advised that, following discussions between the NIO and the MOD, the defence secretary had reduced the "notice to move" times for troops warned for possible service in Northern Ireland.[50] As mentioned earlier, on the 19th Mason had authorized the move of the first Spearhead Battalion to the province. They began deploying on the 20th, and troops cleared barricades later that night.[51]

That same day Director of Military Operations Maj. Gen. William Scotter told the CGS (Gen. Hunt) that he had talked to Lt. Gen. King that morning, and that King had remarked "that Mr. Rees must decide on his philosophy for dealing with the Protestants. Did he want to hammer them or was he prepared to negotiate on some of the matters in dispute?"[52] The subtext of this was that the GOC was frustrated by a lack of guidance from his political master. This may explain Robert Fisk's claim that, by day four of the strike, rumours were circulating among the press that the army felt Rees was "mishandling the situation."[53]

Late the following afternoon (21 May), the ministerial committee of Northern Ireland (IRN) met to discuss the situation. Rees acknowledged that the security forces were "heavily stretched." The reinforcements had allowed them to keep main roads open, but minor roads were still being blocked in many places. In order to encourage the executive to issue its statement on Sunningdale as soon as possible, the army was removing roadblocks in some hard-line Protestant areas. The UDR had been called out to relieve the regular army of some duties, but more troops were needed.[54] The GOC reported the next day that he was pleased by the turnout of the UDR and that its "confrontation" with Protestant militants had gone "extremely well," though what he meant by that was not stated.[55] Service technicians also were standing by to run the power stations, but they would require the help of middle management, who were likely to walk out if the army arrived. In that case, as many as five additional battalions might be needed to protect the stations from sabotage. This would have a serious impact on the army, disrupting training and requiring the redeployment of further forces from Germany. Wilson, in summing up IRN's deliberations, acknowledged the strain on the military, but the committee invited Mason to arrange for the deployment of an additional battalion to the province.[56]

The MOD acted quickly on the committee's direction. As already noted, on the 22nd it ordered the dispatch of the next Spearhead Battalion to the province, with the advance party departing that evening.[57] At the same time Minister of State Stanley Orme was trying to reassure representatives from the Confederation of British Industry that the security forces could handle the situation. He told them: "Technical troops were available to the Government and were currently being trained in Northern Ireland but the decision to commit them to the power stations was absolutely critical because once embarked on that course there could be no turning back. If the timing was wrong there was a real possibility that the workers would sabotage existing generating plants."[58] He explained that two more battalions were being sent to Northern Ireland and that, "if a confrontation was necessary then the Government was ready for it."[59]

The mood in London was less resolute than Orme suggested. Bernard Donoughue, who ran the policy unit at 10 Downing Street, says that the advice from Whitehall (including the Home Office and the NIO) was universally pessimistic. "Even the normally reliable Cabinet Office seemed to lose its nerve."[60] Lt. Gen. King and Field Marshal Sir Michael Carver (the CDS) had doubts about the wisdom of involving the army in maintaining essential services, such as distributing oil.[61] Earlier in the day on 22 May, Gen. Hunt had "expressed astonishment" when King told him that Rees would not be in the province until the 27th.[62] That afternoon King told CGS Hunt that the UDA was massing for a march on Stormont, that he had asked for political guidance, and that he hoped the police would break up the march "in the first instance."[63] Yet, there is no record that he received any guidance on that matter.

On the morning of the 23rd the chief of staff from HQNI attended a meeting of the Northern Ireland executive, ministers, and civil servants, who "painted a desperate picture with most of the essential services under extreme pressure."[64] When the IRN committee met that day, the SSNI praised the army for doing an "excellent job" clearing barricades, and Gen. Hunt, who had just returned from Ulster, told them that "most of the barricades would soon be down."[65] However, he added several cautionary notes: that public support for the strike was growing, and that the UWC's calls for the Royal Ulster Constabulary and the Ulster Defence Regiment to refuse to fulfil their duties would likely be effective among the RUC Reserve. The operation of Aldergrove airport as well as the telephone network were at risk. He said that the army was in contact with the Ulster Defence Association, which wished to avoid a confrontation with the troops. If the army intervened to break the strike, Gen. Hunt said, "confrontation and violence would probably follow. The army would be sucked into an endless situation and greatly increased numbers of soldiers would be required to run the territory."[66] Bew says that "it became very difficult to think of any military strategy that would have broken it [the strike] without serious loss of life, with incalculable consequences."[67]

Hunt's remarks are intriguing on several levels. He clearly intended to force his political masters in London to face some harsh realities. Opening roads was one thing; rolling back the strike was something quite different, and in his view the strike was gaining momentum, not the opposite. His comments to this effect put the ball squarely in the cabinet's court. But his assessment of the potential consequences of asking the army to break the strike was clearly also intended to put the brakes on any rash decision by the politicians. Fortunately, as Rees had indicated, there never was any question of the government asking it to do so. Finally, Hunt's acknowledgment that the army was in contact with the UDA, the muscle behind the strike, is significant. At a time when the government was refusing to negotiate with the UWC, the army was keeping a back channel open, presumably with the government's approval, since the NIO was doing the same.[68] Under the circumstances it probably was a sound tactic; it provided a useful mechanism for "de-conflicting" army and UDA actions to prevent any escalation of violence that neither side wanted. But it raises larger and more troubling questions: Did it serve inadvertently as a channel through which the UDA could continue to intimidate the government by threats of a greater insurrection? Did the army rely on such threats to support its strategic/political arguments about the need to avoid conflict with the Protestant militants?

The former may have been the case. Perhaps emboldened by the government's inaction, the UWC had issued a public call to "Loyalist Ulstermen and women" serving in the army, the UDR, and the RUC "not to allow themselves to be used as a political jackboot to their fellow countrymen who are seeking to re-establish democracy."[69] This was nothing short of a call to disobey orders, if not to outright mutiny.[70] Yet, there is no record that the PM or any other senior British official responded to this provocation.

Donoughue says that in a meeting at Chequers, the country house of the prime minister, between Wilson, Faulkner, and their top advisers on 24 May, all agreed to take a firm stand against the militants.[71] But in the official record there was no talk of confronting the strikers. While Faulkner warned that, with every hour that passed without firm action by the British government, the UWC was gaining political ground, the most that the government was willing to discuss was the possible use of troops to run power stations and to distribute petrol. And with respect to the power stations, Wilson was hesitant to commit troops because the middle management staff might refuse to work with them and the result would be even less electrical power. Indeed, that same day the head of the Electrical Power Engineers Association bluntly told Wilson that if troops were introduced into the power stations, its members would walk off the job, rendering the stations inoperable. Defence Secretary Mason concurred in the PM's assessment. In short, the assertion of government authority with respect to running the power stations might yield a pyrrhic victory. There was, however, more confidence about and agreement on the feasibility of using troops to distribute petrol. If they were available and there was no sabotage by UWC supporters, Faulkner thought army distribution of petrol to essential users would succeed. He did not think the council would force a confrontation, but he acknowledged that it might change its tactics and disrupt another essential sector.[72]

Although a paper prepared for the cabinet meeting on the evening of the 24th described the strike as "an attempt by extremists to establish a form of neo-Fascist government,"[73] and acknowledged that if the government did nothing the executive would fall, it did not propose any dramatic action. It ruled out using troops to "run the country" and proposed instead "a major political and publicity campaign" to show the government's support for the executive, and "some action on the ground to show moderate opinion that Her Majesty's Government and the Executive have the will to govern and are capable of influencing events."[74] But action was to be limited to oil/petrol distribution. That plan aside, the obvious reluctance to use the military to break the strike was at least politically consistent for a governing party that claimed the loyalty of and carried the banner for Britain's working class.[75]

When cabinet convened that evening, Wilson described the political situation in Ulster as "dangerous." The UWC, he said, supported by Protestant political and paramilitary groups "were dictating the course of events." They had closed most factories, and shops were open only with their permission. They were controlling the distribution of food and fuel, the output of power stations was reduced, and many government officials were unable to get to work due to lack of transport. The power-sharing executive had urged that the army take over distribution of oil and fuel at twenty-one service stations. Military technicians were available to work in power stations, "but it was doubtful whether the Army personnel would be able to run the stations without the supervision of middle management ... who might be unwilling to continue to work."[76]

In line with the note for cabinet, neither Rees nor Wilson was suggesting that action on oil and petrol be accompanied by action at the power stations "at this stage." Mason said that if the government decided to take over distribution of oil and petrol, military drivers and technicians could be sent quickly. But he warned cabinet that the operation would make heavy demands on the army: they would have to protect supplies in transit and at service stations. Furthermore, they would not be able to distribute more petrol than the UWC was doing. He added: *"It would not be possible for the armed forces to take over the running of the country if the UWC secured the withdrawal of labour generally."*[77]

Mason confirmed that the military could not run the power stations if middle management withdrew, and he noted that troops at gas stations would also need supervision. He also advised that the CGS was concerned about whether it was right to use troops for tasks of this kind in a situation where life and limb was not being threatened. The PM, summing up, said that cabinet agreed that the army should distribute oil and petrol to service stations and protect them and also should deliver needed chemicals to the Londonderry gas works. It also should undertake an immediate study of the feasibility of the army delivering food to Catholic areas. He asked Mason to issue the necessary instructions to King to carry out the approved actions.[78] It was left to Rees and King to decide on the timing of Operation Flare, as the oil/petrol operation was called. In a telephone call to the CLF, Gen. Hunt stressed that the GOC "should bring home the realities of Op Flare to SSNI."[79] But exactly what he meant by that is unclear.

The following day, Rees told Wilson that "we had now reached the point of final decision." He reminded the PM that "yesterday intelligence reports had put off a decision by making it clear that the UWC would knock out power stations if troops acted over oil supplies."[80] If the cabinet's decisions were indeed being influenced by intelligence on the UWC's threats, this lends weight to the idea that the army's "back channel" to the UDA was an unintentional "two-way street," serving the purposes of the UDA as much as those of the army.

If the government felt that the loyalty or integrity of the army were in doubt, it is not apparent in these discussions. In spite of the UWC's call to mutiny and the CGS's expressed concerns, there is no hint that the PM, the defence secretary, or any member of cabinet had any reason to believe that the army would refuse to carry out the mission assigned to it by cabinet. As noted earlier, the army had conducted an arrest operation against the Protestant paramilitary groups on the night of 25/26 May. While the records cited here say little about it, it is possible to suggest several aims of that action. First, taking key UDA and UVF leaders out of their command roles at that juncture may have limited the militants' ability to disrupt Operation Flare. Second, it sent a warning shot across the bow of the militant groups, reminding them that if things got rough they were up against a powerful force that could find and suppress them quickly and efficiently, with force if necessary. That said, there probably was an element of bluff in this exercise of escalation dominance, since the army's ability to use its power was entirely dependent on the will of the GOC, the PM, and cabinet, all of whom were reluctant to confront the militants. This may explain why, in its comments to the press about the arrest operation, the government did not link it to the strike, instead tying it to long-standing efforts to suppress Protestant sectarian violence.[81] It was a thinly veiled exercise in public relations, however, as the timing of the operation could not be lost on anyone.

The arrests may explain in part why Operation Flare went smoothly on 27 May.[82] Moreover, once it got underway the army displayed no lack of enthusiasm for it. In fact, the CGS remarked that it had "got out of control." The director of army staff duties had received a warning order for an additional thirty heavy truck drivers, and the DMO said that some in HQNI seemed "determined to produce a better petrol service than the UWC."[83]

Despite this success, at a meeting with the CGS that day the GOC had said that the options now open to the government were "almost unlimited." By this he meant that the government was "over a barrel," the executive was likely to fall, and the government could not defeat the strikers "who now smelt victory." He said that Rees was "coming around to accept the situation."[84] All the Northern Ireland permanent undersecretaries wanted direct rule restored, he said. The options King discussed with Gen. Hunt included a new executive to succeed the present one when it fell; direct rule, but with an assembly; removing the army from the province; or keeping the present executive going with the help of the army, which, he suggested "might do better at running essential services than we expected." But even the last scenario would result in great hardship for the population, possibly leading to "pitched battles and armed rebellion." The GOC blamed the NIO for failing to take the Protestant threat seriously. Calling for an offensive against the IRA after the strike ended, he concluded by saying that "*at all costs we must remain friends with the Protestants.*"[85]

That final sentence could be seen as confirming the suspicions of the former executive and the media that the army's leadership had refused to act against the strike, and that it did so out of political sympathy with the UWC. While the intent of that comment certainly is open to that interpretation, it more likely reflected operational pragmatism than political motives. The army's primary task was defeat of the IRA, and that consumed most of the troops deployed in the province. Using them to put down a strike and/or to provide essential services would undercut the primary mission. Furthermore, the tasks associated with the strike could have been taken on only at the expense of Britain's commitment of land forces to NATO, a situation that was both logistically challenging and politically problematic. Yet, it is telling that, in spite of King's reservations, the arrest operation had gone ahead, giving the lie to the notion that the army had refused to confront the Protestant militants.

That action aside, the army's counter-insurgency mission required the cooperation of the RUC, which still was a predominantly Protestant force. Neither King nor Hunt wanted to fight a "two-front war" against both the IRA and Protestant militants, in a situation where they would lack public support on either side and could not count on the police. Faulkner later wrote that he felt the army had "grossly exaggerated ... the likelihood of getting involved in a shooting war with the UDA if they took action against the barricades and the roving gangs."[86] But there was genuine concern about the attitude of RUC members towards the strike. In a 20 May conversation with Wilson, Rees described them as "much more wobbly ... very wobbly."[87] Four days later Rees asked Faulkner directly whether he thought the RUC would remain loyal. Faulkner said he would be "amazed" if they did not, but he admitted that he had received reports that they were not "enthusiastic" and said that experience suggested that "their instinct was always to avoid confrontation."[88] That evening Rees told the cabinet that the reliability of the RUC was "in doubt."[89] So, the UWC's appeal to mutiny may have had some impact on the RUC.

In any case, the government never asked the army to break the strike, only to undertake a limited fuel distribution operation. As far as the prime minister was concerned, that operation had not been delayed because of any pressure from the army.[90] However, after the strike ended the PM conceded that, this action aside, the army was "virtually powerless to maintain essential services. Even if they had no security duties – their main and abiding role – a few thousand soldiers cannot stand in for a hundred thousand or more who are on strike. On sheer numbers they could not do so *even if they possessed the necessary skills.*"[91]

Here Wilson identified a central problem, which was confirmed by subsequent studies of the military's experience during the strike. A 1975 NIO paper on contingency planning for the province noted that specialists from all three services would have been required to maintain essential services during the UWC strike. And even if they had been available, which they were not, they would have needed training on the installations they were required to operate.[92] The MOD elaborated on the NIO study, stating that the kinds of specialists needed to run all the essential services during the strike "were unavailable in such numbers because the Services do not specialise in all the relevant trades."[93] The ministry added that

the armed services have the expertise and capacity only to help provide essential services at very little above the health and safety level … They can in no way maintain or restore normal services throughout the whole province, nor would it be appropriate for them to become involved, for instance, in the sale and distribution of food stuffs … The armed services can make an effective contribution only if some managerial supervision remains available. They are not in a position to provide even a reduced level of service on their own.[94]

In the minutes of the first cabinet meeting after the strike (13 June), there is no discussion of the use of the army during the strike or of any problems related to it. The cabinet's only concern was with the next political steps to be taken to resolve the constitutional crisis. Reflecting on the crisis in a 1992 interview, Sir Frank Cooper, a former permanent undersecretary with the Northern Ireland Office, wondered whether the government could have made strike collapse "if the police had acted more decisively and if the army had been brought in more effectively."[95] He did not say what he thought that more effective use might have been.

The official records cited here make it clear that there was extensive civil-military debate over the best way to deal with the strike. During these discussions the politicians and the army did not always agree, though eventually they reached a consensus on what could be done. The concerns that animated the army – the lack of clear political guidance, the desire to avoid a two-front war – were legitimate operational issues, and the army leadership was well within its professional mandate to raise them. Yet, even where there was disagreement, at no time did the army refuse to do what the government asked of it. Thus, the official records give no indication of a crisis. That said, they may be incomplete and may have been edited to smooth over major differences. Still, if there had been a fundamental disagreement or showdown between the army and the politicians, it seems likely that senior figures would have remarked on it at the time or later. While Wilson's personal papers are not yet available to scholars, his memoirs make no mention of any army refusal to follow political direction;[96] nor does his authorized biography.[97] Likewise, Field Marshal Lord Carver, the CDS at the time, makes no reference to the strike in his memoirs, let alone to any problem with the army's actions during the events. So, much like the Curragh "mutiny," the civil-military crisis over the UWC strike seems to reside largely in the realm of myth. But this raises the question: if there was no crisis, then how did the myth arise in the first place? This is more difficult to assess than determining the facts of the army's performance during the crisis and the political reasons behind it.

SOURCES OF THE CRISIS MYTH

All of the official deliberations regarding the strike took place behind closed doors. Cabinet and committee meetings, and meetings between London and Stormont officials, were conducted in secret, as were communications among them. The same applied to the army and the MOD. But the British press covered the strike extensively for the duration, and it is clear that some reporters were remarkably well informed about the decision-making process, whether from press releases, army briefings, interviews with officials and army officers, parliamentary speeches, or off-the-record sources.[98] In short, collectively London, Lisburn, and Stormont leaked like a sieve. Official sources pushed their own agendas and defended their positions, which often were at odds with each other. And there is no doubt that the press put its own spin on the information and views it received, if only to make stories more newsworthy. But reporters were not privy to all of the crucial details and subtle nuances of the debates, leaving them to draw conclusions that are not sustained by the evidence now available. Even at this far remove, it is difficult to disaggregate facts from speculation, and rumour from editorial or political spin.

With its reputation under scrutiny in the aftermath of the strike, the army was determined to trace the source of the rumours that it had defied its political masters. Its suspicions initially fell on W.F.K. Thompson, a retired brigadier turned correspondent for the *Daily Telegraph* who retained close ties to the army. On 25 May he asserted that the government had decided "*to use the army to break the strike* to the extent of maintaining social services."[99] He added that since the majority of moderate Protestants probably disagreed with the strike but were equally opposed to the Sunningdale Agreement, the government "*in ordering the Army to break the strike* are in effect asking them to coerce the majority of the people in Northern Ireland."[100] He went on to say that the CGS had warned the government of possible consequences of action by the army. Thompson's army pedigree seemed to lend credibility to his claim. The same day the Manchester *Guardian* claimed that the cabinet had decided "to break the Ulster strike, whatever the consequences."[101] As the record shows, both of these stories were wrong. Moreover, the army felt that Thompson's column and similar ones in other papers "allegedly based on authoritative sources" had strengthened the UWC's resolve.[102] They certainly reinforced the narrative that Sunningdale was anti-democratic.

If Thompson was a culprit he was not alone, even in his own paper. Also on 25 May, *Daily Telegraph* reporters James Allan and James Wightman wrote that the army was "reluctant" to take over running essential services.[103] Allan and Wightman said that Gen. Hunt had warned the PM that using the army "against the will of the majority" could deepen the crisis into a "doomsday scenario."[104] Without saying so explicitly, these two stories, taken together with others in rival papers, suggested a serious civil-military split over handling the strike.[105] The notion of a showdown between the generals and the politicians gained additional traction from an account supposedly written by a serving officer and published after the strike in the magazine of the right-wing Monday Club.[106] The author asserted that "the unwillingness of the army to act to bring about the end of the strike (on the quite reasonable grounds that there was little or nothing it could do within the concept of minimum force) and *the subsequent confrontation between the army and the politicians*, must be the most significant event of recent years. *For the first time the army decided it was right and the politicians had better toe the line.*"[107] It was a serious charge, suggesting insubordination at the very least, mutiny at worst. And if it was correct it pointed to perhaps the most serious crisis in British civil-military relations since the Curragh Incident.

In his account of the strike, Robert Fisk alluded to suggestions about army-political discord made by SDLP ministers in the executive. Fisk himself drew attention to what he regarded as "fraternization" between army personnel on the street and members of Protestant paramilitary gangs who were enforcing the strike. There can be no doubt that there was contact between them, since photographic evidence shows it. Moreover, as noted earlier, the army maintained a back channel to the UDA, and troops negotiated with the association for the removal of barricades.[108] That may have been what Fisk and press photographers were seeing. Whether it amounted to fraternization is more difficult to determine. If the army's aim was to remove barricades without resorting to force, then talking to UDA members was unavoidable. It reflected pragmatic operational practice based on the realities of the situation on the streets.

As already discussed, Lt. Gen. King himself had told the CGS that "we" – meaning the army and probably the government too – had to remain "friends" with the Protestants. Without identifying a source, Fisk alluded to a telephone call between Rees and King in which Rees agreed that the Protestants should not be provoked. The army should not give them an excuse for over-reaction. Yet, "it was not an instruction, nor did King take it as such."[109] This ambiguous assertion leaves open to question whether it was Rees or King who was more concerned about keeping the Protestants as "friends," and which one was guiding that policy. Certainly, in his capacity as SSNI, Rees would have had a strong motive for keeping them on his side. King, by contrast, had indicated that he was prepared to "hammer them" if given guidance to do so, and, once given the go-ahead, he launched the successful arrest operation on May 25th. In his own defence when asked later why he did not order the army to break the strike, Rees replied, "We couldn't do a Prague. You can't put down a popular uprising by killing people. We're not Russia."[110] In an interview in August 1974 Lt. Gen. King said the virtually same thing.[111]

Having raised the ghost of Curragh, even if he attributed it to others, Robert Fisk retreated from it. He wrote that the army "neither disobeyed orders nor superceded its power."[112] That should have put the matter to rest. But the damage had been done; the whiff of mutiny hung in the air like a bad odour. Other observers picked up the scent, hinting at sinister motives and behaviour. In his book *Fourteen May Days*, Don Anderson says that many former members of the executive put a great deal of stock in the Monday Club article.[113] Yet, if the cabinet and other records are accurate, then it was incorrect, as were the *Daily Telegraph* stories. The government had not ordered the army to break the strike, and the army had not refused to do so. In fact, even before the army raised its concerns, the government displayed no enthusiasm to confront the strikers and was well aware that the army had neither the numbers nor the appropriate skilled personnel to run the vital services in the province. Consequently, it was prepared to use troops only for removing barricades, for an arrest operation against the paramilitary groups, and for a limited fuel-distribution operation. None of these were seen as breaking the strike or as likely to end it. So how Thompson and others reached the conclusions they did remains something of a mystery.

The army clearly was not an objective player in this situation: it wanted to clear its name. There was no formal enquiry into the matter, but there was a quiet effort behind the scenes to get to the bottom of it. Brigadier W.T. MacFarlane, the army's director of press relations, and John Groves, the chief of public relations at the MOD, determined that Thompson had been in Northern Ireland on the 22nd, returning to London on the 23rd. While in the province he almost made the army press office at HQNI his home, but he had not received any interviews or press briefings there on what advice the CGS had given to the prime minister. MacFarlane also reported that James Allan, who was working with Thompson in Belfast, had called the HQNI press office on the

23rd, saying that "they" had heard from London that the CGS was advising the PM against using the troops. So, if there had been a leak about
that issue, the *Daily Telegraph* reporters believed it originated in London. The *Guardian* lent weight to this, quoting Defence Secretary
Mason as the source on the army's "serious doubts and fears." He supposedly had said that army officers were "very unwilling to become
further embroiled in the situation, and unwilling to begin the first
strike-breaking operation in Northern Ireland since the troubles
began."[114] Mason did raise the army's concerns; it was his job to do so.
But those words do not appear in the minutes of the IRN meeting on
the 23rd. Either the *Guardian* was reporting an incorrect rumour or
the minutes have been edited to remove any hint of discord.

The London "leak," if such there was, had attracted a great deal of
media attention in Belfast. Groves and the CDS (who later asked Gen.
King about this) determined that the media assembled in Belfast on
the 25th had anticipated some major military action in the wake of
Wilson's speech that evening, even to the point of believing that it
would begin at 10 p.m. When that did not occur, speculation began.
Reporters began to interview soldiers, who explained that they were
standing by for an operation but had received no orders. Carver said
that an "experienced journalist could certainly have deduced that the
operation was not particularly welcome."[115] Fisk floated a rumour in
the *Times* on the 27th that the GOC had flown to Chequers and that
the use of troops was hotly debated there. He cited "sources at Stormont" to say that Mason had argued against using the army. This
tends to confirm the *Guardian* story.[116]

Overlooked in this version of events is the fact that there *was* an
army operation on the night of the 25th: the arrest of Protestant paramilitary leaders. It was a major operation but not the one everyone
seemed to be expecting, and was carried out overnight. Moreover, in
arguing against the use of the army, Mason was not simply parroting
the army's position; he was supporting the position already decided
by Wilson and Rees.

Lt. Gen. King was even more explicit in laying blame. In a letter to
Sir Michael Cary, the PUS at the MOD, he said the talks at Chequers on
the 24th between the PM and three members of the executive "were
extensively leaked."[117] He said that Gerry Fitt of the SDLP "certainly
phoned Belfast with a full report shortly after the talks finished and
this, I know, was passed to the press."[118] He felt that this report gave

the impression that Wilson had agreed to support the executive by deploying the army quickly into the fuel-distribution role. When that didn't happen immediately, the media – which King felt had gone out on a limb on the issue – had to come up with an explanation.[119]

Field Marshal Carver was equally blunt. He wrote to Mason saying that "it is impossible to escape the conclusion that the Army authorities have been unreasonably criticized."[120] Like King, he placed the blame squarely on the SDLP, "who had reasons of their own to keep the press informed" of what they mistakenly thought was the British government's policy. He also cast suspicion on other non-military sources, specifically citing the Northern Ireland civil service, which, he believed, passed on everything they knew to the Protestant militants.[121] Interestingly, as important as the issue seemed to be to him at the time, he did not repeat these concerns or allegations in his memoirs.

If these assertions are correct, then it is difficult to dismiss the army's complaints simply as special pleading. But this is not to suggest that it was wholly blameless either. The GOC had given an unattributable interview to the *Sunday Times* on the 23rd in which he had discussed some of the considerations he had to take into account, and a Lt. Col. Warren Sillitoe had spoken to a reporter from the *Evening Standard*. While Groves felt that the latter's interview was unwise and had resulted in inaccurate quotes, in his interviews for television and radio Sillitoe was very circumspect. He refused to be drawn on the question of whether the army had counselled against being used in a strike-breaking role. He also stated that if the secretary of state decided to use the army to keep the power stations going, it would "wholeheartedly carry out that instruction to the best of our ability."[122] Its performance during the petrol-distribution operation validated Sillitoe's assertion. But the interviews were immediately overshadowed by the fall of the executive and the UWC's outright victory the following day, and so the interviews were not sufficient to shake the image of an army in paralysis or in opposition to government policy.

SUMMATION

The UWC strike presented the government and the army with the most challenging problem of civil-military command and control since internment, perhaps even since the decision to deploy troops in 1969. As a minority government, the Wilson administration was in a weak position and was uncertain how to deal with the strike. The military – the army in particular – lacked the resources to provide essential services and was concerned about being drawn into a two-front war against Protestant militants as well as the IRA. As a result, the potential for a serious crisis between the generals and the politicians was very high. Reporting at the time, and accounts written later, suggested that such a crisis actually occurred. Some of these hinted at a near mutiny by the army.

The evidence examined in this chapter, based largely on the official record (which, it must be acknowledged, may be incomplete or carefully edited), offers a less alarmist perspective. It allows us to demystify the events surrounding the strike, at least insofar as they reflect the positions of – and relations between – the government and the army. First, the Wilson government never ordered the army to break the strike. The most it asked of the army was to remove barricades (an action that was only temporarily effective), provide a limited petrol-distribution capacity, and arrest leaders of the paramilitary groups. Second, the army never refused to do what the government requested. It carried out all three of these tasks. If there was any hesitation to take on the strikers, it seems to have been within the cabinet. Third, there is no evidence of a confrontation between the politicians and the generals. Perhaps unfamiliar with what was, after all, a secret and convoluted decision-making process, Stormont politicians and the press may have mistaken the civil-military debates for a showdown. The closest thing to a serious disagreement was Lt. Gen. King's comment that SSNI Rees needed to decide whether to "hammer" the Protestants or to negotiate with them, suggesting that he felt a lack of political guidance. Yet no one challenged or repudiated him on that point; his comment passed unremarked. Even more telling is the fact that in spite of his views on the need for good relations with the Protestants, King did not hesitate to order the arrest of their militant leaders and members. Moreover, the army apparently carried out fuel distribution with great enthusiasm.

The evidence presented here suggests that the government's options in using the army during the strike were limited by its numbers and capacity and by the government's desire to avoid a direct armed confrontation with the strikers, not by any unwillingness on the army's part to follow orders. The notion of a civil-military confrontation over the strike seems to have originated with the media, which drew credible, albeit exaggerated, conclusions from their own observations and from leaks by disgruntled members of the executive. Thus, unless we learn that there has been a massive conspiracy of silence on this matter, and barring the discovery of credible evidence to the contrary, the myth of the alleged civil-military crisis over the Ulster Workers Council strike can be put to rest.

Conclusion

In the introduction to this book, I noted that Peter R. Neumann's study of the conflict in Northern Ireland, *Britain's Long War*, makes two significant observations about the command and control of the army's actions there. He says first that the consensus on the army's role was weakened by "Westminster's tendency to remove itself from the execution of the military instrument, which meant that the government exercised less political control of the security forces than necessary."[1] He then asserts that "there was a tendency to delegate controversial security decisions from Cabinet or ministerial level to other actors or institutions who were thought to judge a particular question on a purely technocratic basis. By doing so, the government avoided responsibility, it distanced itself from events in the province and protected itself from accusations of partisanship."[2] The evidence presented in this book does not support such a blanket indictment. The civil-military command and control relationship was complex, multifaceted, and dynamic, and thus requires a more nuanced assessment.

First, before assessing the civil-military command relationship itself, we must recognize that the Northern Ireland conflict presented the British government and the army with a unique and difficult political-military problem. The conflict was evolving continuously in the period covered in this study. It began in 1968–69 with communal violence between majority Protestant unionists and the marginalized minority of Catholic nationalists. By 1971–72 it had evolved into a protracted nationalist insurgency that employed terrorism with the aim of forcing Britain to abandon the province as a prelude to unifying it with the Irish republic. Finally, in 1974 efforts to resolve the conflict through a power-sharing government led to a political insurrection in the form of a general strike that was supported – willingly or otherwise – by the majority of the Protestants and that defeated this conflict resolution initiative. Although the Labour and Conservative governments in London both sought to distance themselves from the conflict, they were drawn in nevertheless and found no political solution that could simultaneously resolve the grievances of the minority and allay the fears of the majority.

To complicate matters further, for nearly three years the political direction of security affairs in the province was divided between London and Stormont, and they did not always agree. Security policy and political/strategic decision making were the subjects of continuous debate between the two governments and within Whitehall. Thus, there was no single, over-arching political strategy guiding the use of the army in Northern Ireland throughout the period. Rather, security policy was in a constant state of flux, influenced by shifting, often short-term political winds in London and Stormont and by changes in the conflict on the ground.

The challenges posed by this conflict were further exacerbated by the fact that neither the government in London nor the military had a firm grasp on the political situation in Northern Ireland at the outset of the Troubles. Intelligence collection and analysis on the province was weak before and after the troops were deployed and remained so throughout most of the period under discussion. This had a deleterious impact on decisions and operations, and thus on relations with the population on both sides of the communal divide. It rendered the internment operation against the IRA largely ineffective, while further alienating the Catholic population and mobilizing them against the army. Likewise, in 1974 London completely misjudged the loyalists' determination to bring down the executive and their willingness to use a combination of civil disobedience and intimidation to do so. The political costs of these errors were significant: they prolonged the armed conflict and set back progress towards a negotiated resolution by at least a decade.

It is also clear that, prior to deploying the army, the governments in London and Stormont did not understand the concept of aid to the civil power (ACP). London had no idea what its constitutional and legal obligations were in that respect to Northern Ireland nor did it understand how the army might be used to meet those obligations.

This should not be surprising: ACP was an antiquated concept. Since the mid-nineteenth century civilian police had largely replaced the army as the primary force for public order in domestic internal security situations. Yet, due to the weakness of colonial police forces, the army had played this role overseas. As a consequence, the army was more familiar with it than were politicians – it had written tactical procedures for riot control. But with respect to Northern Ireland, even the military and the Ministry of Defence were uncertain about the process for requesting ACP and about what responding to a request would entail. There was concern that the military might have to act before the appropriate political authorities could be consulted and give their approval. This could place both the military and its political masters in some degree of legal jeopardy. These concerns were not resolved before the troops deployed, and the MOD and the army had to draft new guidelines on the fly to suit the unique situation.

The army had encountered most of these forms of conflict during the campaigns that attended the withdrawal from empire, and it had developed a body of "best practices" – if not a formal doctrine – to deal with them.[3] These were far from perfect, and did not always succeed in the colonial/imperial context, but were used overseas without much interference or second guessing from London.[4] The Northern Ireland conflict, however, was occurring within the boundaries of the United Kingdom. It was subject to direct political as well as constant media scrutiny. Army methods that could be employed without much fuss in the jungles of Malaya or the desert wastes of South Arabia were not necessarily applicable to or appropriate on the streets of Londonderry (Derry) or Belfast. Moreover, there was nothing in extant doctrine that told the army how to act when confronted with a political insurrection such as the Ulster Workers' Council strike. Its room for manoeuvre at that time was limited by a lack of political guidance, which, when it finally came, arrived too late to change the outcome.

The first six years of the conflict (1968–74) forced the politicians and the generals onto a steep learning curve. That it was a mutual learning process did not make it any easier; neither side emerged unscathed. If ever there was a conflict meant to test British civil-military relations (CMR) this was it.

Yet, in spite of these problems and of disagreements and strains arising from the conflict and the learning process, the official record and

the extant literature suggest that the civil-military relationship survived intact. Contrary to Neumann's view, throughout the first five
years of the conflict the political leadership *was* in charge. At no time
did the army or the civil service usurp the decision-making power of
their political masters; politicians ran the war. London set the terms
of reference under which the army operated. It imposed operational
and command decision-making constraints (the requirement to refer
back to the MOD, CGS/CDS, and the minister) to ensure that the army
was not an autonomous actor but an instrument of policy that was
decided – as much as possible – in London. What the British government wanted was to control the use of the army, because London –
not Stormont – was responsible for its actions and would have to
answer for them if/when things went wrong. That said, while the
political leadership provided broad, if sometimes inconsistent, guidance to the army regarding the political and military goals of the operations, and approved major operations such as Demetrius and Motorman, at the tactical level the army ran the show. Generally speaking,
the closer troops and their commanders were to the action, the less
political interference and more tactical discretion they had.

Nevertheless, political considerations predominated, and military
concerns and plans were subordinated to them. Army commanders
and staff at all levels had to take them into account because, as Field
Marshal Michael Carver acknowledged, the conflict was rooted in politics and could not be resolved or managed by military means alone.
As a result, the army's role was as much political as it was military, perhaps more so. Its every action was freighted with potential political
consequences. The concept of the "strategic corporal" was not articu-
lated until the 1990s, but it captured the situation in Northern Ireland
accurately. The decisions and actions of junior leaders could – and did
– have consequences out of proportion to their rank.[5] Bloody Sunday
is a case in point. This reality explains the politicians' determination to
keep military activity under their control, even to the extent of trying
to micromanage tactical dispositions (as Lt. Gen. Freeland alleged) and
how AVREs should be used in Operation Motorman. These things lay
well beyond their professional purview and expertise.

That said, it is important to recognize that civil-military command
and control was not a straightforward, top-down system, with the
politicians simply issuing instructions and the army carrying them
out. Rather, the process of developing security policy and translating

it into operations was interactive, mediated by the role of committees, the influence of senior civil servants, and the importance of personalities, both civilian and military. Committees are central to the Westminster model of cabinet governance. Cabinet often delegates decision-making power to them, and did so in the Northern Ireland case. But this did not allow cabinet to evade collective responsibility for controversial decisions, as Neumann suggests. Rather, the committees provided a secure forum for key cabinet ministers to discuss freely the difficult problems or choices confronting the government. It was in such committees that the military shared its expertise, stated its position, and learned what steps the political leadership had in mind. Finally, committees were small enough that they could achieve consensus. Failing that, they could facilitate the prime minister's generating a decision, or imposing one by way of summing up – and both Wilson and Heath did the latter frequently.

At the same time, the committees were not disconnected from the other parts of the policymaking system. This book highlights the significant (some critics would say excessive) influence of senior civil servants,[6] in particular those within the Cabinet Office, the Home Office, the Northern Ireland Office, and the Ministry of Defence.[7] Through their intimate daily access to the PMs and/or their ministers, whom they served as professional advisers and trusted aides, and through their role in preparing discussion papers and selecting and offering comments on those submitted through them, they were able to help shape committee agendas and discussions, and thus to help steer the outcomes by delineating options to be considered.[8] The Cabinet Office provided secretaries to the cabinet committees; they prepared the minutes and served as the institutional memory. The official sources on Northern Ireland illuminate clearly the active role and significant influence of long-serving, experienced professional civil servants such as Burke Trend, Philip Allen, and Arthur Hockaday.

This brings us to the importance of personalities. It is difficult to escape the conclusion that these mattered a great deal, even if it is hard to prove in an empirical sense. Wilson's and Heath's leadership styles differed greatly: Wilson the quiet negotiator who sought to avoid confrontation; Heath more blunt and assertive. Wilson's conciliatory style was apparent in the tone of his meeting with Terence O'Neill and William Craig in November 1968, in his effort to mollify Richard Crossman by appointing him to the cabinet committee, and in his desperate search for ways to avoid involvement in the province's conflict in the spring of 1969. Similarly, during the 1974 UWC strike Wilson was reluctant to approve any action that might lead to a confrontation with the militants. When he finally approved army action, it was too late to affect the outcome. In fairness to Wilson, it must be noted that during the strike he was constrained by the fact that he was leading a minority government.

Heath, unfettered by the constraints of minority rule, took a more engaged, even bold, approach, shown in his leading role in the discussions with Stormont preceding the internment operation, in his rapid decision to appoint an inquiry into the Bloody Sunday massacre, in his willingness to face down Brian Faulkner over the law and order issue, and thus to approve direct rule when Faulkner refused to yield, and in his efforts to forge a bipartisan political solution (the Sunningdale Agreement). This is not to say that his approach always succeeded. On the internment decision in August 1971, Faulkner outmanoeuvred Heath, which may explain Heath's "hard-nosed" stance over the control of law and order in March 1972.

Denis Healey was an activist, details-oriented defence secretary, while Carrington by his own admission took a more laissez-faire approach to leading the MOD.[9] It was Healey who insisted in late 1968 that the government needed a proper legal view of aid to the civil power. Early in 1969 he was quick to correct Callaghan's ad hoc thinking about direct rule. In spring 1969 he demonstrated an incisive grasp of the implications of withdrawing troops from Ulster. And, over the issue of continued use of the B-Specials in the fall of that year, Healey did not hesitate to confront the army high command when he felt they were not keeping him properly informed.

If by contrast Carrington took a less "hands on" approach to managing the MOD, he nonetheless had the PM's ear and was an influential voice in decision making on military and security matters. In January 1971 he flatly refused to grant Stormont any power to direct army operations. He stood shoulder to shoulder with Generals Tuzo and Carver in opposing internment in July 1971. It was Carrington who insisted that Faulkner accept responsibility for internment, to deflect blame away from the army. But his less focused approach to management of the MOD and the military allowed controversial in-depth interrogations to proceed, because he did not probe too deeply into the methods he had approved.

Roy Mason has been described as a "pugnacious" man with an "aggressive style,"[10] but that reputation was earned largely on the basis of his tenure as the secretary of state for Northern Ireland, which came after the period under study. Those qualities were less obvious when he was defence secretary while the Wilson government wrestled with the UWC strike. Siding with both the PM and the CGS, he acquiesced with the restrained approach to the crisis.

James Callaghan may have inherited a ministry with only nominal responsibility for Ulster's affairs, but as the crisis deepened in 1968–69 he made the province his priority. One of his first and wisest actions in this regard was to request an assessment of the situation from MI5. And where Wilson seemed obsessed with finding any way to avoid a military commitment to the province, Callaghan showed a firmer grasp on the dilemma the conflict posed for the British government. In meetings with Stormont, Callaghan was the iron fist inside Wilson's velvet glove. Thus, in August 1969 the PM left it to Callaghan to read the riot act to James Chichester-Clark and his ministers when they appeared to treat cavalierly the political implications of requesting troops. However, he over-reached his authority when he tried to give orders to Lt. Gen. Freeland.

By contrast, if Sir Frank Cooper's memory is accurate, Callaghan's Conservative successor at the Home Office, Reginald Maudling, was inclined to take a hands-off approach to Northern Ireland. At the height of the internment debate, he sent mixed signals to Faulkner about the need for such a step, and fumbled an invitation to him to come to London to discuss it. He later acquiesced in the approval of in-depth interrogation. Like Carrington he did not inquire too closely into the specifics of the proposed action. He did, however, make to cabinet in March 1972 a persuasive case for direct rule, based on a prescient assessment that the conflict would continue to engage the army for a long time and that the Ulster Catholics would never see Stormont as an impartial arbiter of law and order. But his permanent undersecretary observed at the time that Maudling seemed only too ready to hand over responsibility for the province's affairs to the new SSNI. Later, Conservative cabinet minister Douglas Hurd claimed that Maudling "hadn't a grip on anything, that was part of the Irish problem too … you had a man who was shrewd and idle."[11]

As SSNI, William Whitelaw and Merlyn Rees also present a study in contrasts. If it were possible, in terms of boldness Whitelaw outshone even his prime minister in asserting his leadership as SSNI. He quickly carved out his fiefdom in the NIO, relying on it for security advice, bringing the D/INT in as his intelligence adviser,[12] and sometimes bypassing Carrington in making policy (such as lifting the ban on marches). Over the reservations of the army leadership, he imposed the low-profile policy on army operations in order to create space for a political initiative. All of this generated some criticism from within the MOD and the army but paid off in the short term, leading to an IRA ceasefire and direct talks with that group. That it did not lead to a political solution at that time had nothing to do with Whitelaw's initiatives and everything to do with the IRA's unpreparedness for serious political negotiations.

Merlyn Rees does not emerge from the 1974 UWC strike with a burnished reputation. The evidence suggests that he shared Wilson's tendency to avoid confrontation. Rees – and the rest of Wilson's cabinet – clearly underestimated the ability of the militants to impose their will by means of a general strike and blatant intimidation. He postponed visiting the province for the duration of the strike and, more important, failed to provide the GOC with political guidance for army operations. Rees seemed to take council of his worst fears, to the point of being rendered ineffectual. Ironically, Lt. Gen. King's views on the government's relations with the Protestants probably unintentionally reinforced Rees's inclination to postpone difficult decisions. But as noted earlier, the government was playing a weak hand with no good options.

By the very nature of the profession, the army does not tend to attract shrinking violets, and those who reach the most senior levels of command usually demonstrate qualities of competence and self-confidence. Those senior officers involved in the Northern Ireland conflict during this period were no exceptions. Carrington had nothing but praise for Carver, Tuzo, and King.[13] Carver's obituary in the *Telegraph* described him as "the cleverest soldier since the Second World War and also one of the most uncompromising senior officers of his generation."[14] The *Guardian* called him "the thinking man's soldier."[15] As chief of the general staff Carver displayed those elements of his character: steadfastly opposing internment on sound military grounds; offering perceptive insights on the political effects of proposed military options in fall 1971; and being unafraid to criticize Whitelaw's low-profile security policy in spring 1972, albeit without being insubordinate.

Apart from noting that he had received a DSO for bravery in action in 1944, it is harder to get a sense of the character of Lt. Gen. Freeland. Despite having been on the job as GOC barely a month, he effectively handled the deployment of troops onto the streets of Londonderry and Belfast in August 1969. Drawing perhaps on his experience in East Africa he was prescient in his observation that the "honeymoon period for the use of troops in a situation like this can be very short-lived."[16] Equally astute was his understanding that intelligence would play a central role in the emerging operation but that it was, at the time, a weak link, and that he, therefore, needed a director of intelligence answerable to him. He also could articulate clearly to his fellow soldiers the problematic dual civil-military command and control relationship in which he found himself. It seems fair to conclude that purely by chance and good fortune the Wilson government found itself with a GOC who proved to be the right man in the right place at the right time.

The *Independent* described Harry Tuzo as "a man of considerable courage, charm, and charisma. He had a sharp intellect, great humour, and could hold an audience spellbound."[17] Desmond Hamill writes that Tuzo was "the first intellectual soldier they [the Stormont cabinet] had ever met. He was much too bright for them."[18] He needed and used all of those qualities during his service as GOC. Upon taking up his position in 1971, he refused to be bullied by Faulkner into taking unsound military measures. Like Carver, he would not compromise on his opposition to internment, which he saw as unnecessary on security grounds, even while understanding the political pressures that would bring it about. In the wake of internment he led efforts to defuse political tensions and to align military methods with political goals. He highlighted for cabinet the need for a clear chain of command under direct rule. Tuzo was quite prepared to raise objections to proposals advanced by his political masters but, like Carver, he did so within the limits of his professional responsibilities.

Frank King has been called "the best and most successful director of operations in Northern Ireland,"[19] an accolade he shares with Harry Tuzo. He was praised even by Merlyn Rees, who said, "you have never played at politics and I have never played at being a soldier; that's why we have got on so well."[20] That statement is surprising, since the evidence shows that, at least during the UWC strike, King – described as "a soldier's soldier"[21] – was not impressed by Rees's indecisiveness and

was not afraid to express his dismay. Nor did he shrink from expressing his views on security policy, even when these did not coincide
with those of the government.

Given this range of personalities and their competing, overlapping,
or intersecting responsibilities, it is not surprising that disputes arose
between the soldiers and the politicians. But personalities alone, especially the brief snapshots provided here, probably do not fully explain
them. Thomas-Durell Young identifies different institutional cultures
as a source of tension between political and military leaders. Politicians, he argues, "thrive on ambiguity and uncertainty," while military
officers, because of the potential for devastating consequences, "seek
clarity of mission and certainty of conditions."[22] This "clash of cultures" was evident in the cases discussed here. The government's
intentions may have been clear to the politicians themselves, but their
direction to the military in support of those goals was not always consistent or sound.

Until it imposed direct rule in March 1972, London's principal
political goal with respect to Ulster was to keep the Stormont prime
ministers and their governments in power, so as to avoid being forced
to run the province itself. This gave Northern Ireland's leaders inor-
dinate influence over London's decisions, an example of the tail wag-
ging the dog that was most obvious in the case of the 1971 internment
decision. The army advised against the operation on the grounds that
it was not necessary and would exacerbate the political and security
situation. But London's fear that Faulkner's government would fall,
leaving it to run the province, drove the decision to approve internment against the army's best professional advice. Throughout the
pre–direct rule period, moreover, the GOC had to refer frequently back
to the CGS and the minister for clarification when Stormont's ideas
about security policy clashed with his and London's understandings.

Similarly, in coordination with direct rule and while he pursued
political openings to the nationalist community, SSNI Whitelaw imposed a low-profile posture on the army. This left it uncertain about its
role and undermined its capacity to provide security, with no certainty
of achieving lasting political gains. Violence escalated, and the army
and the public suffered more casualties. Equally frustrating, at this
time the CGS felt that the new SSNI and the Northern Ireland Office
were sidelining the defence secretary and, *inter alia*, the army, on some
security matters.

By contrast, during the 1974 UWC strike the government in London was indecisive, leaving the army without any political or strategic guidance through most of the crisis. As the crisis deepened, the government prevaricated. By the time it authorized action against the loyalist insurgents, it was too late to prevent the fall of the power-sharing executive. The government's hesitation could be attributed to its minority status and to its misreading of the loyalists' determination and power. SSNI Rees was also uncertain about the reliability of the RUC, whose cooperation against the IRA was essential. He was reluctant to risk that cooperation by forcing that force to choose sides. Contrary to allegations, there is no evidence to suggest that the army leadership refused to follow the government's direction, or that Wilson's government ever thought it might do so.

Yet, where Neumann's analysis was correct beyond question was Heath's appointment of Lord Widgery to conduct the first inquiry into Bloody Sunday. This was a transparent effort to delegate the handling of a highly controversial issue onto an institution outside of government. Doing so allowed the government to avoid direct responsibility, to distance itself from the tragic events, and to protect itself from accusations of partisanship. While in these respects Heath's motives were clearly political and self-serving, they were not completely without a sound policy basis. It is doubtful that any kind of in-house inquiry would have put to rest the controversy and the clamour for justice. Moreover, Heath had a legitimate concern that any inquiry not undermine the morale of the army, whose effective performance was vital to maintaining internal security in the province at a time when violence was escalating. In that regard the inquiry was a success. The army continued to perform its duties effectively to the extent that political strictures (such as the low-profile policy) allowed. However, Widgery's report was widely criticized for failing to sufficiently hold the army to account for its actions that day. Consequently, the legacy of Bloody Sunday dogged all efforts at restoring security and achieving a political solution. Thus, it seems fair to say that Heath's Widgery gambit was at best only a partial success.

Turning to the army, while it observed its professional boundaries most of the time, it could not avoid straying into matters that normally lay properly within the political domain. Gen. Tuzo engaged in political discussions with both Stormont's leaders and its opponents. Gen. Carver's assessment of the situation and of security policy options in fall 1971 could not avoid raising political aspects, since each option would have political consequences that would – in turn – affect the security situation and the actions of the security forces. And as GOC in 1974, Lt. Gen. King made a thoroughly political point when he asserted that the government had to keep the Protestants on its side, even if he was speaking mostly with the security situation (especially the reliability of the RUC) in mind. Yet, his political stance had not prevented him from ordering his troops to arrest the Protestant militant leaders twenty-four hours earlier, and the following day the army carried out the petrol-distribution operation with efficiency and enthusiasm.

What the foregoing demonstrates is the blurring of the political-military boundaries that occurs in internal wars. It was impossible for politicians or military leaders to make political or security policies and decisions in isolation from each other or without impinging on each other's professional domains. The two dimensions were linked inextricably. Moreover, the army's role within the command and control process for Northern Ireland supports Hew Strachan's argument, as it was thoroughly engaged, both professionally *and* politically, in this process. This also validates Morris Janowitz's theory that, as armies become more professional, they become more political. As I note in the introduction, Amos Perlmutter would argue that the army could not have been otherwise and have performed its job effectively because, along with the political leaders and bureaucrats, its senior generals are part of the triad that makes and implements national security policy. The other two partners *need* the army to be politically active because they require its specialized knowledge and expertise in certain areas. This need predisposes senior generals to "behavior that can be construed as political" precisely because they sit at the apex of policymaking and decision making.[23] In the Northern Ireland conflict, the generals had both a necessary voice and a deciding role, and with these came political involvement and influence.

Yet, it is clear that the soldiers and civilians did not always agree on policy or on the courses of action to be taken. What is notable is that such disagreements did not cause a crisis in British civil-military relations. Even when they disagreed, the politicians and generals continued to work together in relative harmony. In discussions with Whitelaw in July 1972, Gen. Carver warned that army frustration could rise if the government failed to exploit quickly the opportunity that Bloody Friday presented. This statement could be construed as not too subtle blackmail. But with the exception of the 1974 Monday Club article discussed in chapter 8, there is no evidence that any senior officers went public or threatened to resign over a major policy dispute with regard to Northern Ireland in this period. The kind of adversarial relationship or competition for power that characterizes Peter Feaver's agency theory of CMR seems to have been absent in this case. So, how can this relatively benign working relationship be explained?

Adopting Strachan's argument, one would point with considerable justification to history – to the body of practices and customs developed over several centuries. The politicians and generals wrestling with Northern Ireland knew the rules of the game and played it accordingly. They relied on long-established, collaborative processes and procedures for civilian leaders to consult the military on matters within its professional competence, to take decisions, and to ensure that those decisions were enacted by the MOD and the military chain of command.[24] These practices seem to lend weight to Rebecca Schiff's theory of concordance, which focuses on dialogue, compromise, and "shared values or objectives" among the military, the political elites, and society. But while there clearly was dialogue and compromise in the civil-military decision-making process, it is harder to make the case for shared values and objectives. The two entities diverged with respect to the latter on several occasions, most notably over internment and arguably over the handling of the UWC strike. The notion of shared values is even more problematic and is difficult to prove or disprove with a high degree of certainty. Schiff's four indicators of concordance are the social composition of the officer corps; the political decision-making process; recruitment methods; and military style, including its professional ethos, and public attitudes towards it. Concordance on these points occurs "in the context of active agreement, whether established by legislation, decree, or constitution, or based on longstanding historical and cultural values."[25]

Strachan's historical analysis supports Schiff's theory at a certain level of generality. As noted in the introduction, Strachan argues, with regard to the army, that its constitutional status has been above reproach, it was well financed through most of the last century, and it remains popular among the citizenry. Historically, the officer corps has been less aristocratic and more representative of wider British society than Huntington and Janowitz believed. The army's legitimacy was never seriously challenged because it had "colonized" British civil society, resulting in a more "militarized" nation. This perspective could be explained by Britain's long period of military national service, which was not abolished until 1962, allowing the military to remake postwar Britain in its own image to some degree. Yet, even though the aristocracy no longer dominated British politics, postwar Britain still had a "governing class." The politicians, civil servants, and generals who oversaw the Northern Ireland conflict were part of it. They generally were well educated, some of them at the same schools and universities. But it would be a mistake to overemphasize the notion that British civil society mirrored the character of its military. Strachan acknowledged in a 2003 article that there remained a significant gap between the two.[26]

That gap was not limited to the public in general; it included some in the political elites. Former MOD civil servant Desmond Bowen, whose service began near the end of the period under study, observes that while politicians appreciate the military's capabilities, versatility, and positive approach to problem solving, this does not mean they "understand the military ethos."[27]

Heath, Whitelaw, Healey, and Carrington clearly did. They had seen active wartime service, and Healey in particular had immersed himself in postwar defence matters. This experience served them well in their relations with the army. But not all politicians and senior civil servants shared this level of familiarity. During the rising crisis in 1968–69 and again during the 1974 strike, it was readily apparent that Wilson, Callaghan, and Rees were less familiar with the military and less comfortable dealing with it. Whitelaw insisted in spring 1972 that the army maintain a low profile while he pursued political initiatives, even though that posture posed operational and morale problems for the army. All of this is by way of saying that, when taken to a more granular level, Schiff's concordance theory cannot be assumed to apply in a universal manner when it comes to shared values.

What the foregoing suggests is that no single CMR theory can explain the British civil-military command and control relationship illuminated by the Northern Ireland cases explored in this book. The British Army of the 1970s met Huntington's criteria for professionalism, but its behaviour defied his concept of "objective control," while remaining committed to a process of civilian supremacy. The inability of the foundational work in the CMR field to provide a theoretical basis to explain this apparent contradiction has forced us to look elsewhere. We can find complementary but partial elements of theoretical explanation in the works of Janowitz, Perlmutter, and Schiff that, taken together, provide insights into British CMR. Janowitz reconciles military professionalism and an army's political role. Perlmutter provides an argument for the necessity of that role. And Schiff identifies the indicators of concordance between an army and its political masters. That none of these by themselves can explain the nature of British CMR calls into question the utility of theory for studying it.

In the absence of theory we are left with the historical record, however imperfect and incomplete. That record suggests that the politicians and generals managed to find some common ground that would guide policy, decisions, and actions. Even if they might have disagreed on their visions of what Britain should look like, there was no disagreement over maintaining the integrity of the state. Likewise, they shared abhorrence for violent protest – terrorism in particular – and a general consensus that it should be repressed rather than rewarded. They were united in their desire to bring the conflict to an end as soon as possible, and in their recognition that it was fundamentally a political problem that ultimately required a political solution. Paradoxically, however, at the outset they also were united – regrettably – in their poor grasp of the Northern Ireland problem. This meant that both found it difficult to tailor military means to political ends.

Yet, they understood the process that was meant to match those ends and means, and they understood and respected each other's place and role in it. Even if there was some blurring of the political-military boundaries, neither exploited that to the other's disadvantage to any great extent. Guided by written procedures and unwritten customs, with conflicts mediated by the machinery of government, they made the command and control system work. Ultimately, the elected civil power remained ascendant, as it should in a liberal democracy. For better or for worse, the politicians defined the mission, and the generals issued the orders to carry it out. But the path from the one to the other was complex, interactive, and dynamic, as much bottom-up as it was top-down.

Glossary

AID TO THE CIVIL POWER (ACP): The procedure by which the national government provides military forces at the request of local/provincial governments to support the efforts of the police to restore public order during serious disturbances.

BRITISH ARMY OF THE RHINE (BAOR): The army's NATO force based in Germany.

B-SPECIALS: The paramilitary arm of the Royal Ulster Constabulary.

CHIEF OF THE DEFENCE STAFF (CDS): The senior officer in the military chain of command and the chief military adviser to cabinet.

CHIEF OF THE GENERAL STAFF (CGS): The senior officer of the British Army.

COMMANDER LAND FORCES (CLF): The senior officer responsible for the planning and operations of army formations and units in Northern Ireland; the CLF worked under the direction of the general officer commanding.

CS: A form of tear gas used for riot control.

DIRECTOR OF OPERATIONS (D/OPS): The in-theatre role of the general officer commanding Northern Ireland from August 1969.

GEN 47: The Heath government's cabinet committee on Northern Ireland, from June 1970 to March 1972.

GEN 79: The Heath government's cabinet committee on Northern Ireland, from March 1972 to February 1974.

GENERAL OFFICER COMMANDING (GOC): The commander of a theatre of operations or of a major deployed force, in this case the senior military officer in Northern Ireland.

G2: The senior army intelligence officer, normally at the battalion or brigade level.

INSPECTOR GENERAL (IG): The head of the Royal Ulster Constabulary.

IRN: The Wilson government's cabinet committee on Northern Ireland, it replaced MISC 238 in 1970.

MILITARY ASSISTANT (MA): The officer assigned to provide administrative support to a senior officer.

MI5: The British security service.

MI6: The British secret intelligence service.

MISC 238: The Wilson government's cabinet committee on Northern Ireland, 1969–70.

MILITARY OPERATIONS 4 (MO 4): The branch within the Directorate of Military Operations at the Ministry of Defence responsible for Northern Ireland.

OFFICIAL COMMITTEE ON NORTHERN IRELAND: The committee of senior civil servants assigned to provide administrative staff support to ministerial committees dealing with Northern Ireland.

ORDERS GROUP (O GROUP): The meeting held before operations during which the unit commander issues orders regarding the operation to subordinates.

ROYAL ULSTER CONSTABULARY (RUC): The Northern Ireland police force during the Troubles.

RULES OF ENGAGEMENT (ROE): Written guidelines specifying the conditions for the use of force as well as levels of force (especially lethal force) permitted in military operations.

SINN FÉIN: The political wing of the Irish Republican Army.

ULSTER DEFENCE REGIMENT (UDR): The army reserve unit raised in and serving only in Northern Ireland, used to assist the regular army on internal security duties. The UDR replaced the B-Specials.

UNITED KINGDOM LAND FORCES (UKLF): The army command responsible for all army units based in the United Kingdom.

YELLOW CARD: A printed copy of the rules of engagement issued to each soldier on internal security operations.

Notes

INTRODUCTION

1 Elliott and Flackes, *Northern Ireland*, 681–7.
2 *Sutton Index of Deaths*, table NI-SEC-05. It should be noted that all tabulations of casualty figures for this conflict have been disputed.
3 O'Leary and McGarry, *Politics of Antagonism*, 12–13.
4 See one effort to assess this: Cost of the Troubles Study, *Final Report*, 38–9.
5 For a partial estimate of financial costs up to 1979, see Smith, "Fin de Siecle, 1972," 20.
6 Chichester and Wilkinson, *The Uncertain Ally*, 54; Dockrill, *British Defence since 1945*, 101.
7 On these security measures, see French, *British Way in Counter-Insurgency*.
8 Smith, *Fighting for Ireland*, 94–109. Sinn Féin members now hold ministerial positions within the Northern Ireland executive, including the position of deputy first minister.
9 Those words formed the title of a 1973 BBC documentary that recorded the experiences of an eight-man infantry section as they trained and then deployed on operations in the province.
10 The quote has been attributed to French prime minister Georges Clémenceau.
11 The online bibliography created by the University of Ulster Conflict Archive on the Internet (CAIN) boasted some 15,700 entries to August 2009.
12 Edwards, "Whipping Boy," 167.
13 *Report of the Bloody Sunday Inquiry*. See also Charters, "Have a Go"; Edwards, "Whipping Boy"; Lafree, Dugan, and Corte, "Impact of British Counterterrorist Strategies"; McCleery, *Operation Demetrius*; Neumann, *Britain's Long War*; O'Halpin, "A Poor Thing but Our Own"; and Sanders, "Operation Motorman."

14 Neumann, *Britain's Long War*, 29.
15 Ibid.
16 Keithly and Ferris, "Auftragstaktik."
17 Neumann, *Britain's Long War*, 29.
18 Campbell and Connolly, "Model for the 'War against Terrorism'" 372, quoted in Edwards, "Whipping Boy," 167.
19 Strachan, *Politics of the British Army*, 1, 10–11.
20 Ibid., 11, 18, 25–6.
21 See, for example, Higley, *Civil-Military Relationships*. The leading scholarly journal in the field, *Armed Forces and Society*, has been published continuously since 1974.
22 Huntington, *Soldier and the State*, 82.
23 On this concept, see Krulak, "The Strategic Corporal."
24 *Report of the Bloody Sunday Inquiry*, vol. 9, chap. 193, paras 4, 7; Public Record Office Northern Ireland (hereafter PRONI), HA 32/3/1, "Conclusions of a Meeting of the Cabinet Security Committee," 17 July 1969; Hennessey, *History of Northern Ireland*, 32–3, 142–5, 148.
25 Cunningham, *British Government Policy*, 1–5; Callaghan, *A House Divided*, 1.
26 Wilson's own memoir of the period, *The Labour Government*, devotes large portions of many chapters to economic problems, such as the devaluation crisis, and to foreign policy issues, such as the Rhodesian Unilateral Declaration of Independence. But the rising violence in Ulster in the fall of 1968 gets only a passing mention (part of one sentence on page 725).
27 For example, the memoir of Heath's defence secretary, Peter Lord Carrington, *Reflecting on Things Past*, 247–50, discusses Northern Ireland in such general terms that it offers no insights useful for this study. That said, it should be noted that the conflict was still ongoing when the memoir was published, and the author was bound by the terms of the Official Secrets Act.
28 Huntington, *Soldier and the State*, viii, 2–3, 82, and Part 3, chap. 12–17.
29 Coffman, "The Long Shadow," 69–70, 81–2; and Desch, "Soldiers, States and Structures," 390.
30 Huntington, *Soldier and the State*, 164, 187, 328–9.
31 Ibid., 83.
32 Janowitz, *Professional Soldier*, viii, 9–10, 12, 285, 342–3, 348, 350, 359, 367–8, 372, 439.
33 Strachan, *Politics of the British Army*, 12.
34 Quoted in ibid., 18–19, 25.

35 Ibid., 128.

36 Ibid., 8–9, 42, 249; Feaver, "Crisis as Shirking," 408–10.

37 Schiff, "Civil-Military Relations Reconsidered," 10, 12.

38 Ibid., 12.

39 Ibid.

40 Ibid., 14–15.

41 Ibid., 12.

42 Strachan, *Politics of the British Army*, 11–16, 25, 263–6. Baynes, *Soldier in Modern Society*, 124, and Yardley and Sewell, *New Model Army*, 49, 56, lend weight to Strachan's argument about the increasingly wide social base of the army, though Yardley and Sewell note that vestiges of the old class system still exist.

43 Strachan, *Politics of the British Army*, 266–7.

CHAPTER ONE

1 National Archives (hereafter NA), CAB 164/877, no. 3M, "Northern Ireland: Background Brief for the Prime Minister, I. Constitution and Machinery," para. 2, 23 June 1970; Cunningham, *British Government Policy*, 1–5; Hennessey, *History of Northern Ireland*, 9, 121–2, 125–6, 136, 138, 139, 143–4, 147, 150, 157–62. See also Birrell and Murie, *Policy and Government*, 12–14, 38.

2 Hennessey, *History of Northern Ireland*, 10, 15, 32–3, 43–53, 105–7, 110–14, 128–33, 141–3, 151, 153, 154, 238–9; Birrell and Murie, *Policy and Government*, 6–7, 144–6, 164–6, 214–15; O'Dochartaigh, *Civil Rights to Armalites*, 3, 48–9, 52–3, 126–7, 311–12, 318–19.

3 *Report of the Bloody Sunday Inquiry*, vol. 9, chap. 193, paras. 4, 7; PRONI, HA 32/3/1, "Conclusions of a Meeting of the Cabinet Security Committee," 17 July 1969; Hennessey, *History of Northern Ireland*, 32–3, 142–5, 148.

4 Cunningham, *British Government Policy*, 1.

5 Ibid.; NA, CAB 164/877, no. 3M, paras 3, 5, 23 June 1970.

6 Cunningham, *British Government Policy*, 1–5; Callaghan, *A House Divided*, 1.

7 See "Right to Be Cautious."

8 On this, see Walles, *British and American Systems*, 98–102; Smith, *Policy-Making in British Government*, 74–5, 79, 84, 86, 87, 90, 92–9; Jordan and Richardson, *British Politics and the Policy Process*, 67, 119–20, 123, 124–5, 126–8, 132–3, 137–40, 151–2; and McIntosh, *Managing Britain's Defence*, 37. For a former prime minister's perspective, see Wilson, *Governance of Britain*, 9, 11, 47–51, 53, 55, 62, 64–5, 66–7, 156–62. Donoughue, *Prime Minister*, 2–6 offers

the perspective of a policy adviser. In respect of the military-political decision making, see Johnson, *Defence by Ministry*, 9.

9 Jordan and Richardson, *British Politics and the Policy Process*, 120, 134–5, 139,
148–9, 158; Beloff and Peel, *Government of the United Kingdom*, 74–5; Wilson, *Governance of Britain*, 78–9; and Donoughue, *Prime Minister*, 10–13, 15,
48, 57.

10 NA, DEFE 13/902, no. 53, note, Trend to Cubbon, "Northern Ireland," 20 February 1969. The "official" committee drafted papers and prepared reports for
the ministerial committee. Sir Philip Allen, the permanent undersecretary
at the Home Office, chaired the official committee.

11 *Report of the Bloody Sunday Inquiry*, vol. 1, chap. 8, para. 8.3.

12 Later it also included the attorney general. NA, CAB 165/949, no. 5, Cabinet
Office, note by the Secretary of the Cabinet, "Ministerial Committee on
Northern Ireland, Composition and Terms of Reference," 11 January 1974.

13 Career details are available online.

14 NA, CAB 134/3778, Ministerial Committee on Northern Ireland, minutes of
meeting, 1 April 1974.

15 *Military Balance*, 19, set the total at 210,000. Baynes, *No Reward But Honour*,
27 provides a much lower figure for 1968 (171,300), but this excludes the
Gurkhas and others recruited outside Britain, which, according to the IISS
report, would add some 22,000 soldiers to his total. Although both would
have drawn on published official figures, this still leaves a wide discrepancy
between them.

16 *Military Balance*, 19; Barnett, *Britain and Her Army*, 492; Blaxland, *Regiments
Depart*, 474; Dockrill, *British Defence*, 82, 86–7, 93–6.

17 Barzilay, *British Army in Ulster*, 1; Hamill, *Pig in the Middle*, 8.

18 Chichester and Wilkinson, *Uncertain Ally*, 150.

19 Ibid., 14–15, 20–3; Baynes, *No Reward But Honour*, 28; Dockrill, *British
Defence*, 95; Blaxland, *Regiments Depart*, 468–74.

20 Huntington, *Soldier and the State*, 8–18. See also Baynes, *Soldier in Modern
Society*, 31, 69.

21 Huntington, *Soldier and the State*, 83; Strachan, *Politics of the British Army*, 1,
10–11.

22 Strachan, *Politics of the British Army*, 11, 18, 25–6.

23 Ibid., 19.

24 Ibid., 7-8.

25 Ibid., 127–32.

26 Beckett, *The Army and the Curragh Incident*, 1, 14.

27 Johnson, *Defence by Ministry*, 9, 104.

28 Strachan, *Politics of the British Army*, 248.

29 Ibid.; Johnson, *Defence by Ministry*, 106–7, 123, 131–2, 142–3. War service information is available online.

30 The DOPC effectively operated in place of the Defence Council, which was supposed to exercise all powers of command and control of administration. Consisting of the defence secretary, the permanent secretary, the chief scientific advisor, the CDS, and the chiefs of the three services, the council was not practical, and met rarely. See Smith, "Command and Control," 312.

31 Johnson, *Defence by Ministry*, 104, 112, 116, 120; Strachan, *Politics of the British Army*, 247.

32 Quoted in Liddell Hart Centre for Military Archives (hereafter LHCMA), Cooper Papers, file – Academic Interviews, 4/1/2, interview with Susan Higgins, 2 April 1992, 6.

33 Ibid. (emphasis added).

34 Within the MOD, short-term operational planning was the responsibility of the assistant CDS (Operations). See Smith, "Command and Control," 315n46.

35 This is shown in the chapters that follow.

36 Hennessey, *Evolution of the Troubles*, 53, citing the testimony of General Sir Robert Ford to the Bloody Sunday Inquiry.

37 Howard, *Central Organization of Defence*, 17, 18, 40–6, 51; Johnson, *Defence by Ministry*, 9. NA, DEFE 4, Chiefs of Staff Committee Meetings, minutes, and DEFE 11 and DEFE 25, COSC Registered Files indicate clearly the wide range of issues that filled the committee's agenda.

38 Their career information is widely accessible online.

39 Johnson, *Defence by Ministry*, 120–1, 153; Strachan, *Politics of the British Army*, 269.

40 Johnson, *Defence by Ministry*, 6, 121, 195; Howard, *Central Organization of Defence*, 23–5, 40, 47.

41 Johnson, *Defence by Ministry*, 6.

42 Ibid., 106, 119, 152, 153; Howard, *Central Organization of Defence*, 20, 21, 23, 24, 40, and Appendix 2, *The British Civil Service*.

43 Howard, *Central Organization of Defence*, 24.

44 *Report of the Bloody Sunday Inquiry*, document KH9, written testimony of Sir Arthur Hockaday, paras. 1–2.

45 Ibid., para. 3. *Report of the Bloody Sunday Inquiry*, document KS3, written testimony of Anthony Stephens, para. 2, places the founding of DS10 in or after November 1971.

46 *Report of the Bloody Sunday Inquiry*, Hockaday testimony, para. 6.

47 Ibid., para. 4.

48 Andrew, *Defence of the Realm*, 602–3; see also, O'Halpin, "A Poor Thing but Our Own," 665–6; NA, CAB 130/422, minutes of a meeting, Cabinet Miscellaneous Committee 244, 25 April 1969.

49 McIntosh, *Managing Britain's Defence*, 36.

50 Ibid., 33, 41, 46.

51 Ibid., 37. This is what McIntosh means by "Prime Ministerial Government."

52 Ibid., 55–6.

53 Johnson, *Defence by Ministry*, 199.

54 Davis, *Prime Ministers and Whitehall*, 3, 8, 159.

55 McIntosh, *Managing Britain's Defence*, 63, 76. "Current policy" refers to both government policy and (on defence matters) initiatives arising from within the MOD. Davis, *Prime Ministers and Whitehall*, 9, quotes a source that describes the postwar civil service as having a "mentality of maintenance."

56 Quoted in McIntosh, *Managing Britain's Defence*, 38.

57 Ibid., 49.

58 Ibid., 33.

59 Ibid., 39–40.

60 Ibid., 40, 49–50, 62–3, 67–8.

CHAPTER TWO

1 See, e.g., Hamill, *Pig in the Middle*, 1–7. Hamill incorrectly identifies the 1st Battalion Prince of Wales' Own Regiment as one of the regular Northern Ireland garrison battalions. In fact, as shown here, it deployed temporarily in April 1969 to guard vital points.

2 NA, DEFE 13/902, no. 68, Statement [to the House of Commons], James Callaghan, "Use of Troops to Safeguard Certain Key Installations in Northern Ireland," 21 April 1969.

3 Taylor, *Loyalists*, 47–50, points out that, although the discrimination was real and blatant, the living conditions of the Protestant and Catholic working classes were equally grim. Hennessey, *History of Northern Ireland*, 127–32 offers a more nuanced analysis of housing discrimination but highlights the more striking employment imbalance.

4 Hennessey, *History of Northern Ireland*, 136–38.

5 Prince, "5 October 1968," 399–404.

6 Quoted in O'Dochartaigh, *Civil Rights to Armalites*, 20. Even the Cameron Commission, convened to examine the events of 5 October and their wider

implications, described the police response as "ill co-ordinated and ill conducted." See Hennessey, *History of Northern Ireland*, 143.

7 O'Dochartaigh, *Civil Rights to Armalites*, 21; Bew, Gibbon, and Patterson, *The State in Northern Ireland*, 170. On the complexity of the events on 5 October, see Prince, "5 October 1968," 398–400, 401–2, 403–5, 408.

8 Hennessey, *History of Northern Ireland*, 142; Moloney, *Secret History of the IRA*, 64. See also Prince, "5 October 1968," 405–6.

9 Prince, "5 October 1968," 408.

10 Quoted in "Brutality Complaint by MPs."

11 Wilson, *The Labour Government*, 844.

12 Quoted in "Brutality Complaint by MPs" (emphasis added).

13 See United Kingdom, *Parliamentary Debates*, Lords, 7 October 1968, "Londonderry Disturbances," vol. 296, cc. 811–15. See also United Kingdom, *Parliamentary Debates*, Commons, 21 October 1968, "Northern Ireland," vol. 770, cc. 882–5.

14 See "Mr. Fitt and the Misfits," 9.

15 "Tough Tactics in Derry," 8. See also "Questions for Ulster," 9, and Marshall, "O'Neill Defends Police Action," 3.

16 Wilson, *The Labour Government*, 844; *Times* (London), 8 October 1968, 1.

17 NA, PREM 13/2847, no. 2, "Note of a Meeting Held at 10 Downing Street," 4 November 1968, 1, 11–12; Wilson, *The Labour Government*, 845–6; *Parliamentary Debates*, Commons, 21 October 1968, vol. 770, cc. 882–5 and 4 November 1968, vol. 772, cc. 491–557.

18 Farrington, "Mobilisation, State Crisis."

19 Ibid., 519, citing Stormont cabinet minutes, 20 November 1968.

20 PRONI, HA/32/2/35, letter from Harold Black, Secretary of the Northern Ireland Cabinet, to J. Greeves, Ministry of Home Affairs, 7 May 1969.

21 Ibid. See also Roberts, "The British Army and Politics," 534–6; Critchley, *Conquest of Violence*, 59–60, 62, 67–8, 73–5, 123–4, 166–71, 177; Fox, "Public Order," 298–301, 303, 305; Deane-Drummond, *Riot Control*, 11–13.

22 French, *British Way in Counter-Insurgency*, 82, points out that, even as late as the mid-twentieth century, no one in the British Army could state definitively what "minimum force" meant.

23 Deane-Drummond, *Riot Control*, 56.

24 Raghaven, "Protecting the Raj."

25 Charters, "From October to Oka."

26 NA, DEFE 13/902, no. 1, letter, Brian Cubbon (Home Office) to Broadbent (MOD), 19 November 1968.

27 Quoted in ibid.

28 NA, DEFE 13/902, no. 2, minute, "Military Assistance to the Northern Ireland Government," by K.T. Nash, AUS (POL), MOD, 20 November 1968.
29 Ibid.
30 NA, CAB 164/576, unnumbered signal, VCGS to GOCNI, 21 November 1968.
31 NA, DEFE 13/902, no. 5, minute, Nash to APS/SSD (Mayne), "Military Aid to the Civil Power in Northern Ireland," 5 December 1968, para. 2.
32 Ibid., para. 3.
33 Ibid., para. 5.
34 NA, DEFE 13/902, no. 9, minute, Mayne (APS/SSD) to Nash, "Military Aid to the Civil Power in Northern Ireland," 6 December 1968.
35 NA, CAB 164/576, unnumbered signal, CGS to GOCNI, 6 December 1968 (emphasis added).
36 NA, DEFE 13/902, no. 11, Mayne to Nash, "Military Aid to the Civil Power in Northern Ireland," 9 December 1968.
37 NA, CAB 164/576, memorandum, CDS to SSD, "Military Aid to the Civil Power in Northern Ireland," 12 December 1968, paras 3, 4, 6, 7 (emphasis added).
38 Ibid., paras 3, 8, 9. The CDS enclosed copies of the two signals already sent to the GOC.
39 Ibid., paras 10, 11, 14.
40 NA, DEFE 13/902, no. 15, minute, Mayne to Healey, "Military Aid to the Civil Power in Northern Ireland," 12 December 1968.
41 Ibid.
42 NA, CAB 164/576, no. 1, letter, Attorney General to SSD, "Military Aid to the Civil Power in Northern Ireland," 13 December 1968 (emphasis added).
43 NA, DEFE 13/902, no. 23, note, Capt. P. White (PSO/CDS) to Private Secy/SSD, "Military Aid to the Civil Authorities in Northern Ireland," 16 December 1968.
44 NA, DEFE 13/902, no. 24, DUS(P) to SSD, "Military Aid to the Civil Authorities in Northern Ireland," 16 December 1968.
45 NA, DEFE 13/902, no. 26, note, Mayne to Healey, 17 December 1968.
46 Ibid.
47 NA, CAB 164/576, no. 2, letter, Healey to Wilson, "Military Aid to the Civil Power in Northern Ireland," 17 December 1968.
48 NA, CAB 164/576, no. 3, note, Trend to Wilson, "Military Aid to the Civil Power in Northern Ireland," 18 December 1968.
49 NA, DEFE 13/902, no. 33, letter, Callaghan to Wilson, "Military Aid to the Civil Power in Northern Ireland," 20 December 1968.
50 Quote from Taylor, *Loyalists*, 57. The Cameron Commission concluded that

the police had failed to provide adequate protection to the marchers. See Hennessey, *History of Northern Ireland*, 151–2, 154–5.

51 Quoted in "Mr. O'Neill Praises Police," 1. See also "Riot in Derry," 1.

52 Andrew, *Defence of the Realm*, 602–3.

53 NA, DEFE 13/902, no. 36, Mayne to White (PSO/CDS), "Military Aid to the Civil Power in Northern Ireland," 27 January 1969.

54 *Parliamentary Debates*, Commons, 28 January 1969, vol. 776, cc. 1103–4.

55 NA, DEFE 13/902, no. 37, Hockaday to Mayne, "Military Aid to the Civil Power in Northern Ireland," 30 January 1969.

56 NA, DEFE 13/902, no. 40, Baker (CGS) to Healey, "Northern Ireland," 7 February 1969, and Annex Scenario 3 "Widespread Riots"; also no. 44, minute, Healey to Wilson, 14 February 1969.

57 NA, DEFE 13/902, no. 53, note, Trend to Cubbon, "Northern Ireland," 20 February 1969.

58 NA, CAB 130/416, minutes, Cabinet Miscellaneous Committee (hereafter MISC) 238 (69), 1st Meeting, 26 February 1969.

59 Andrew, *Defence of the Realm*, 603; See also O'Halpin, "A Poor Thing but Our Own," 664–6, 668; written testimony of the former head of General Staff Intelligence at HQ Northern Ireland, document 2241, *Report of the Bloody Sunday Inquiry*. He says the JIC first established an Ulster Working Group and that the Northern Ireland Current Intelligence Group succeeded it in the autumn. The CIG was responsible for considering and producing an assessment on intelligence from all sources.

60 Hennessey, *History of Northern Ireland*, 161. For a Labour Party perspective on these events, see Wilson, *Labour Government*, 847–8, and Callaghan, *A House Divided*, 13–14.

61 PRONI, HA/32/2/35, letter, Black to Greeves, 7 May 1969.

62 Taylor, *Loyalists*, 59–62. The truth about who was behind the bombings came out later that year, when several of the perpetrators were arrested for the crime. However, only one was convicted.

63 NA, DEFE 13/902, no. 68, "Callaghan Statement," 21 April 1969; NA, CAB 130/416, minutes, MISC 238(69) 2nd meeting, 21 April 1969; Imperial War Museum (hereafter IWM), Freeland Papers, box 79/34/3, binder, IS Operations Northern Ireland, 3–4. Cited with permission. The brigade comprised two infantry battalions, an armoured reconnaissance squadron, and supporting elements.

64 NA, DEFE 13/902, no. 74, minute, Hockaday to Private Secretary/Secretary of State for Defence, "Northern Ireland," 24 April 1969, and no. 79, minute, Mayne to Military Assistant/CGS, "Northern Ireland," 25 April 1969; NA, CAB

130/416, minutes, MISC 238(69), 3rd meeting, 25 April 1969, and paper, MISC 238(69) 4, "Northern Ireland General Appreciation of the Situation, Memorandum by the Secretary of State for the Home Department," 1 May 1969, para. 3(b). See also IWM, Freeland Papers, IS Operations Northern Ireland, 3–4.

65 Crossman, *Diaries*, 453.

66 Ibid., 463.

67 NA, CAB 130/416, minutes, MISC 238, 2nd meeting, 21 April 1969, and CAB 130/422, minutes, MISC 244, 2nd meeting, 25 April 1969; NA, DEFE 13/903, no. 29, minute, CGS to Secretary of State for Defence, 19 May 1969; Andrew, *Defence of the Realm*, 604. One of the two was future MI5 director general Stella Rimington. See Rimington, *Open Secret*, 105–6.

68 Both quotes are from Crossman, *Diaries*, 478.

69 NA, CAB 130/416, minutes, MISC 238(69), 4th meeting, 29 April 1969.

70 Ziegler, *Wilson*, 345.

71 NA, DEFE 11/699, Chiefs of Staff Committee Registered Files, no. E154, "Northern Ireland: Memorandum to Secretary Chiefs of Staff Committee," by Arthur Hockaday (Assistant Under-Secretary General Staff), 9 May 1969, paras 1–2, 7–8.

72 Ibid., paras 2, 4, 8.

73 NA, DEFE 11/699, no. E166, "Northern Ireland: Draft Memorandum by the Secretary of State for Defence," 16 May 1969, paras 3–6; no. E170, "Annex to Minute 4, Amendments to D/DS6/7/153/44 Dated 19 May 1969," Part 1 to COS 21st Meeting (69), 20 May 1969.

74 NA, DEFE 11/699, no. E166, "Northern Ireland: Draft Memorandum," 16 May 1969, paras 8–9.

75 NA, DEFE 11/699, no. E 173, "Northern Ireland: Draft Memorandum by the Secretary of State for Defence," 21 May 1969, para. 8.

76 NA, DEFE 13/903, no. 37, note, Hockaday to Private Secretary/Secretary of State for Defence, "Northern Ireland," 28 May 1969.

77 NA, DEFE 13/903, no. 57, "Brief on MISC 238 (69)5, Paper by Secretary of State for Defence," 15 July 1969. The debate over withdrawal of British troops is not addressed in either Wilson's or Callaghan's memoirs.

CHAPTER THREE

1 NA, CAB 130/416, Cabinet committee minutes, MISC 238 (69), 2nd meeting, 21 April 1969, 1–3.

2 Ibid., 3.

3   NA, CAB 130/416, minutes, MISC 238 (69), 4th meeting, 29 April 1969, 1–3.

4   NA, CAB 130/416, Cabinet paper MISC 238(69) 4, "Northern Ireland: General
     Appreciation on Intervention, Memorandum by the Secretary of State for
     the Home Department," 1 May 1969, 3.

5   NA, PREM 13/2843, Prime Minister's Office, no. 7A, note of a meeting held at
     10 Downing Street, 21 May 1969, 1–2.

6   IWM, Freeland Papers, binder, IS Operations Northern Ireland, 4. Cited with
     permission of the IWM. Every effort was made to seek permission of the
     original copyright holder, who could not be located.

7   Edwards, "Whipping Boy," 168.

8   NA, DEFE 11/699, no. E140, minute, CDS to Secretary of State for Defence,
     "Command Arrangements for Northern Ireland," and E140/1, message, MOD
     to HQNI, "Command Arrangements for Northern Ireland," both 1 May 1969.

9   PRONI, HA 32/2/35, enclosure to letter, Harold Black to J.E. Greeves (Home
     Affairs), 7 May 1969 (emphasis added).

10 NA, DEFE 11/700, no. 259, "DMO Brief 84/69 Northern Ireland, for Chiefs of
     Staff Committee Meeting," 29 July 1969; no. 263, "Intelligence on Northern Ire-
     land," attachment to minute, Callaghan to Wilson, 30 July 1969; no. 268, note,
     DCDS (I) to VCDS, 4 August 1969; and minute, Brigadier General Staff (Intelli-
     gence), no. 323, "Current Weaknesses in Northern Ireland Special Branch," 18
     August 1969; DEFE 13/903, no. 29, minute, CGS to Secretary of State for
     Defence, 19 May 1969, and no. 60, letter, Freeland to Baker, 15 July 1969.

11 Moloney, Secret History, 65.

12 O'Dochartaigh, Civil Rights to Armalites, 91. See also, CAIN, Chronology, entry
     for 12 July 1969; Hennessey, History of Northern Ireland, 163, makes reference
     to disturbances in Derry, Belfast, and Dungiven on the 12th.

13 CAIN, Chronology.

14 NA, DEFE 11/700, no. C255, signal, MOD to HQNI, "Use of Helicopters in Sur-
     veillance Role by RUC," 25 July 1969, and no. E259, "DMO Brief no. 84/69
     Northern Ireland for COSC meeting 29 July 1969," para. 7.

15 NA, DEFE 11/700, no. E256, "Revised Draft Memorandum, Approved by Min-
     ister (Administration)," 28 July 1969; no. E258, Confidential annex to COSC
     meeting 31(69), held 29 July 1969, item 3; no. E259, "DMO Brief no. 84/69";
     no. E262, Note, Hockaday to secretary COSC, 30 July 1969; and no. 263/13,
     signal, CDS to HQNI, 31 July 1969.

16 Hennessey, History of Northern Ireland, 164; "Petrol Bombs Used"; and
     Chartres, "Belfast Violence Erupts," 1, 8.

17 "Mob Violence in Ulster," Times, 4 August 1969, 9; also Chartres, "Fears That
     Troops May Be Called In."

18 NA, DEFE 11/700, no. E269, letter, Brian Cubbon (personal secretary to the
    home secretary) to A.M. Halls (private secretary to the prime minister), 4
    August 1969; PRONI, CAB 4/1458, "Discussion on Possible Use of Troops in
    Aid of the Civil Power Arising Out of Disturbances in Belfast, 2–3 August
    1969" (note by Harold Black), 7 August 1969, 1.
19 PRONI, CAB 4/1458, 2.
20 Ibid.
21 Clare, "Ulster Premier Refuses," 1.
22 "Ban the Marches," 9.
23 PRONI, CAB 4/1458, 2–3.
24 Ibid., 3.
25 Ibid., 4.
26 Ibid., 4–5.
27 NA, DEFE 11/700, no. E272/1, letter, Chichester-Clark to Callaghan, 6 August
    1969, 1.
28 Ibid., 2–3.
29 NA, PREM 13/2843, no. 20, Cubbon to Gregson, 6 August 1969, 2.
30 NA, CAB 164/577, item 5M, note of a meeting at the Home Office, 8 August
    1969, 2. In the event, that is exactly how the B-Specials were used a few days
    later.
31 Ibid.
32 Ibid., 2–4.
33 Ibid., 5–6; NA, DEFE 11/700, no. E275, letter, Brian Cubbon to Peter Gregson
    (PS/PM), 8 August 1969, 1.
34 NA, CAB 164/577, item 5M, 7–9. The minister (A) told Secretary Healey on
    12 August that no one in the Home Office or MOD thought that limiting
    London's intervention to law and order only was practicable. See NA, DEFE
    13/903, no. 74/1, minute, "Northern Ireland," Minister (A) to Secretary of
    Defence, 12 August 1969.
35 NA, DEFE 11/700, no. E276, record of a meeting held in the minister (A)'s
    office, 8 August 1969.
36 Ibid. For the letter, see NA, DEFE 11/700, no. 277, Douglas Harvey, head DS6
    to Robin North, Home Office, 11 August 1969.
37 Quoted in Jackson, "Mr. McAteer Calls for Help," 1.
38 Ibid.
39 "Ulster's Failure of Leadership."
40 Hennessey, *History of Northern Ireland*, 164. O'Dochartaigh, *Civil Rights to
    Armalites*, 115, 118–19 concedes that Catholic youths instigated the violence

against the parade. Catholics had also erected barricades and apparently prepared many petrol bombs before the march.

41 O'Dochartaigh, *Civil Rights to Armalites*, 119–29. Taylor, *Loyalists*, 66–69
describes the violence in Belfast. The IRA killed two, and Protestant militants killed one.

42 *Times* (London), 14 August 1969, 7, 15 August, 1; *Guardian* (Manchester),
13–16 August 1969, 1.

43 Jackson and Hoggart, "Stormont Back Today," 1.

44 NA, DEFE 11/700, no. E291/1, note of a meeting at R.A.F. St. Mawgan, 14
August 1969, 1–3.

45 Crossman, *Diaries*, 621.

46 NA, DEFE 11/700, no. E292/1, letter, Hattersley to Callaghan, "Northern Ireland," 14 August 1969, 1–2.

47 Wood, "Wilson in Talks," 1.

48 "Official Statement," 6.

49 IWM, Freeland Papers, IS Operations Northern Ireland, 7, 9, 10.

50 Eveleigh, *Peacekeeping*, 6–7. The author, who served two tours in Northern
Ireland as a battalion commander, relied on the Scarman Tribunal report
(1972) for his chronology.

51 Hennessey, *Evolution of the Troubles*, 6–7.

52 IWM, Freeland Papers, IS Operations Northern Ireland, 11–12; NA, DEFE
11/700, no. E283, minutes, COSC, 32nd meeting/69, item 1, "Northern Ireland," 14 August 1969, and no. E303, CDS to Minister (A), "SITREP, Northern
Ireland," 15 August 1969, 1–2.

53 "How Long a Stay for the Troops?" and "A Gamble for Peace in Derry."

54 Wood, "Wilson in Talks."

55 Wood, "Forces Facing a Long Stay," 1.

56 "What the Troops Mean," 7.

57 Ibid.

58 Ibid.

59 NA, PREM 13/2483, Joint Intelligence Committee Ulster Working Group
paper JIC(A) (69) (UWG) 5, "Northern Ireland," 19 May 1969, para. 19 refers
to the Ministerial Security Committee, the Internal Security Committee,
and the Protective Security Committee.

60 PRONI, HA 32/3/2, Government of Northern Ireland, "Instruction from the
Prime Minister," 15 August 1969, and CAB 4/1465, Cabinet Conclusions, 20
August 1969. Attendees varied over time. See NA, DEFE 11/701, nos. E 490,
509, "Conclusions of a Meeting of the Joint Security Committee," 25, 29 Sep-

tember 1969. The director of intelligence and the UK representative to Stormont also attended regularly. JSC meetings are discussed in the full text of a speech by the Northern Ireland PM in "Major Chichester-Clark Indicts Eire," 8.

61 *Report of the Bloody Sunday Inquiry*, vol. 1, chap. 7, para. 73. If Crossman's diary (622–3) is correct, cabinet met on the afternoon of the 18th and Wilson's meeting with Chichester-Clark followed it immediately. They announced their agreement on television that evening. The formal document was not promulgated officially until the next day.

62 *Report of the Bloody Sunday Inquiry*, vol. 1, chap. 8, para. 9; NA, DEFE 11/700, no. E334, "Record of a Meeting in the Secretary of State's Room on 20 August to Discuss Northern Ireland," item 7; and NA, CAB 164/577, no. 12, Memorandum by Graham Angel (principal private secretary, Home Office), "Northern Ireland," 21 August 1969, item 3. See also, Patterson, "The British State," 497.

63 "Responsibility for Law and Order in Northern Ireland," note by the chairman of the Official Committee, 10 December 1971, cited in *Report of the Bloody Sunday Inquiry*, vol. 9, chap. 193, para. 25 (emphasis added).

64 Charters, "From Palestine to Northern Ireland," 197.

65 NA, DEFE 11/700, no. E291/1, 2–3.

66 NA, DEFE 11/700, no. E334, "Record of a Meeting in the Secretary of State's Room," 20 August 1969, para. 5.

67 NA, DEFE 11/700, no. E339, Signal, Acting CDS to GOCNI, "Directive for the General Officer Commanding Northern Ireland," 22 August 1969.

68 Ibid.

69 *Report of the Bloody Sunday Inquiry*, document G0, vol. 9, chap. 193, "Note of a Meeting Between the Prime Minister and the Prime Minister of Northern Ireland on Tuesday, 19th August 1969," p. 5. See also NA, DEFE 11/700, no. 325/1, "Northern Ireland ... Brief for S of S," 18 August 1969.

70 See, e.g., UK, War Office, *Keeping the Peace (Duties)*, 44–6; UK, War Office, *Keeping the Peace, Part 1*, 59, 62; UK, MOD, Defence Council, *Land Operations*, 69–71. See also Kitson, *Low Intensity Operations*, 71, 73–4, 95, 99–100. But this was not always achieved in practice: see French, *British Way in Counter-Insurgency*, 28–31.

71 NA, DEFE 11/700, no. E323, minute, Brigadier D.J. Willison (BGS INT) to CGS, 18 August 1969.

72 NA, CAB 130/444, Cabinet paper 244(70)5, "Security Intelligence Organization in Northern Ireland: Memorandum by the Security Service," to the Official Committee on Northern Ireland, 6 May 1970, 1–3.

73 See NA, CAB 164/877, no. 1, Cabinet, Northern Ireland Committee, minutes of meeting, 22 June 1970, 4; and *Report of the Bloody Sunday Inquiry*, vol. 1, chap. 8, document GIAAB, "Directive for the General Officer Commanding Northern Ireland as Director of Operations," 4 February 1971. It told him that he would deal with the Northern Ireland government on intelligence matters "through the machinery of the Joint Security Committee." But the director of intelligence at the time of Bloody Sunday made no mention of the ISC in his testimony to the Saville Inquiry.

74 IWM, Freeland papers, box 79/34/3, file – Exile! February–June 1971, sub-file Letters to and from the Chief of the General Staff, "CGS Record of a Discussion with GOC Northern Ireland," 21 August 1969, 4.

75 IWM, Freeland papers, clutch file Northern Ireland, 1969–1971, file 1, GOC's Conference, 2 September 1969, "Talk to Commanders," 2 September 1969, 4. See also NA, DEFE 11/700, no. E334, para. 8.

76 NA, DEFE 11/700, item 357, note, BGS (INT), 29 August 1969, including directive to the GOC, and Annex A "Terms of Reference for the Director of Intelligence Northern Ireland." The terms of reference were approved by the CGS, DCDS (I), and the full JIC. See also DEFE 13/921, no. 2, note, R.A. Custis, Assistant Private Secretary to the Secretary of State for Defence, to AUS (GS), 7 March 1972, "GOC's Directives, 1971–1973." The directive was drafted by the COSC.

77 *Report of the Bloody Sunday Inquiry*, document KD2.1, written testimony of former director of intelligence for Northern Ireland to the Bloody Sunday Inquiry. This may have been the same D/INT appointed in 1969, although he told the inquiry that he took up the position in 1970 after three months as SLO.

78 NA, PREM 13/2844, attachment to no. 5, "Northern Ireland Statement Released 14.8.69," states clearly that troops would be withdrawn as soon as law and order was restored.

79 *Report of the Bloody Sunday Inquiry*, vol. 9, chap. 193, para. 3.

80 Ibid., para. 5.

81 Quoted in Douglas-Home, "British Troops May Become Targets," 8.

82 "What Way Out for Ulster?" (emphasis added).

83 Douglas-Home, "British Troops May Become Targets."

84 IWM, Freeland Papers, clutch file, Northern Ireland, 1969–1971, General Sir Ian Freeland, "Staff College Lecture 9 December 1970," 1.

85 NA, PREM 13/2844, unnumbered note of a telephone conversation between the prime minister and the defence secretary, 20 August 1969.

86 Ibid.

87 NA, CAB 164/577, no. 20, Hooper (Cabinet Office) to Allen, 4 September 1969.

88 NA, PREM 13/2844, no. 22, letter Hooper to Allen, 22 August 1969, with draft memo on Northern Ireland.

89 NA, CAB 164/577, no. 15, letter, Allen to Hooper, 27 August 1969.

90 NA, CAB 164/577, no. 16, letter, Dunnett (MOD) to Hooper, 27 August 1969, and no. 36M, note, Cairncross to Hooper, "Home Office Northern Ireland Department," October 1969.

91 IWM, Freeland Papers, Staff College lecture, 1–2.

92 IWM, Freeland Papers, file – Miscellaneous Papers, letter, Freeland to the Rt Hon. James Callaghan, MP, 7 September 1973.

93 *Report of the Bloody Sunday Inquiry*, document KB1, written testimony of Sir Kenneth Bloomfield.

94 Ibid.

95 *Report of the Bloody Sunday Inquiry*, document KC15, written testimony of Brian Cummings.

96 Ibid. The GSU was created when the Stormont PM also took responsibility for Home Affairs. It was supposed to have a security-planning role but its role in developing security policy was circumscribed. Like the JSC, it focused on matters such as prisons and policing, but not on operational issues.

97 Ibid.

98 *Report of the Bloody Sunday Inquiry*, vol. 9, chap. 193, document G0, "Note of a Meeting," para. 3. (The original can be found at NA, PREM 13/2844, no. 5.)

99 Ibid., para. 4.

100 Ibid., para. 5.

101 Ibid. See also "What Way Out for Ulster?" and Mounter, "Peace Talks at Stormont," 1, for press commentary on the B-Specials.

102 *Report of the Bloody Sunday Inquiry*, vol. 9, chap. 193, document G0, "Note of a Meeting," para. 7.

103 Ibid.

104 Ibid., 7–8.

105 NA, PREM 13/2844, note of a telephone conversation between the prime minister and the defence secretary, 20 August 1969.

106 IWM, Freeland Papers, file – Exile! February–June 1971, sub-file – Letters to and from the Chief of the General Staff, "CGS Record of a Discussion with the GOC Northern Ireland," 21 August 1969, 1–3; NA, PREM 13/2844, unnumbered letter, Healey to Wilson, 22 August 1969.

107 IWM, Freeland Papers, sub-file – Letters to and from the Chief of the Gener-

al Staff, "CGS Record of a Meeting of the Northern Ireland Cabinet Security Committee," 21 August 1969.

108 NA, DEFE 47/7, no. E8, note, Hugh Ellis-Rees, Head of C2 (AD), MOD, to PUS (A), "Legal Position of the GOC Northern Ireland," 29 August 1969. This is an MOD commentary on the adviser's message.

109 Ibid.

110 NA, DEFE 11/701, no. E533, minute, Healey to Baker, "Northern Ireland," 3 October 1969.

111 Ibid.

112 NA, DEFE 11/701, no. E533/2, minute, Baker to Healey, 3 October 1969.

113 Ibid.

114 Ibid.

115 NA, DEFE 11/701, no. E534/2, record of a meeting, "Northern Ireland," 3 October 1969. On the change in riot control policy, see DEFE 11/701, no. E 509, "Conclusions of a Meeting of the Joint Security Committee," 29 September 1969.

116 NA, DEFE 11/701, no. E534/2.

117 Ibid., no. 561/2, note, MA/VCGS to Mayne (APS/defence secretary), "Northern Ireland," 8 October 1969, and no. 561/3, note, Mayne to MA/VCGS, "Northern Ireland – Arming of Army Personnel with Batons," 8 October 1969.

118 NA, CAB 164/577, no. 49, "Extract from a Note of a Meeting on Northern Ireland," 10 December 1969. See the new terms of reference for the civil adviser (September 1971) in NA, DEFE 47/7, and discussed in the next chapter.

119 NA, DEFE 11/702, no. 639, letter, Freeland to Baker, 17 October 1969, and no. 665, signal, CDS to GOC, 24 October 1969; *Report of the Bloody Sunday Inquiry*, vol. 9, chap. 193, para. 26.

120 NA, PREM 13/2848, "Home Secretary's Meeting with the Prime Minister of Northern Ireland," 18 November 1969, 2; IWM, Freeland Papers, file – Exile!, sub-file Letters to and from the Chief of the General Staff, letter, Baker to Freeland, 24 November 1969 (emphasis added). See also Hennessey, *Evolution of the Troubles*, 16.

121 Hennessey, *Evolution of the Troubles*, 17; Patterson, "British State and the Rise of the IRA," 500.

122 See remarks by Sir Knox Cunningham, *Parliamentary Debates*, Commons, 13 October 1969, vol. 788, cc. 91.

123 Ibid., 13 October 1969, vol. 788, cc. 47–164; 14 October 1969, vol. 788, cc. 203–5; 13 November 1969, vol. 791, cc. 626–743.

124 Ibid., 13 October 1969, vol. 788, cc. 148.
125 Ibid., cc. 156.

CHAPTER FOUR

1 McCleery, *Operation Demetrius*, 19, 22; English, *Armed Struggle*, 139–41;
Moloney, *Secret History*, 102; *Report of the Bloody Sunday Inquiry*, vol. 1, chap.
8, paras 62–3. Early official statistics vary slightly from the standard narrative, showing 337 arrested and 94 released. See NA, CJ4/56, no. 53, note, P.
Leyshon to Howard-Drake, "Internment," 16 August 1971. Lafree, Dugan,
and Corte, "The Impact of British Counterterrorist Strategies," 26, gives a
total of 1,981 for the whole internment period. McCleery, *Operation
Demetrius*, 22, provides a different total: 2,447 detained, 934 released
between 9 August 1971 and 14 February 1972, leaving 1,523 in long-term
detention. Cabinet noted the recruiting boost for the IRA: NA, CAB 128/48/2,
Annex to Cabinet Minutes CM (71) 47, 21 September 1971.
2 *Report of the Bloody Sunday Inquiry*, vol. 1, chap. 8, paras 66–70. The European Court of Human Rights later ruled that the techniques used amounted to inhuman and degrading treatment but not torture.
3 Kennedy-Pipe, *Origins of the Present Troubles*, 55, 57, 59; Hennessey, *History of
Northern Ireland*, 195–8; English, *Armed Struggle*, 141.
4 United Kingdom, Ministry of Defence, *Operation Banner*, para 220.
5 Kennedy-Pipe, *Origins of the Present Troubles*, 55, 58; English, *Armed Struggle*,
141.
6 French, *British Way in Counter-Insurgency*, 79, 81–2, 87–8, 110–12, 116, 162–6.
On the image of detention, see Carruthers, *Winning Hearts and Minds*.
7 Finn, *Constitutions in Crisis*, 54–5, 68.
8 Kissane, "Defending Democracy," 157–8, 172. Internment was one of a number of emergency powers (such as military courts) that the Irish government
used immediately after the civil war and again during the 1930s.
9 McCleery, *Operation Demetrius*, 14–16.
10 Finn, *Constitutions in Crisis*, 57.
11 LHCMA, Cooper papers, 4/1/2 file – Academic Interviews, 2 April 1992, 9;
Bew and Patterson, *British State and the Ulster Crisis*, 34, 42; Hennessey, *Evolution of the Troubles*, 28.
12 LHCMA, Cooper Papers, Academic Interviews, 10.
13 Hennessey, *Evolution of the Troubles*, 31.
14 IWM, Freeland Papers, 79/34/4, file – Miscellaneous Papers, letter, Freeland to
Callaghan, 7 September 1973.

15 Hennessey, *Evolution of the Troubles*, 33.

16 Patterson, "British State and the Rise of the IRA," 493, lays some of the blame on the UK representatives in Northern Ireland. He argues that their advice led London to give priority to political reform over counter-insurgency, creating the best possible conditions for the growth of the PIRA.

17 O'Dochartaigh, *Civil Rights to Armalites*, 202–5, 215, 219, 230, 232–7; Hamill, *Pig in the Middle*, 45–7; Smith, *Fighting for Ireland*, 95–99. McCleery, *Operation Demetrius*, 6, says the 1970 search yielded 100 firearms, 100 home-made bombs, 250 pounds of explosives, and 21,000 rounds of ammunition. There was some debate over the legality of the curfew. See Hennessey, *Evolution of the Troubles*, 42, and Campbell and Connolly, "Model for the 'War against Terrorism,'" 343–5, 347–51, 353–4, 362–71 See also the quote from Maj. Gen. A.J. Dyball in Heather, "British Army in Northern Ireland," 91n. 47.

18 Quoted in Hennessey, *Evolution of the Troubles*, 64. Interestingly, Farrar-Hockley's assertion that the situation was not war stands in stark contrast to later assertions that this episode and the Northern Ireland campaign in general was seen as a model for the post-9/11 "war on terrorism." See Campbell and Connolly, "Model for the 'War against Terrorism,'" 341–3.

19 NA, CAB 128/48/2, Confidential Annexes to Cabinet Minutes (71) 15th and 16th meetings, 18, 22 March 1971. Hennessey, *History of Northern Ireland*, 184–5, 187–9.

20 See his appointment speech, as quoted in Hennessey, *History of Northern Ireland*, 189–90.

21 NA, CJ 4/40, no. 10, despatch, Howard Smith to Maudling, 11 June 1971, 1–3. See also the HO intelligence summary of the same day: NA, PREM 15/477, HONIP (71) 23 "Northern Ireland: Political Summary for the Period 4–10 June 1971," 11 June 1971, para. 1. Hennessey, *History of Northern Ireland*, 193, notes that in the first seven months of 1971, 55 people had been killed and over 600 hospitalized in more than 300 explosions and 320 shootings.

22 PRONI, CAB 9/G/89/2, "Note of a Meeting in the Prime Minister's Room," 22nd April 1970.

23 Ibid.

24 Ibid.

25 Hamill, *Pig in the Middle*, 39; O'Dochartaigh, *Civil Rights to Armalites*, 179–80. While most sources assert that the searches and curfew of July 1970 ended the "honeymoon" between the army and the Catholics, O'Dochartaigh suggests that those events marked only the end of a more gradual erosion of mutual tolerance. Hennessey, *History of Northern Ireland*, 174–5, notes

that IRA sniping had provoked the searches. On Porter's resignation, see CAIN, *Chronology*, entry for 26 August 1970.

26 NA, DEFE 13/676, no. 1, letter, Hockaday to Allen, 9 November 1970, 1. A handwritten marginal note by Hockaday to the defence secretary says that Carrington concurred with the GOC's position.

27 Ibid., 2.

28 Ibid. (emphasis added).

29 NA, DEFE 13/676, no. 2, loose minute, Hockaday to Private secretary/Secretary of State, "Northern Ireland – Authority for Searches," 12 November 1970; no. 3, minute, Stephens (APS/Secretary of State) to Hockaday, "Northern Ireland – Authority for Searches," 20 November 1970; no. 6, minute, Hockaday to Woodfield (Home Office), "Northern Ireland – Authority for Searches," 23 November 1970.

30 NA, DEFE 13/676, no. 19, letter, Maudling to Chichester-Clark, 2 December 1970.

31 Ibid.

32 NA, DEFE 13/676, no. 29, minute, Stephens to Hockaday, "Northern Ireland: Searches," 15 January 1971.

33 Hennessey, *Evolution of the Troubles*, 61–2, citing the official record of the meeting.

34 Ibid., 62.

35 Ibid., 58–61.

36 NA, DEFE 4/253/4/1 COSC meeting, 26 January 1971, 1 (emphasis added).

37 NA, DEFE 5/188/14, COSC paper 14/71, "Directive for the General Officer Commanding Northern Ireland as Director of Operations," 9 February 1971, para. 4 (emphasis added).

38 Ibid., para. 5 (emphasis added).

39 NA, CAB 128/48/2, Confidential Annexes to Cabinet minutes, CM (71) 15, 18 March 1971.

40 NA, DEFE 4/255/2, Confidential Annex to COSC Meeting, COS (71) 11, 23 March 1971.

41 NA, CAB 128/48/2, CM (71) 15, 18 March 1971.

42 Faulkner, *Memoirs*, 80. He expected progress in limiting the movement of terrorists, cutting their supply lines, and gathering intelligence.

43 McCleery, *Operation Demetrius*, 10, 15, 16.

44 *Report of the Bloody Sunday Inquiry*, vol. 1, chap. 8, para. 35.

45 PRONI, CAB 4/1535, conclusions of a meeting of the cabinet, 20 July 1970, item 3 (1).

46 NA, PREM 15/475, no. 6, Home Office brief, "Internment in Northern Ireland," attached to note, Graham Angel (PS/Home Office) to Robert Armstrong (PS/PM), 12 February 1971.

47 *Parliamentary Debates*, Commons, 8 February 1971, vol. 811, cc. 35; *Parliamentary Debates*, Lords, 11 February 1971, vol. 315, cc. 245.

48 NA, PREM 15/475, no. 6, "Internment in Northern Ireland."

49 Ibid.

50 Ibid.

51 Quoted in Hamill, *Pig in the Middle*, 45. See also Moloney, *Secret History*, 95–6.

52 NA, PREM 15/475, no. 7, "Note for the Record: Northern Ireland," 13 February 1971, 4–6.

53 Hennessey, *Evolution of the Troubles*, 73–4; McCleery, *Operation Demetrius*, 7.

54 NA, CAB 134/3011, paper NI (71) 4, "Internment," 15 March 1971, para. 4.

55 Ibid., para. 6.

56 Ibid., para. 5.

57 Ibid., paras 7–8.

58 PRONI, HA 32/3/6, note of a meeting in London, 16 March 1971.

59 NA, CJ 4/56, nos 1a and 1b, note from box 500 [MI5] to Robin North (Home Office), 16 March 1971, and undated brief, "Internment." On Operation Anvil, see French, *British Way in Counter-Insurgency*, 116.

60 NA, CJ4/56, no. 1b. A response from the Home Office could not be found in this file or elsewhere.

61 NA, PREM 15/477, note of a meeting held at 10 Downing Street, 1 April 1971, 3 (emphasis added).

62 Ibid., 3–4. In his *Memoirs*, 117, Faulkner claims that he had spoken out against internment when the option had come up for discussion several times during Chichester-Clark's term.

63 NA, PREM 15/477, no. 3A, note, Trend to Heath, "Northern Ireland," 8 April 1971.

64 Hamill, *Pig in the Middle*, 55; Moloney, *Secret History*, 100; Hennessey, *Evolution of the Troubles*, 96.

65 "Sustained Campaign of Violence," 13. O'Dochartaigh, *Civil Rights to Armalites*, 266, says this was part of a deliberate effort by the Provisional IRA, which may have brought or sent in two men to Londonderry to escalate the violence.

66 *Report of the Bloody Sunday Inquiry*, vol. 1, chap. 8, para. 36.

67 *Parliamentary Debates*, Commons, 29 July 1971, vol. 882, c. 160. Paisley had

also posed multiple questions on 1, 6, 20, and 30 July, and again later on 4 and 5 August. Likewise, Bernadette Devlin had asked questions on the situation on 12, 13, and 15 July.

68 Faulkner, *Memoirs*, 119.

69 McCleery, *Operation Demetrius*, 15; Hennessey, *Evolution of the Troubles*, 112.

70 PRONI, HA 32/2/54, "Internment – Note of a Meeting Held in Room 406, Home Office, Whitehall on Thursday 15th July 1971," 15 July 1971. Faulkner, *Memoirs*, 117, says that Special Branch and military intelligence had drawn up lists of potential detainees early in 1971.

71 PRONI, HA 32/2/54, "Contingency Plan for Internment." The document is relatively brief and is not dated, so it is not certain that this is the plan drafted for the 20 August meeting. See also PRONI, HA 32/2/54, "Letter Concerning Meeting at the Home Office in London on the Subject of Internment," 21 July 1971. It states that the plan would have a number of appendices, including a joint army-police operational plan. These appendices are not attached to this document.

72 PRONI, HA 32/2/54, "Contingency Plan for Internment."

73 *Report of the Bloody Sunday Inquiry*, vol. 1, chap. 8, paras 35, 37. See also NA, PREM 15/478, no. 1, letter, Stephen (MOD) to Gregson (PS/PM), 21 July 1971.

74 LHCMA, Ramsbotham Papers, box – Speeches, 1982–1995, file – Articles and Talks by Field Marshal Lord Carver, 1971–1996, Lt. Col. David Ramsbotham, "Internment," undated, 1. Although undated, the document refers to the Special Provisions Act of June 1973 and thus was written sometime after that date. See also Faulkner, *Memoirs*, 118.

75 NA, CJ 4/56, no. 1, Smith to Woodfield (Home Office) and Sir Stewart Crawford (FCO), "Internment," 20 July 1971. Smith said that Faulkner had told him that morning of his change of heart on internment.

76 Jones, "Mr Faulkner Makes Appeal," 1, and "Sustained Campaign of Violence," 13. Seamus Cusack and Desmond Beattie, shot by the army on 8 and 9 July respectively, were the first fatal victims of the violence in Londonderry: O'Dochartaigh, *Civil Rights to Armalites*, 266–7, 270.

77 NA, CAB 128/48/2, Confidential Annexes to Cabinet Minutes 1971, annex to CM (71) 40, 22 July 1971.

78 Ibid.

79 Ibid. (emphasis added).

80 According to the *Report of the Bloody Sunday Inquiry*, the Cabinet Committee on Northern Ireland was referred to as GEN 47. Cabinet minutes also refer to IRN, which was the ministerial committee on NI that predated it.

Ramsbotham's "Internment" has the CGS meeting a "Ministerial" committee on Northern Ireland on 3 August. It is not clear whether the delegated authority referred to in the *Report of the Bloody Sunday Inquiry* was of a "blanket" nature or only for the prime minister and the home, foreign, and defence secretaries for the duration of the parliamentary recess, as implied in NA, CAB 128/48/2, annex to CM (71) 44, 16 August 1971, 1.

81 LHCMA, Ramsbotham, "Internment," 1–2. See also NA, PREM 15/478, Stephen to Gregson, 21 July 1971.

82 Quoted in Stanhope, "Army Adopts New Role," 1; Carver, *Out of Step*, 405–6. The Government of Ireland Act 1949 reaffirmed Ulster's status within the United Kingdom in light of the Irish Republic's 1948 declaration of its own status as a republic, thereby taking it out of the Commonwealth.

83 Carver, *Out of Step*, 406; Hennessey, *Evolution of the Troubles*, 114–15; Stanhope, "Army Adopts New Role"; NA, CAB 128/48/2, annex to CM (71) 40, 2; LHCMA, Ramsbotham, "Internment," 2. Both English, *Armed Struggle*, 140, and Moloney, *Secret History*, 101, say that the IRA had some degree of warning about the internment operation.

84 NA, CJ 4/56, no. 18, R.J. Andrew (PS/Secretary of State) to PS/Minister of State, "Northern Ireland," 3 August 1971, para. 4. Stanhope, "Army Adopts New Role" says only six remained in custody at the end of the first day.

85 NA, CJ 4/56, no. 5, note for the record, 28 July 1971.

86 Ibid.

87 Ibid.

88 NA, PREM 15/478, no. 5, NI (71) 7, "Memorandum to the Prime Minister: Northern Ireland Committee (NI (71)7," 28 July 1971, para. 7.

89 Ibid., paras 8–9.

90 *Report of the Bloody Sunday Inquiry*, Confidential annex to minutes of cabinet ministerial committee on Northern Ireland, NI (71) 8, 29 July 1971, 2.

91 Ibid.

92 *Parliamentary Debates*, Commons, 29 July 1971, vol. 822, cc. 791–801, and 2 August 1971, cc. 1084–1150; *Parliamentary Debates*, Lords, 29 July 1971, cc. 638–46; "Unions Claim," 1; "Mr. Heath Returns," 1.

93 Chartres, "Sinn Fein Intend Action," 1.

94 *Parliamentary Debates*, Commons, 5 August 1971, vol. 822, cc. 1871–1900.

95 Ibid. The possible need to recall Parliament was mentioned.

96 NA, CJ 4/56, no. 18, R.J. Andrew (PS/SSD) to PS/Minister of State, "Northern Ireland," 3 August 1971, 1–2.

97 Heath, *Course of My Life*, 428.

98 NA, CJ 4/56, no. 15A, note by Hockaday, "Northern Ireland – Internment," 2 August 1971. The minute was copied to the Home Office.

99 Ibid.

100 Ibid.

101 Ibid.

102 Andrew, *Defence of the Realm*, 553.

103 NA, CJ 4/56, no. 19, minute, W.K. White (Western European Department) to Sir Stewart Crawford (DUS/FCO), "Northern Ireland," 3 August 1971, 1–2.

104 Ibid., 3.

105 Ibid.

106 LHCMA, Ramsbotham, "Internment," 2.

107 NA, CJ 4/56, no. 17, "Northern Ireland – Internment: Report by Officials," 3 August 1971,

108 Ibid.

109 NA, CJ 4/56, unnumbered note, Hockaday to Allen, 5 August 1971.

110 NA, CJ 4/56, unnumbered copy of "Annex B: The Intelligence Implications."

111 IWM, Oral History, Clive Marcus Brennan, reel 15.

112 NA, CJ 4/56, no. 20, "Message to the Prime Minister of Northern Ireland from the Home Secretary," 4 August 1971.

113 Ibid.

114 NA, CJ 4/56, no. 23, note, R.J. Andrew (MOD) to Graham Angel (HO), 4 August 1971.

115 Ibid. Faulkner, *Memoirs*, 119, says that he called Maudling on the 4th to request a meeting.

116 NA, PREM 15/478, no. 23, note, Armstrong to Heath, 4 August 1971.

117 Ibid.

118 LHCMA, Ramsbotham, "Internment," 2–3.

119 NA, CJ 4/56, no. 24, telegram, UK Rep. Belfast to private secretary, Home Office, 5 August 1971.

120 Ibid.

121 *Report of the Bloody Sunday Inquiry*, vol. 1, chap. 8, paras 39–41, supported by the minutes of the GEN 47 committee meeting, 5 August 1971.

122 NA, PREM 15/478, no. 25, "Northern Ireland: Note of a Meeting Held at 10 Downing Street," 5 August 1971, 1–2.

123 Ibid., 2.

124 Ibid., 3.

125 Ibid.

126 This is what Heath told Burke Trend after the meetings with Faulkner had

concluded. See NA, PREM 15/478, no. 26, note, Trend to Armstrong, 6 August 1971.

127 LHCMA, Ramsbotham, "Internment," 4.

128 Ibid. Ramsbotham says that the British representative to the Northern Ireland government also attended, but his name does not appear in the official record. He may have mistakenly identified Kenneth Bloomfield (deputy secretary of the Stormont cabinet), who did attend, as such. The note of the meeting does not show the role of the GOC and the CGS, but that document itself may not be a complete record. Likewise, Faulkner, *Memoirs*, 120, says that Shillington was called in with the GOC and CGS and stated that the time for internment had arrived. An email from Lianne Smith, archives services manager, King's College London Archives, to the author, 11 August 2016, provided some comments on this paragraph from Lord Ramsbotham that clarified the sequence of events during the day.

129 NA, CJ 4/56/101, "Operational Instruction 2/71," 6 August 1971; Hennessey, *Evolution of the Troubles*, 123, 130–1.

130 LHCMA, Ramsbotham, "Internment," 3–4. PIRA leader Sean MacStiofan later claimed that a sympathizer in the Ministry of Home Affairs gave the group forewarning of the operation. See Hennessey, *Evolution of the Troubles*, 216; email, Smith to author, 11 August 2016.

131 LHCMA, Ramsbotham, "Internment," 4; Carver, *Out of Step*, 409; Hennessey, *Evolution of the Troubles*, 129.

132 PRONI, CAB 4/1607, letter, Government Security Unit, Northern Ireland to D. Johnston, assistant chief constable, RUC, 18 August 1971.

133 Quoted in Hennessey, *Evolution of the Troubles*, 129.

134 McCleery, *Operation Demetrius*, 20–1.

135 Ibid., 21.

136 Ibid., 18, 20.

137 Ibid., 45.

138 PRONI, CAB 4/1610, note of a meeting held at Chequers, 19 August 1971.

139 Faulkner, *Memoirs*, 121.

140 Maudling, *Memoirs*, 184.

141 Ibid.

142 Hennessey, *Evolution of the Troubles*, 132–8, 142–3.

143 Cited in ibid., 210–11.

144 NA, CAB 128/48/2, CM (71) 44, confidential annex to cabinet minutes, 16 August 1971; *Report of the Bloody Sunday Inquiry*, vol. 1, chap. 8, paras 56, 58. See also the following documents in the *Report*: E7, Bew, "Historical Back-

ground to Bloody Sunday: Report to the Bloody Sunday Tribunal," 15–16; G1, 8 Infantry Brigade, "Operational Directive 3/71," 2 July 1971; and G41, "Future Military Policy for Londonderry: An Appreciation of the Situation by CLF," 14 December 1971, paras 3–4. Document G44A, "Commander 8 Brigade's Brief for CGS on Derry," 17 December 1971, mentioned lack of intelligence. See also document G44, "CGS Report on Visit to Northern Ireland, 15–17 December 1971," 20 December 1971, 3, para. 8, and Moloney, *Secret History*, 101–2. O'Dochartaigh, *Civil Rights to Armalites*, 271, 281, says that, with internment removing the older leadership of the Provisional IRA, the younger generation took control of the movement.

145 McCleery, *Operation Demetrius*, 32, 57.

146 Geraghty, *The Irish War*, 47–50.

147 Hennessey, *Evolution of the Troubles*, 153, citing a DEFE 23 document from the National Archives.

148 McCleery, *Operation Demetrius*, 61; NA, CAB 130/522, item 6, GEN 47 (71), minutes, 6th meeting, 18 October 1971. The number of personnel involved is from Hennessey, *Evolution of the Troubles*, 155.

149 NA, DEFE 47/7, E32, Hockaday to Balneil (minister of state), 13 September 1971.

150 Carver cited in Geraghty, *The Irish War*, 47, and in Hennessey, *Evolution of the Troubles*, 159–60.

151 Hennessey, *Evolution of the Troubles*, 154, citing a DEFE 23 document from the National Archives.

152 NA, DEFE 47/7, item E34, Balneil to Carrington, 16 September 1971.

153 Ibid.

154 Ibid.; Carrington quoted in NA, CAB 130/522, item 6.

155 Geraghty, *The Irish War*, 51–2; Hennessey, *Evolution of the Troubles*, 216–20.

156 Quoted in *Report of the Bloody Sunday Inquiry*, vol. 1, chap. 8, paras 66–8, citing the original sources.

157 Ibid., chap. 8, para. 67.

158 NA, CAB 128/48/2, CM (71) 47, 21 September 1971.

159 Ibid., and CM (71) 49, 12 October 1971.

CHAPTER FIVE

1 *Report of the Bloody Sunday Inquiry*, vol. 1, chap. 5, para. 4, and vol. 8, chap. 154, para. 1.

2 Ibid., vol. 1, chap. 4, paras 16–20.

3 McKittrick and McVea, *Making Sense of the Troubles*, 77–8; Hennessey, *History of Northern Ireland*, 206; English, *Armed Struggle*, 151–2.

4 Finn, *Constitutions in Crisis*, 74.

5 *Report of the Bloody Sunday Inquiry*, vol. 1, chap. 8, paras 56, 58, and document G41, "Future Military Policy for Londonderry: An Appreciation of the Situation by CLF," 14 December 1971, paras 3–4. Document G44A, "Commander 8 Brigade's Brief for CGS on Derry," 17 December 1971, mentioned lack of intelligence. See also document G44, "CGS Report on Visit to Northern Ireland 15–17 December 1971," 20 December 1971, p. 3, para. 8. See also O'Dochartaigh, *Civil Rights to Armalites*, 279–80.

6 *Report of the Bloody Sunday Inquiry*, vol. 1, chap. 8, paras 62–3; Moloney, *Secret History*, 102–3.

7 *Report of the Bloody Sunday Inquiry*, vol. 1, chap. 8, paras 71–6.

8 Ibid., paras 93–8.

9 *Report of the Bloody Sunday Inquiry*, document E6, Arthur, "Historical Background to Bloody Sunday," 28.

10 Ibid., 32.

11 French, *British Way in Counter-Insurgency*, 95–6, 103–4. This was true even in Malaya, where Gen. (later Field Marshal) Templer held the civilian post of high commissioner.

12 *Report of the Bloody Sunday Inquiry*, document E7, Bew, "Historical Background to Bloody Sunday," 15.

13 *Report of the Bloody Sunday Inquiry*, document G1, 8 Infantry Brigade, "Operational Directive 3/71," 2 July 1971.

14 Ibid.

15 Ibid.

16 *Report of the Bloody Sunday Inquiry*, document E7, Bew, "Historical Background," 15–16.

17 O'Dochartaigh, *Civil Rights to Armalites*, 274–5, 277–8, makes it clear that the sterile statement of army policy issued in July did not accord with the ugly reality of search operations and clashes with rioting civilians.

18 *Report of the Bloody Sunday Inquiry*, document E7, Bew, "Historical Background," 17–18. The quoted portion comes *Report of the Bloody Sunday Inquiry*, document G15, cabinet committee on Northern Ireland minutes of meeting, 6 October 1971.

19 *Report of the Bloody Sunday Inquiry*, document E7, Bew, "Historical Background," 19–20, citing the minutes of the 7 October meeting between Heath and Faulkner.

20 *Report of the Bloody Sunday Inquiry*, document G14AAA, 86.9, Robert Armstrong (principal private secretary to the prime minister) to R.J. Andrew (MOD), 30 September 1971.

21 *Report of the Bloody Sunday Inquiry*, document G14B, "Northern Ireland – Appreciation of the Security Situation as at 4th October 1971," 86.8.

22 Ibid., 86.9.

23 Ibid.

24 Ibid., 86.7

25 Neumann, *Britain's Long War*, 56; French, *British Way in Counter-Insurgency*, 82, 84.

26 See the description of army searches and use of CS gas in O'Dochartaigh, *Civil Rights to Armalites*, 277–9.

27 *Report of the Bloody Sunday Inquiry*, document G14B, "Northern Ireland," 86.8–12.

28 Ibid., 86.12–13.

29 Ibid., 86.13–14.

30 Ibid., 86.14–15.

31 Minutes of the meeting quoted in McKittrick and McVea, *Making Sense of the Troubles*, 74.

32 NA, CAB 128/48/2, annex to CM (71) 49, 12 October 1971.

33 *Report of the Bloody Sunday Inquiry*, document G23, "Commander Land Forces Directive for Future Internal Security Operations," para. 5.

34 Ibid., para. 1.

35 Ibid., paras 1–2.

36 Ibid., para. 3.

37 Ibid., para. 6.

38 Ibid., paras 8–9.

39 Ibid., para. 8, items a–e.

40 Ibid., para. 9.

41 Ibid., para. 11. It was also to jam and possibly eliminate Radio Free Derry.

42 Ibid., document G27, "Operational Directive 4/71," para. 1, a 4.

43 Ibid., para. 5, a 1–4.

44 Ibid., para. 5, b 1–3.

45 Ibid., para. 5, c 1–5.

46 Ibid., para. 6.

47 See the CGS's reports to GEN 47 Committee in November, December, and January in *Report of the Bloody Sunday Inquiry*, documents G32, G34, G34A, G35, G37A, G38, G38A, and G62, and in document B1279 (Brigadier MacLel-

lan's draft statement to the Widgery Inquiry, 1972). Details of the violence in Londonderry can be found in various intelligence summaries for December 1971 and January 1972 in *Report of the Bloody Sunday Inquiry*, documents G36AA, G37A, G42A, G44C, G45AA, G45B, G50AA, G51, G60B, G61, G64, G65, G67, G72, G80, and G99. See also O'Dochartaigh, *Civil Rights to Armalites*, 278–9.

48 *Report of the Bloody Sunday Inquiry*, document G41, 14 December 1971.

49 Ibid.

50 *Report of the Bloody Sunday Inquiry*, vol. 1, chap. 9, paras 116–18, 121–2, 162.

51 The JSC had approved a renewal of the ban for one year on 13 January, and the Stormont cabinet passed it five days later: Hennessey, *Evolution of the Troubles*, 248; *Report of the Bloody Sunday Inquiry*, vol. 1, chap. 9, para. 188.

52 The lone dissenter was RUC Chief Superintendent Frank Lagan, whose division was responsible for Derry. He thought the march should be allowed to proceed, and that stopping it would lead to violence. Hennessey, *Evolution of the Troubles*, 254.

53 *Report of the Bloody Sunday Inquiry*, vol. 1, chap. 9, para. 322.

54 Ibid., para. 323

55 Ibid., para. 332.

56 Ibid., para. 286.

57 Ibid., para. 333.

58 Ibid., para. 340 (my emphasis).

59 Hennessey, *Evolution of the Troubles*, 259.

60 *Report of the Bloody Sunday Inquiry*, vol. 1, chap. 9, para. 341; Jackson, "Army Says Shooting Began," *Guardian*, 6.

61 *Report of the Bloody Sunday Inquiry*, vol. 1, chap. 9, para. 342

62 Ibid., chap. 8, para. 22 and chap. 9, para. 45. Since the GOC was a member of the JSC and the CLF was not, the D/Ops Committee was one formal forum in which they could exchange views. They also met privately on a regular basis, at which times the CLF would inform the GOC of operational plans and actions, and the GOC would keep the CLF apprised of matters discussed with Stormont and the CGS.

63 Ibid., chap. 9, paras 124, 222, 226, 228–30.

64 Hamill, *Pig in the Middle*, 91; *Report of the Bloody Sunday Inquiry*, vol. 1, chap. 9, paras 205–13, 218, 220–4.

65 Hennessey, *Evolution of the Troubles*, 262.

66 Ibid., 249.

67 *Report of the Bloody Sunday Inquiry*, vol. 1, chap. 9, paras 664–5.

68 Ibid.

69 *Report of the Bloody Sunday Inquiry*, document G95.

70 Charters, "Have a Go," 202–29.

71 *Report of the Bloody Sunday Inquiry*, document G83.

72 Ibid., document G85.

73 *Report of the Bloody Sunday Inquiry*, vol. 1, chap. 9, para. 665.

74 Ibid., paras 676–78.

75 Ibid., para. 679.

76 Ibid., para. 680.

77 Ibid., para. 713.

78 Quoted in Hennessey, *Evolution of the Troubles*, 259.

79 *Report of the Bloody Sunday Inquiry*, document KH4, 6, written testimony by Sir Edward Heath. He had checked his memory against the minutes of the GEN 47 meeting. See also Heath's testimony on day 283.

80 *Report of the Bloody Sunday Inquiry*, document KH4, 7.

81 O'Dochartaigh, *Civil Rights to Armalites*, 284.

82 "As the Smoke Clears in Derry," 4.

83 LHCMA, Ramsbotham Papers, file – Bloody Sunday, 1–2. There was no written record of Carrington's call, and Ramsbotham himself was not with him at the time, so his written account relied on Carver's memory.

84 Ibid., with quotes from Father Denis Bradley, MP Bernadette Devlin, Eddie McAteer, and an unnamed MP. Hennessey, *Evolution of the Troubles*, 230–1; English, *Armed Struggle*, 150–1; McKittrick and McVea, *Making Sense of the Troubles*, 76–7; Sanders and Wood, *Times of Troubles*, 121–2.

85 Quoted in "13 Killed," 1.

86 Quoted in Hoggart, "Bogsiders' Bitter Condemnation," 1.

87 *Parliamentary Debates*, Commons, 31 January 1972, vol. 830, cc. 33–43.

88 *Report of the Bloody Sunday Inquiry*, document G9A, "Note of a Meeting Held at Chequers, 19 August 1971," 2.

89 *Report of the Bloody Sunday Inquiry*, document KH4, written testimony of Sir Edward Heath, 10 January 2003, 7.

90 Ibid. Curiously, under cross-examination during his oral testimony, Heath contradicted himself and asserted that maintaining the morale of military was not a factor in deciding upon an inquiry. See *Report of the Bloody Sunday Inquiry*, oral testimony of Sir Edward Heath, day 286.

91 Ibid.

92 Aitken, "Widgery Alone on Derry Tribunal," 1. See also *Parliamentary Debates*, Commons, 1 February 1972, vol. 830, cc. 241–4, 267–8, 271–3, 276–9, 282, 289–90.

93 Hennessey, *Evolution of the Troubles*, 299.
94 Widgery, *Report of the Tribunal*, introduction, para. 6, and Appendix B.
95 LHCMA, Ramsbotham papers, Bloody Sunday, 1.
96 Ibid., 3.
97 Widgery, *Report of the Tribunal*, summary of conclusions, paras 8 and 11.
98 Ibid., paras 1–3 and 7; McKittrick and McVea, *Making Sense of the Troubles*, 78; English, *Armed Struggle*, 152–3; Hennessey, *Evolution of the Troubles*, 305–7.
99 LHCMA, Ramsbotham Papers, Bloody Sunday, 4.
100 Ibid., 1.
101 The JSC meeting of 27 January was informed of plans to deal with the march, but had no say in drafting those plans. See PRONI, HA 32/3/7, 27, "Conclusions of a Meeting of the Joint Security Committee, 27 January 1972.

CHAPTER SIX

1 Kennedy-Pipe, *Origins of the Present Troubles*, 63.
2 *Report of the Bloody Sunday Inquiry*, document KH4, Heath, written testimony, 10 January 2003, 5. A 1971 Home Office report suggests that Faulkner recognized Britain's reluctance to impose direct rule and leveraged it to prolong British support for his position. See *Report of the Bloody Sunday Inquiry*, document G1AA.19.1.8, Howard Smith, "Report to the Home Secretary," 10 June 1971, See also NA, CAB 128/48/2, Confidential Annexes to Cabinet Minutes 1971, annex to CM (71) 40, 22 July 1971.
3 NA, CAB 130/422, cabinet paper CP Misc 244(69)1, "Northern Ireland: Contingency Planning. Memorandum by the Home Office," 16 September 1969, 1.
4 Ibid.
5 NA, CAB 130/444, Cabinet Miscellaneous Committees, "Contingency Planning for Direct Rule in Northern Ireland," 6 May 1970, 4.
6 Ibid. Northern Ireland already had a governor, the Crown's representative in the province.
7 NA, CAB 128/48/2, Confidential Annex to Cabinet Minutes CM (71) 13, 9 March 1971.
8 NA, CAB 134/3011, NI (71)1, Ministerial Committee on Northern Ireland, minutes of a meeting, 10 March 1971, 2. The committee included the prime minister, the home, defence, and foreign secretaries, and the chancellor of the Exchequer.

9 Ibid., 3.

10 NA, DEFE 5/188/13, COSC 13 (71), note by the secretary, COSC, "Contingency Planning to Cover the Possibility of Direct Rule in Northern Ireland," 9 February 1971.

11 Ibid.

12 Ibid., and Annex A, "Contingency Planning for Direct Rule in Northern Ireland."

13 Annex A, "Contingency Planning for Direct Rule in Northern Ireland."

14 Ibid.

15 Ibid.

16 Ibid.

17 Ibid.

18 NA, CAB 134/3011, NI (71) 3, Ministerial Committee on Northern Ireland, minutes of a meeting, 17 March 1971, 5. Maudling had sent instructions on 12 March to have parliamentary counsel draft the alternative bill: CAB 134/3011, CP NI (71) 3, "Contingency Planning for Direct Rule: Memorandum by the Home Secretary," 12 March 1971, 1.

19 NA, CAB 164/1174, "Northern Ireland: Ministerial Dispositions in the Event of Direct Rule," note by Sir Philip Allen to Burke Trend, 25 March 1971.

20 NA, CAB 128/48/2, annex to CM (71) 40, 22 July 1971.

21 NA, CAB 128/48/2, annex to CM (71) 47, 21 September 1971, 1.

22 Ibid., 1–2.

23 NA, DEFE 4/261/3, Confidential Annex to Minutes COSC Meetings, COSC (71) 36, 26 October 1971, "Direct Rule in Northern Ireland – Contingency Planning." The concerns about Home Office responsibilities were not specified.

24 Ibid. The VCDS said that, if the COSC agreed, he would approach the PUS for support on this.

25 NA, CAB 134/3417, Official Committee on Northern Ireland: Sub-Committee on Contingency Planning, NIO [C] (71) 1st meeting, minutes, 3 November 1971, 1. On the subcommittee's terms of reference, see CAB 134/3417, NIO [C] (71)1, Official Committee on Northern Ireland: Sub-Committee on Contingency Planning, "Composition and Terms of Reference: Note by the Secretary of the Cabinet," 27 October 1971. P.J. Woodfield from the Home Office chaired the subcommittee, with members representing the Foreign Office, MOD, JIC, and Cabinet Office.

26 NA, CAB 134/3417, Official Committee on Northern Ireland: Sub-Committee on Contingency Planning, NIO [C] (71) 1st meeting, minutes, 3 November 1971, 1–3.

27 NA, CAB 134/3417, 2nd meeting, minutes, 12 November 1971.

28 Ibid., 3rd meeting, minutes, 1 December 1971.

29 NA, CAB 134/3417, NIO [C] (71) 4, "Military Contingency Plans: Note by the Secretaries," 24 November 1971.

30 NA, CAB 134/3417, NIO [C] 72, "Report by the Joint Intelligence Committee: The Probable Reactions to the Introduction of Direct Rule in Northern Ireland," 18 January 1972.

31 NA, CAB 129/162/1, cabinet paper CP (72) 26, Memorandum by the Secretary of State for the Home Department, 3 March 1972.

32 Ibid.

33 Ibid. (emphasis added).

34 Ibid.

35 Hennessey, *Evolution of the Troubles*, 326–29.

36 NA, CAB 128/48/3, Confidential Annex to CM (72) 13, 7 March 1972, 5 (emphasis added).

37 NA, CAB 128/48/3, Confidential Annex to CM (72) 14, 9 March 1972, 1.

38 Ibid.

39 LHCMA, Ramsbotham Papers, box – Speeches 1982–1995, file – Articles and Talks by Field Marshal Lord Carver, 1971–1996.

40 Ibid.

41 NA, DEFE 13/921, GOC's Directives 1971–1973, note, R.A. Custis (assistant permanent secretary to the secretary of state for defence), 7 March 1972.

42 NA, DEFE 13/921, item 8, note, CGS to Permanent Under-Secretary (to the permanent secretary) to the Secretary of State for Defence, re Directive to GOC NI, 9 March 1972 (emphasis added).

43 Ibid.

44 Ibid. (emphasis added).

45 Ibid. (emphasis added).

46 Ibid. (emphasis added).

47 LHCMA, Ramsbotham Papers, file – Direct Rule and Motorman. The CGS also visited the GOC in the province on 13 March to discuss the range of possible options.

48 NA, CAB 128/48/3, Confidential Annex to CM (72) 15, 14 March 1972.

49 NA, DEFE 13/921, item 9, minute, Minister of State for Defence to Secretary of State for Defence, 14 March 1972.

50 Ibid.

51 Ibid.

52 NA, DEFE 13/921, item 9 (attachment), note from Deputy Under-Secretary to Secretary of State for Defence (undated).

53 Ibid.

54 NA, DEFE 13/921, item 11, note, D.R.J. Stephen (AUS/GS) to Assistant PS/SSD, 14 March 1972.

55 NA, DEFE 13/921 item 15, handwritten note, Stephen to Private Secretary to Permanent Under-Secretary, "N. Ireland – Departmental Organisation," 15 March 1972.

56 Ibid.

57 Ibid.

58 NA, DEFE 13/921, item 14, minute, Permanent Under-Secretary to Secretary of State for Defence, 15 March 1972.

59 Ibid.

60 NA, DEFE 13/921, item 12, minute, Balneil to Carrington, 16 March 1972.

61 Ibid.

62 NA, DEFE 13/921, item 13, minute, Stephen to PS/PUS, "Northern Ireland – Chain of Command," 17 March 1972.

63 Ibid.

64 Ibid.

65 Ibid.

66 NA, DEFE 13/921, item 18, minute, PUS/SSD to CGS, "The Responsibilities of the GOC and the Secretary of State in the Event of the appointment of a Secretary of State for Northern Ireland," 20 March 1972.

67 Ibid., 1.

68 Ibid., 2.

69 Ibid., 2–3.

70 Ibid., 3.

71 Ibid.

72 NA, DEFE 13/921, item 19, draft letter to Burke Trend (undated), Northern Ireland – Chain of Command.

73 NA, CAB 128/48/3, Confidential Annex to CM (72) 18, 23 March 1972; Whitelaw, *Memoirs*, 80. See also Hennessey, *History of Northern Ireland*, 207; McKittrick and McVea, *Making Sense of the Troubles*, 80–1.

74 NA, CAB 128/48/3, Confidential Annex to CM (72) 18, 23 March 1972. The announcement of this also would include a declaration of intent to hold a plebiscite and to end internment.

75 Whitelaw, *Memoirs*, 82–3.

76 Kennedy-Pipe, *Origins of the Present Troubles*, 62.

77 LHCMA, Ramsbotham Papers, "Direct Rule and Motorman," 1.

78 NA, DEFE 13/921, item 20, "Directive for the General Officer Commanding Northern Ireland as Director of Operations," 23 March 1972, 1.

79 Ibid., 2.
80 Ibid.
81 Ibid.
82 Hennessey, *Evolution of the Troubles*, 208–9; McKittrick and McVea, *Making Sense of the Troubles*, 78–9, 82–3.

CHAPTER SEVEN

1 NA, DEFE 24/718, item E54/3, HQ Northern Ireland, "Operational Summary for the Week Ending Wednesday 2 August 1972, Annex B Operation Motorman," 2 August 1972. The Order of Battle shows 20 regular army infantry battalions plus 2 companies, 2 Royal Marine Commandos, elements of 4 artillery regiments (in an infantry role), 6+ armoured squadrons, 9 Ulster Defence Regiment (UDR) battalions, plus supporting elements. This amounted to 21,000 British regulars and 9,000 part-time members of the UDR. The UDA was a Protestant loyalist militia.
2 NA, DEFE 24/718, item E52/2, HQ Northern Ireland, "SITREP on Operation Motorman as at 310700A," 31 July 1972; item E54/3, "Annex B Operation Motorman."
3 Moloney, *Secret History*, 117; Smith, *Fighting for Ireland*, 110; O'Dochartaigh, *From Civil Rights to Armalites*, 287–88; Kennedy-Pipe, *Origins of the Present Troubles*, 70; Bennett, "From Direct Rule to Motorman," 522.
4 See the range of critiques cited in Bennett, "From Direct Rule to Motorman," 512.
5 Neumann, *Britain's Long War*, 78, 80, cites dramatic contrasting figures: 2,598 shooting incidents in the province in the three weeks before Motorman, and only 380 in the same period after. See also McKittrick and McVea, *Making Sense of the Troubles*, 326, table 1 (which is based on a previously published source). See also Kennedy-Pipe, *Origins of the Present Troubles*, 65; Smith, *Fighting for Ireland*, 110; Moloney, *Secret History*, 118; Bennett, "From Direct Rule to Motorman," 522.
6 NA, CAB 130/560, Cabinet Committee on Northern Ireland (GEN 79), minutes, 15th meeting, 2 May 1972, 1.
7 Ibid., minutes, 16th meeting, 5 May 1972, 3.
8 Bennett, "From Direct Rule to Motorman," 512–13.
9 CAB 130/560, GEN 79, minutes, 15th meeting, 2 May 1972, 1. Whitelaw himself used the term "low profile" in referring to the military's operations.
10 Whitelaw, *Memoirs*, 107. See also Neumann, *Britain's Long War*, 80; Moloney,

Secret History, 112; and see statistics for one week in June provided by CGS in CAB 130/560, GEN 79, minutes, 21st meeting, 16 June 1972, 1.

11 NA, CAB 130/560, GEN 79, minutes, 15th meeting, 2 May 1972, 2.

12 Ibid., minutes, 18th and 19th meetings, 18, 25 May 1972.

13 Ibid., 19th meeting, 25 May 1972, 5–6.

14 English, *Armed Struggle*, 155–56; Moloney, *Secret History*, 111–12. The brief reduction in violence is noted in NA, CAB 128/50/25, cabinet conclusions, 4 May 1972, 3.

15 Moloney, *Secret History*, 116.

16 NA, PREM 15/1009, note of a meeting with representatives of the Provisional IRA, 21 June 1972, www.cain.ulst.ac.uk, accessed 16 June 2015.

17 Whitelaw, *Memoirs*, 99–100; NA, CAB 130/560, GEN 79, 21st meeting, 16 June 1972, 2–3.

18 Moloney, *Secret History*, 112, 114.

19 Ibid., 114–15; McKittrick and McVea, *Making Sense of the Troubles*, 85.

20 English, *Armed Struggle*, 24–5, 106–7, 114–15, 157–8; Moloney, *Secret History*, 79; Smith, *Fighting for Ireland*, 67, 102–9, 178–83. Whitelaw, *Memoirs*, 99–100, described the meeting as a "non-event." He said little of substance about it to the next cabinet committee meeting. See NA, CAB 130/560, GEN 79 minutes, 25th meeting, 10 July 1972, 1.

21 LHCMA, Ramsbotham Papers, File – Articles and Talks by Field Marshal Lord Carver, 1971–1996, "Direct Rule and Motorman," para. 9; NA, CAB 130/560, GEN 79 minutes, 25th meeting, 10 July 1972, 1; English, *Armed Struggle*, 158; Smith, *Fighting for Ireland*, 109.

22 Moloney, *Secret History*, 117, claims that it actually was planned before the truce to pressure the British to negotiate. After the truce it was meant to show the IRA "was still in business but it backfired badly." They had overestimated how quickly the security forces could respond to multiple bombs in such a short space of time.

23 English, *Armed Struggle*, 158–9; Moloney, *Secret History*, 114, 116–18; NA, CAB 130/560, GEN 79 minutes, 25th meeting, 10 July 1972, 3; LHCMA, Ramsbotham Papers, "Direct Rule and Motorman," undated c. 1972, para. 9.

24 LHCMA, Ramsbotham Papers, box – Speeches, 1982–1995, file – Articles and Talks by Field Marshal Lord Carver, 1971–1996, memorandum, CGS to Secretary of State for Defence, "The Army's Aims in Northern Ireland," 30 May 1972, 1.

25 Ibid., "Summaries of Visits to NI by CGS," no. 8, "Visit to NI – 24 May 1972."

26 Carver, *Out of Step*, 421.

27 LHCMA, Ramsbotham Papers, "Direct Rule and Motorman," para. 7.

28 Ibid., para. 2.

29 Ibid.

30 LHCMA, Frank Cooper Papers, 4/1/2, File – Academic Interviews, [with Susan Higgins, 2 April 1992], 7.

31 Sanders, "Operation Motorman," 474.

32 NA, DEFE 4/266/4, confidential annex to COS (72) 12, 27 March 1972.

33 Bennett, "From Direct Rule to Motorman," 517–19.

34 NA, CAB 130/560, GEN 79, minutes, 15th meeting, 2 May 1972, 2; Carver, *Out of Step*, 421; Hamill, *Pig in the Middle*, 105–7. In one month early in the direct rule period the army suffered 28 killed and over 100 wounded.

35 NA, CJ 4/135, interdepartmental meetings on intelligence, security, and information policy in Northern Ireland, items 2, 7, 8, and 15, notes of meetings, 7, 14, and 21 April and 2 May 1972. See also comments by the CGS in NA, CAB 130/560, GEN 79, minutes, 15th meeting, 2 May 1972, 2, and 18th meeting, 18 May 1972, 2. Bennett, "From Direct Rule to Motorman," 519.

36 LHCMA, Ramsbotham Papers, "The Army's Aims in Northern Ireland," 1.

37 Ibid.

38 Ibid., 1–2.

39 Ibid., 3.

40 Ibid. In fact, the Official IRA had announced a truce on the 29th. The PIRA followed suit on 22 June.

41 Ibid., 4.

42 Ibid.

43 LHCMA, Ramsbotham Papers, "Summaries of Visits to NI by CGS," no. 9, "Conversation with GOC – 15 June 1972."

44 Ibid.

45 NA, CAB 128/48/3, Confidential Annex to CM (72) 31, 22 June 1972, 1–2 (emphasis added).

46 LHCMA, Ramsbotham Papers, "Direct Rule and Motorman," para. 9.

47 NA, CAB 128/48/3, Confidential Annex to CM (72) 36, 13 July 1972, 2 (emphasis added).

48 Ibid. (emphasis added).

49 Bennett, "From Direct Rule to Motorman," 521.

50 NA, CAB 164/1100, "Northern Ireland Contingency Planning Operation Folklore," unnumbered item, "Brief for CGS re Northern Ireland – Visit of GOC," 14 July 1972, 5 says the CLF had drafted his plan as of 7 July; item 1, memo, Hockaday to Trend, "Northern Ireland Contingency Planning Some

Hypothetical Scenarios," 13 July 1972, and item 2, letter, Hockaday (Cabinet Office) to Sir Kenneth Jones (Home Office), 14 July 1972; NA, DEFE 24/718, loose minute and attachment, A.W. Stephens (DS 10) to DUS(P), 6 May 1974. This document was drafted during work on the Northern Ireland narrative several years after Motorman. Hockaday's scenarios ranged from "patience and reconciliation" to "clobbering" the paramilitary groups separately or together, and to Ulster independence and withdrawal of troops.

51 NA, CAB 164/1100, Hockaday to Jones, 14 July 1972.
52 NA, CAB 164/1100, "Northern Ireland Contingency Planning," 1.
53 Ibid.
54 NA, CAB 164/1100, Hockaday to Jones, 14 July 1972.
55 NA, DEFE 5/188/13, COSC Memorandum 13/71, "Contingency Planning to Cover the Possibility of Direct Rule in Northern Ireland," note by the secretary to COSC, 9 February 1971, and report at Annex A.
56 NA, CAB 164/1100, "Brief for CGS re Northern Ireland – Visit of GOC," 14 July 1972, 1–3, 20–1.
57 Ibid.
58 LHCMA, Ramsbotham Papers, "Summaries of Visits to NI by CGS," no. 14, "Steering Brief to VCDS and VCGS – 13 July 1972." This would have entailed deploying all available troops from UK Land Forces as well as stripping away many from BAOR, which would have been politically difficult within NATO.
59 Ibid.
60 NA, DEFE 24/718, loose minute and attachment, Stephens to DUS(P).
61 NA, CAB 164/1100, "Brief for CGS re Northern Ireland – Visit of GOC," 14 July 1972, 12–13.
62 Charters, British Army and Jewish Insurgency, 118–24; Hoffman, Anonymous Soldiers, 315–17. Hoffman cites official and private papers not previously available.
63 French, British Way in Counter-Insurgency, 115–16.
64 Loose minute and attachment, Stephens to DUS(P), 6 May 1974.
65 Ibid.
66 Ibid.
67 NA, CAB 164/1100, "Brief for CGS re Northern Ireland – Visit of GOC," 14 July 1972, 5. The Cabinet Office proposed that the initiative take the form of a constitutional conference: CAB 164/1100, "Annex D – A Fresh Political Initiative Following a[n] intensive Military Operation" (undated draft).
68 NA, CAB 164/1100, "Northern Ireland Contingency Planning – Report by Officials," 22 July 1972.

69 Ibid., see annexes A–D.

70 NA, CAB 164/110, memo, Trend to Heath, "Northern Ireland: Contingency Planning," 23 July 1972.

71 Ibid., 1–2.

72 NA, CAB 164/1101, item 4, COSC, Defence Operational Planning Staff, DOP 529/72 (Final –2nd ed.), "Contingency Plan for a State of Emergency in Northern Ireland: Plan by the Defence Operational Planning Staff," 31 July 1972; item 11, letter, Hockaday to Jones, "Northern Ireland Contingency Planning," 22 August 1972; item 14, letter, Hockaday to Jones, "Northern Ireland Contingency Planning," 14 September 1972; CAB 130/561, GEN 79 (72) 28, "Contingency Planning Northern Ireland – A Note by the Secretaries," Cabinet Office, 6 December 1972, and attached report by officials. The CAIN website reproduces an FCO document from 16 November 1973 that shows that the plan was still under discussion at that time.

73 See, e.g., *Times* (London), 22 July 1972, 1, 2, 13; *Guardian* (Manchester), 22 July 1972, 1; 24 July 1972, 1, 10. See also quote from the *Daily Telegraph* in Smith, *Fighting for Ireland*, 110. Newspaper coverage was disrupted from the 24th to 27th by wildcat strikes in sympathy with striking dock workers, a labour dispute that was seen as a more serious crisis than the violence in Northern Ireland.

74 NA, CAB 164/1100, memo, Trend to Heath, "Northern Ireland: Contingency Planning," 23 July 1972, 2.

75 Ibid., 2.

76 NA, DEFE 24/718, item E29, loose minute (Coaker) on plan for Motorman, 23 July, and annex.

77 NA, CAB 130/560, confidential annex, minutes, GEN 79, 28th meeting, 24 July 1972, 2 (emphasis added).

78 Ibid., 2. See also NA, DEFE 24/718, item E 37/3, "Report of CGS Visit to Northern Ireland," 24–25 July 1972, 1, para. 1.

79 NA, CAB 130/560, confidential annex, minutes, GEN 79, 28th meeting, 24 July 1972, 2 (emphasis added).

80 Ibid., 2–3.

81 Ibid., 3.

82 Ibid.

83 NA, CAB 164/1100, Trend to Heath, "Northern Ireland: Contingency Planning," 23 July 1972.

84 *Parliamentary Debates*, Commons, 24 July 1972, vol. 841, cc. 1327.

85 Ibid., cc. 1329.

86 Ibid., cc. 1331.

87 Ibid., cc. 1333.

88 Ibid., cc. 1336–38, 1346, 1352, 1371, 1373, 1378–79.

89 Ibid., cc. 1385–87.

90 NA, DEFE 24/718, E37/3, "CGS Visit to Northern Ireland – 24–25 July 1972," 1, para. 2 a.

91 Ibid.

92 Ibid., 2, para. 3.

93 Ibid., 3, paras 4–5.

94 Ibid., 3–4, para. 6c.

95 Ibid.

96 Ibid., 4, para. 8.

97 Ibid., 6, para. 14.

98 Ibid., 6–7, paras 15–17.

99 Ibid., 7, para. 18.

100 Ibid., 8, para. 19.

101 Ibid.

102 Ibid., 4, para. 8, and item E33, "Note for the Record. Northern Ireland: Contingency Plan for Operation against Creggan and Bogside," 24 July 1972.

103 NA, DEFE 24/718, item E35, A.W. Stephens (head of DS10) to AUS (GS) and attachment "Pros and Cons," 25 July 1972.

104 Ibid.

105 Ibid.

106 NA, DEFE 24/718, item E36, note, "Northern Ireland Contingency Planning," 26 July 1972.

107 NA, DEFE 24/718, Stephens to AUS (GS) and attachment "Pros and Cons."

108 NA, DEFE 24/718, item E37/2, "Draft Paper by Secretary of State for Defence: Army Operations in Northern Ireland," 26 July 1972, para. 2.

109 Ibid., para. 4.

110 NA, CAB 130/560, confidential annex, minutes, GEN 79, 30th meeting, 27 July 1972, 1; DEFE 24/718, item E41, minute by A.W. Stephens, "Northern Ireland: Re-Occupation of No-Go Areas and Action against Provisional IRA," 27 July 1972.

111 NA, DEFE 24/718, item E39/1, "DMO to CGS, loose minute, Gen 79 Meeting – 27 July 1972 – Op Motorman."

112 NA, CAB 130/560, confidential annex, minutes, GEN 79, 30th meeting, 27 July 1972, 2.

113 Ibid.

114 NA, DEFE 24/718, item E43, "Telegram DMO to GOC," 27 July 1972.

115 NA, DEFE 24/718, item E46, "Commander Land Forces' Directive for Operation Motorman," 27 July 1972, para. 2.

116 Ibid., para. 4.

117 Ibid., para. 5.

118 Ibid., para. 13b.

119 Ibid.

120 Ibid., para. 22.

121 NA, DEFE 24/718, item E48, letter, CGS to GOC Northern Ireland, 28 July 1972.

122 NA, DEFE 24/718, item E49, telegram, DMO to GOC Northern Ireland, 28 July 1972.

123 NA, DEFE 24/718, item E49/2, minute, Lt. Col. D.J. Ramsbotham (MA to CGS), "GEN 79 and Telephone Conversation CGS/GOC Northern Ireland," 28 July 1972.

124 Charters, *British Army and Jewish Insurgency*, 2–3.

CHAPTER EIGHT

1 Taylor, *Loyalists*, 128.

2 Anderson, *Fourteen May Days*, 13, 20, 21, 31, 32, 39, makes it clear that the UDA was the real power behind the UWC.

3 Hennessey, *History of Northern Ireland*, 230.

4 Aveyard, "We Couldn't Do a Prague," 91. Prague refers to the Soviet invasion of Czechoslovakia in 1968.

5 NA, PREM 16/146, Prime Minister's Office, unnumbered, Northern Ireland Office, "Summary of Political Events in Northern Ireland, 9–16 May 1974," 2.

6 Quoted in Taylor, *Loyalists*, 129.

7 "Loyalist Strike Called Off," 1.

8 Taylor, *Loyalists*, 130–1. See also Anderson, *Fourteen May Days*, 30–2, 39.

9 McKittrick and McVea, *Making Sense of the Troubles*, 103, 105; Fisk, *Point of No Return*, 56, 63, 73–4, 77, 81–2, 88, 95, 126.

10 PRONI, COM 58/1/305, "The May 1974 UWC Strike: A Review by the Department of Commerce," 3 July 1974, 1.

11 Faulkner, *Memoirs*, 263.

12 United Kingdom, Ministry of Defence, *Operation Banner*, chap. 2, 11, para. 230 (emphasis added).

13 Hamill, *Pig in the Middle*, 148. See also Fisk, *Point of No Return*, 151.

14 PRONI, OE/2/23, minutes of executive meeting, 17 May 1974.

15 NA, PREM 16/146, unnumbered item, "Record of Conversation between PM and SSNI," 17 May 1974. Rees did not specify if these were to be military personnel or civilian power station workers.

16 See *Parliamentary Debates*, Commons, 20 May 1974, cc. 32–4.

17 NA, PREM 16/146, no. 6, "Note by Lord Bridges," 16 May 1974; and CAB 134/3778, Ministerial Committee on Northern Ireland, minutes, 2nd meeting, 21 May 1974. Fisk, *Point of No Return*, 87, says that most of the technical specialists were from the Royal Navy.

18 NA, PREM 16/146, no. 11, letter, Nicholls to Bridges, 20 May 1974.

19 NA, PREM 16/146, unnumbered document, "Record of a Telephone Conversation between the Prime Minister and the Secretary of State for Northern Ireland," 20 May 1974, 1.

20 NA, CAB 134/3778, Ministerial Committee on Northern Ireland, minutes, 2nd meeting, 21 May 1974; Hamill, *Pig in the Middle*, 150. On 22 May in the Commons, Rees identified six areas where barricades had been removed. See *Parliamentary Debates*, Commons, 22 May 1974, c. 379.

21 NA, PREM 16/147, no. 1D, letter, David Omand (MOD) to Bridges, 22 May 1974.

22 NA, PREM 16/148 no. 2, "Record of Conversation between the Prime Minister and the Secretary of State for Northern Ireland," 26 May 1974, 2. Fisk, *Point of No Return*, 203, says the operation took place less than six hours after Wilson's speech on the 25th. Ironically, the UDA and UVF had been removed from the list of proscribed organizations on the eve of the strike. See "Police Hold 18 in Belfast," 1, and "No Union with South," 2. In the House on 3 June, Rees described it simply as a "security operation." See *Parliamentary Debates*, Commons, 3 June 1974, c. 881.

23 Hamill, *Pig in the Middle*, 153.

24 Fisk, *Point of No Return*, 92.

25 Beckett, *The Army and the Curragh Incident*, 1, states unequivocally that calling the Curragh incident a mutiny is erroneous.

26 Ibid., 4–5.

27 Ibid., 12–15, 22. When the government later repudiated the terms of reinstatement offered to Gough and others, the secretary of state for war, J.E.B. Seely, and the chief of the Imperial General Staff, Field Marshal Sir John French, were forced to resign.

28 Ibid., 25–9.

29 Bew and Patterson, *The British State and the Ulster Crisis*, 67.

30 Anderson, *Fourteen May Days*, 44–5; Faulkner, *Memoirs*, 263.

31 Quoted in Aveyard, "We Couldn't Do a Prague," 92.

32 Kennedy-Pipe, *Origins of the Present Troubles*, 71–2. I have not found a record of any such message in the official files.

33 McKittrick and McVea, *Making Sense of the Troubles*, 104–6.

34 Hennessey, *History of Northern Ireland*, 216–21.

35 Ibid., 221–6.

36 Ibid., 227–8; Taylor, *Loyalists*, 121–2.

37 NA, CAB 128/54/11, Confidential Annex to Cabinet Conclusions (74) 11, cabinet conclusions, minute 1, 10 April 1974.

38 Ibid.

39 NA, PREM 16/145, no. 18, note, John Hunt to PM, 11 April 1974.

40 The House adjourned on 24 May, to resume on 10 June, but it was recalled one week early specifically to deal with the crisis. See remarks by Rees in the Commons: *Parliamentary Debates*, Commons, 3 June 1974, c. 878

41 PRONI, OE/2/24, minutes of executive meeting, 20 May 1974.

42 PRONI, OE/2/25, minutes of executive meeting, 21 May 1974.

43 Ibid.

44 PRONI, OE/2/27, minutes of executive meeting, 22 May 1974.

45 PRONI, OE/2/32, minutes of executive meeting, 28 May 1974.

46 NA, PREM 16/145, no. 9, "Prime Minister's Statement in the House of Commons," 1 April 1974.

47 NA, PREM 16/146, no. 6, note by Lord Bridges, 16 May 1974.

48 Ibid., no. 8, minute, Nicholls (MOD) to Bridges, 16 May 1974.

49 NA, PREM 16/146, unnumbered document, "Note of a Meeting at the Northern Ireland Office," 17 May 1974. Who attended this meeting and made that decision is not recorded.

50 NA, PREM 16/146, no. 10, minute, Nicholls to Robin Butler, Personal Secretary to the PM, 17 May 1974.

51 Ibid., no. 11, letter, Nicholls to Bridges, 20 May 1974, and unnumbered document, "Record of a Telephone Conversation between the Prime Minister and the Secretary of State for Northern Ireland," 20 May 1974.

52 NA, DEFE 70/204, item 12, note, DMO to CGS, 20 May 1974.

53 Fisk, *Point of No Return*, 87. See also McKittrick, *Despatches from Belfast*, 48.

54 NA, CAB 134/3778, Ministerial Committee on Northern Ireland, minutes, 2nd meeting, 21 May 1974.

55 NA, DEFE 70/204, item 27, office note, "Record of a Conversation between CGS and GOC Northern Ireland," a.m. 22 May 1972.

56 Ibid.

57 NA, PREM 16/147, no. 1D, letter, Omand to Bridges, 22 May 1974.

58 NA, PREM 16/148, unnumbered, "Note of a Meeting between the Minister of State for Northern Ireland and a Deputation from the Confederation of British Industry at Stormont Castle," 22 May 1974.

59 Ibid.

60 Donoughue, *Downing Street Diary*, 130.

61 NA, DEFE 70/204, "Record of a Conversation between CGS and GOC Northern Ireland," a.m. 22 May 1972.

62 Ibid.

63 NA, DEFE 70/204, item 26, office note, "Record of a Conversation on the Pickwick between the CGS and GOC Northern Ireland," 22 May 1974.

64 Ibid., item 36, office note, "Notes of a Meeting between CGS and GOC Northern Ireland Held at HQ Northern Ireland," 23 May 1974 (record dated 28 May).

65 NA, CAB 134/3778, minutes of meeting, 23 May 1974.

66 Ibid.

67 Quoted in Aveyard, "We Couldn't Do a Prague," 92.

68 Craig, "Laneside," 304–5.

69 Quoted in NA, PREM 16/147, unnumbered telegram, Prime Minister's Office to Wilson (at Chequers), 24 May 1974.

70 Speaking in the Commons on the adjournment motion on 23 May, Captain L.P.S. Orr (member for South Down) described the situation in the province as "but one step short of civil war." *Parliamentary Debates*, Commons, 23 May 1974, c. 629.

71 Donoughue, *Downing Street Diary*, 130. Curiously, he placed this meeting at the start of the strike, not on the 24th.

72 NA, PREM 16/147, no. 10, "Record of a Conversation between the Prime Minister and the Chief Executive at Chequers," 24 May 1974, 1–6; unnumbered letter, Lyons to Wilson, 24 May 1974. MPs such as Gerry Fitt, who demanded that the army take over and run the power stations, seemed unaware of the army's limited capacity to do so. See *Parliamentary Debates*, Commons, 23 May 1974, c. 638.

73 NA, CAB 129/177, no. 16, note for cabinet, 24 May 1974, enclosed with note from the secretary to the cabinet (John Hunt), 1.

74 Ibid.

75 Aveyard, "We Couldn't Do a Prague," 91.

76 NA, CAB 128/54/18, Cabinet Conclusions, minute 1, 24 May 1974.

77 Ibid. (emphasis added).

78 Ibid.

79　NA, DEFE 70/204, item 38, office note, "Record of a Meeting between S of S and CGS 2145 Hrs Friday 24 May and Subsequent Telephone Call between CGS and CLF."

80　NA, PREM 16/148, "Record of a Conversation between the Prime Minister and the Secretary of State for Northern Ireland at RNAS Caldrose, Penzance," 26 May 1974, 1.

81　"Police Hold 18 in Belfast," 1, and "No Union with South," 2.

82　NA, PREM 16/148, no. 2C, telegram, NIO to PM, 27 May 1974.

83　NA, DEFE 70/204, item 44, "Notice of a Discussion in the CGS's Office 1700 Hrs Tuesday 28 May 74"; see also item 70, letter, King to Hunt, 30 May 1974.

84　NA, DEFE 70/204, office note, "Record of the CGS's Visit to Northern Ireland," 27 May 1974.

85　Ibid.

86　Faulkner, *Memoirs*, 263.

87　NA, PREM 16/146, unnumbered document, "Record of a Telephone Conversation between the Prime Minister and the Secretary of State for Northern Ireland," 20 May 1974, 1.

88　NA, PREM 16/147, no. 10, "Record of a Conversation between the Prime Minister and the Chief Executive at Chequers," 24 May 1974, 4.

89　NA, CAB 128/54/18, Cabinet Conclusions, minute 1, 24 May 1974.

90　NA, PREM 16/148, unnumbered, Note for the Record, 29 May 1974, 2–3.

91　Ibid., no. 10A, note by the Prime Minister to Robert Armstrong (Principal Private Secretary), 30 May 1974 (emphasis added).

92　DEFE 11/876, Ian M. Burns, NIO to J.D. Bryans, Cabinet Office, 17 June 1975.

93　Ibid., letter, Johnson (Secretary to the Chief of Staff, MOD) to Ian M. Burns, NIO, 24 June 1975.

94　Ibid. Rees had made essentially the same point in the House on 22 May 1974. See *Parliamentary Debates*, Commons, 22 May 1974.

95　LHCMA, Cooper papers, file – Academic Interviews, 4/1/2, Higgins interview with Cooper, 2 April 1992, 4.

96　Wilson, *Final Term*, 74–7.

97　Ziegler, *Wilson*, 465–6, devotes less than a page to the strike and provides no insights on this issue.

98　See, e.g., "Ulster Leaders Meet Wilson" 1, and "Government decides on firm policy," 1; "Army Ready to Break," 1, and "Troops to Break Strike," 1.

99　NA, DEFE 70/204, unnumbered item, copy of Thompson's column from 25 May 1974 (emphasis added).

100 Ibid.

101 "Troops to Break Strike," 1.

102 NA, DEFE 70/204, item 50, note, Mason to PUS MOD, 29 May 1974.

103 Ibid., copy of Allan/Wightman article in item 81, minute, Brigadier W.T. MacFarlane, Director Public Relations (Army) to Military Assistant to CGS, 3 June 1974.

104 Ibid.

105 Other newspapers picked up on these themes. See NA, DEFE 70/204, item 65, John Groves, Chief of Press Relations, MOD to Private Secretary to Secretary of State for Defence, 31 May 1974.

106 The Monday Club was a lobbying group within the Conservative Party known for its hard-line Tory policies.

107 Quote from Anderson, *Fourteen May Days*, 44 (emphasis added).

108 Fisk, *Point of No Return*, 145–9.

109 Ibid., 72.

110 Quoted in Taylor, *Loyalists*, 132.

111 Ibid., 131.

112 Fisk, *Point of No Return*, 102.

113 Anderson, *Fourteen May Days*, 44–5; Faulkner, *Memoirs*, 263.

114 NA, DEFE 70/204, item 65, Groves to PS to Secretary of State for Defence, 31 May 1974, and item 81, minute, MacFarlane to MA to CGS, 3 June 1974; "Troops to Break Strike."

115 NA, DEFE 70/204, item 51, note, PUS to Mason, 30 May 1974.

116 Ibid., item 65, Groves to PS to Secretary of State for Defence, 31 May 1974.

117 Ibid., un-numbered item, King to Cary, 3 June 1974.

118 Ibid.

119 Ibid.

120 NA, DEFE 70/204, item 85, letter, Carver to Mason, 6 June 1974.

121 Ibid.

122 NA, DEFE 70/204, Groves to PS to Secretary of State for Defence, 31 May 1974, plus transcript of Sillitoe interviews.

CONCLUSION

1 Neumann, *Britain's Long War*, 29.

2 Ibid.

3 The most recent iteration of such doctrine, *Land Operations*, vol. 3, *Counter-Revolutionary Operations*, based on the most recent campaign experience in

South Arabia, had been published at the end of August 1969, barely a fort-
night after troops deployed in Belfast and Londonderry.

4 On their limitations, see French, *British Way in Counter-Insurgency*.

5 Krulak, "The Strategic Corporal."

6 Davis, *Prime Ministers and Whitehall*, xv, notes that, during the 1960s and
1970s, questions were raised about "whether the senior civil service wielded
too much power."

7 Davis says that the MOD was supported by "informed and high quality technocratic civil servants," ibid., 9.

8 Ibid., 159, 165.

9 Carrington, *Reflecting on Things Past*, 250.

10 "Lord Mason of Barnsley Obituary," *Guardian*.

11 Quoted in Davis, *Prime Ministers and Whitehall*, 142.

12 Charters, "Have a Go," 210–11.

13 Carrington, *Reflecting on Things Past*, 217, 249, and his written testimony in
Report of the Bloody Sunday Inquiry, document KC6.

14 "Field Marshal Lord Carver," *Telegraph*.

15 "Field Marshal Lord Carver," *Guardian*.

16 Quoted in *Times* (London), 19 August 1969, cited in Heather, "British Army
in Northern Ireland," 53.

17 "Obituary: General Sir Harry Tuzo," *Independent*.

18 Hamill, *Pig in the Middle*, 46.

19 "General Sir Frank King," *Times*.

20 Ibid.

21 "General Sir Frank King," *Herald Scotland*.

22 Young, "Military Professionalism in a Democracy," 23.

23 Strachan, *Politics of the British Army*, 18–19, citing Perlmutter, and 25, 128.
See also Bowen, "The Political-Military Relationship," 273.

24 Bowen, "Political-Military Relationship," 273; Strachan, *Politics of the British
Army*, 266–7 and chap. 1.

25 Schiff, "Civil-Military Relations Reconsidered, 12, 14–15.

26 Strachan, "The Civil-Military 'Gap' in Britain," 43–50, 53.

27 Bowen, "Political-Military Relationship," 277.

Bibliography

ARCHIVAL SOURCES

Imperial War Museum (IWM)

Oral History, Colonel Clive Marcus Brennan, 27190
Papers of Lieutenant-General Sir Ian Freeland, 26258

*Liddell Hart Centre for Military Archives,
King's College, London (LHCMA)*

Papers of Sir Frank Cooper
Papers of General David [Baron] Ramsbotham

Public Record Office of Northern Ireland (PRONI),
found at Conflict Archive on the Internet, at www.cain.ulst.ac.uk

CABINET
CAB 4/1458, 1465, 1535, 1607, 1610, Cabinet Conclusions, 1968–1972
CAB 9/G/89/2, Cabinet Secretariat: Ulster Defence Regiment

DEPARTMENT OF COMMERCE
COM 58/1/305, Department of Commerce: Requisition of Petrol Distribution, 1974

MINISTRY OF HOME AFFAIRS
HA/32/2/35, Security Use of Army, 1968–1971
HA 32/2/54, Internment, Policy, Security

HA 32/3/1, Minutes of Cabinet Security Committee, May–August 1969

HA 32/3/2, Minutes of Joint Security Committee, August–December 1969

HA 32/3/6, Minutes of Joint Security Council, January–October 1971

HA 32/3/7, Minutes of Joint Security Committee, January–June 1972

NORTHERN IRELAND EXECUTIVE

OE/2/23–32, Minutes of the Northern Ireland Executive, May 1974

United Kingdom National Archives (NA)

CABINET OFFICE

CAB 128/48/2–3, Confidential Annexes to Cabinet Minutes, 1971–72

CAB 128/50/25, Cabinet Conclusions, 1972

CAB 128/54/11, Confidential Annex to Cabinet Conclusions, 1974

CAB 128/54/18, Cabinet Conclusions, 1974

CAB 129/162, Cabinet Memoranda, 1972

CAB 129/177, Cabinet Memoranda, 1974

CAB 130/416, Minutes, Miscellaneous Committee 238, 1969

CAB 130/422, Papers, Miscellaneous Committee 244, 1969

CAB 130/444, Papers, Miscellaneous Committee 244, 1970

CAB 130/522, Minutes of Meetings, Cabinet Committee on Northern Ireland (GEN 47), 1971–72

CAB 130/560, Confidential Annex to Minutes, Cabinet Committee on Northern Ireland (GEN 79), 1972

CAB 134/3011, Minutes, Ministerial Committee on Northern Ireland, 1970–71

CAB 134/3417, Official Committee on Northern Ireland: Sub-Committee on Contingency Planning, 1971–72

CAB 134/3778, Minutes and Memoranda, Ministerial Committee on Northern Ireland (IRN), 1974

CAB 164/576–77, Registered Files, Ministerial and Official Committees, 1969–70

CAB 164/877, Subject Files, Situation in Northern Ireland, 1970–71

CAB 164/1100–101, Subject Files, Northern Ireland Contingency Planning, Op Folklore, 1972

CAB 164/1174, Contingency Planning for Direct Rule, 1970–72

CAB 165/949, Ministerial Committee on Northern Ireland: Composition and Terms of Reference, 1970–74

HOME OFFICE

CJ 4/40, Registered Files, Papers for Meetings, Ministerial Committee on Northern Ireland, 1971

CJ 4/56, Registered Files, Internment in Northern Ireland, 1971

CJ 4/101, Registered Files, Detention in Northern Ireland, Army Instructions Concerning Administration and Security, 1971

MINISTRY OF DEFENCE

DEFE 4/253, Minutes, Chiefs of Staff Committee Meetings, 1971

DEFE 4/255, Confidential Annexes, Chiefs of Staff Committee Meetings, 1971

DEFE 4/261, Minutes, Chiefs of Staff Committee Meetings, 1971

DEFE 4/266, Confidential Annexes to Chiefs of Staff Committee Meetings, 1972

DEFE 5/188/13, Memoranda, Chiefs of Staff Committee, 1971

DEFE 5/188/14, Papers, Chiefs of Staff Committee, 1971

DEFE 11/699, Registered Files, Chiefs of Staff Committee, May–July 1969

DEFE 11/700, Confidential Annexes to Chiefs of Staff Committee Meetings, July–August 1969

DEFE 11/701–2, Confidential Annexes to Chief of Staff Committee Meetings, September–October 1969

DEFE 11/876, Registered Files, Chiefs of Staff Committee, Northern Ireland Contingency Planning for Essential Services, 1975

DEFE 13/676, Registered Files, Minister's Office, 1970–71

DEFE 13/902, Registered Files, Minister's Office, Northern Ireland, 1968–69

DEFE 13/903, Registered Files, Minister's Office, Northern Ireland, April–August 1969

DEFE 13/921, Registered Files, Minister's Office, Northern Ireland, GOC's Directives, 1971–73

DEFE 24/718, Registered Files, Defence Secretariat Branches, Northern Ireland Contingency Planning, Operation Motorman, 1972

DEFE 25, Registered Files, Chiefs of Staff Committee, Aid to the Civil Power Policy, 1972–73

DEFE 47/7, Registered Files, 2nd Permanent Under-Secretary of State, Emergencies Northern Ireland, 1969–73

DEFE 70/204, Registered Files, Chief of the General Staff, Northern Ireland, General, 1974

NORTHERN IRELAND OFFICE

CJ 4/135, Interdepartmental Meetings on Intelligence, Security and Information Policy – Correspondence and Administrative Papers, 1972

PRIME MINISTER'S OFFICE

PREM 13/2843–48, Minutes, Meetings, Memoranda, Northern Ireland Disturbances, Law and Order, 1968–69
PREM 15/475–78, Correspondence and Papers, Internal Situation in Northern Ireland, 1970–71
PREM 15/1009, Correspondence and Papers, Situation in Northern Ireland,
1972
PREM 16/145–48, Correspondence and Papers, Situation in Northern Ireland, March–June 1974

PUBLISHED SOURCES

Aitken, Ian. "Widgery Alone on Derry Tribunal." *Guardian* (Manchester), 2
February 1971
Anderson, Don. *Fourteen May Days: The Inside Story of the Loyalist Strike of
1974.* Dublin: Gill and Macmillan, 1994
Andrew, Christopher. *Defence of the Realm: The Authorized History of MI5.*
Toronto: Viking, 2009
"Army Ready to Break Ulster Fuel Blockade." *Guardian* (Manchester), 24
May 1974
"As the Smoke Clears in Derry the Question Is: Who Fired First?" *Times*
(London), 1 February 1972
Aveyard, Stuart C. "'We Couldn't Do a Prague': British Government
Responses to Loyalist Strikes in Northern Ireland, 1974–77." *Irish Histori-
cal Studies* 39, no. 153 (2013): 91–111
"Ban the Marches." *Times* (London), 5 August 1969
Barnett, Corelli. *Britain and Her Army, 1509–1970.* New York: William Mor-
row, 1970
Barzilay, David. *The British Army in Ulster.* Vol. 1. Belfast: Century Books,
1973
Baynes, John. *No Reward But Honour: The British Soldier in the 1990s.* Lon-
don: Brassey's, 1991
– *The Soldier in Modern Society.* London: Eyre Methuen, 1972
Beckett, Ian F.W., ed. *The Army and the Curragh Incident, 1914.* London: The
Bodley Head, 1986

Beloff, Max, and Gillian Peel. *The Government of the United Kingdom: Political Authority in a Changing Society*. New York: W.W. Norton, 1980

Bennett, Huw. "From Direct Rule to Motorman: Adjusting British Military Strategy for Northern Ireland." *Studies in Conflict and Terrorism* 33, no. 6 (2010): 511–32

Bew, Paul, and Henry Patterson. *The British State and the Ulster Crisis: From Wilson to Thatcher*. London: Verso, 1985

Bew, Paul, Peter Gibbon, and Henry Patterson. *The State in Northern Ireland, 1921–72*. Manchester: Manchester University Press, 1979

Birrell, Derek, and Alan Murie. *Policy and Government in Northern Ireland: Lessons in Devolution*. Dublin: Gill and Macmillan, 1980

Bland, Douglas L. "A Unified Theory of Civil-Military Relations." *Armed Forces and Society* 26, no. 1 (1999): 7–26

Blaxland, Gregory. *The Regiments Depart: A History of the British Army, 1945–1970*. London: William Kimber, 1971

Bowen, Desmond. "The Political-Military Relationship on Operations." In *British Generals in Blair's Wars*, edited by Jonathan Bailey, Richard Iron, and Hew Strachan, 273–79. Farnham, UK: Ashgate, 2013

The British Civil Service: Permanent Secretaries and Other Senior Appointments Since 1900, http://www.gulabin.com/britishcivilservants/pdf/Senior %20Civil%20Servants.pdf, accessed 1 July 2013

"Brutality Complaint by MPs." *Times* (London), 7 October 1968

Callaghan, James. *A House Divided: The Dilemma of Northern Ireland*. London: Collins, 1973

Campbell, Colm, and Ita Connolly. "'A Model for the 'War against Terrorism'? Military Intervention in Northern Ireland and the 1970 Falls Curfew." *Journal of Law and Society* 30, no. 2 (2003): 341–75

Carrington, Peter Lord. *Reflecting on Things Past: The Memoirs of Peter Lord Carrington*. New York: Harper and Row, 1989

Carruthers, Susan L. *Winning Hearts and Minds: British Government, the Media, and Colonial Counter-Insurgency*. Leicester: Leicester University Press, 1995

Carver, Michael. *Out of Step: The Memoirs of a Field Marshal*. London: Hutchinson, 1989

Charters, David A. *The British Army and Jewish Insurgency in Palestine, 1945–47*. Houndmills, UK: Macmillan, 1989

– "From October to Oka: Peacekeeping in Canada, 1970–1990." In *Canadian Military History: Selected Readings*, ed. Marc Milner, 368–93. Toronto: Copp Clark Pitman, 1993

- "From Palestine to Northern Ireland: British Adaptation to Low-Intensity Operations." In *Armies in Low-Intensity Conflict*, ed. David A. Charters and Maurice Tugwell, 169–249. London: Brassey's, 1989
- "Have a Go: British Army/MI5 Agent-Running Operations in Northern Ireland." *Intelligence and National Security* 28, no. 2 (2013): 202–29

Chartres, John. "Belfast Violence Erupts as Orangemen March." *Times* (London), 4 August 1969
- "Fears That Troops May Be Called In." *Times* (London), 4 August 1969
- "Mob Violence in Ulster." *Times* (London), 4 August 1969
- "Sinn Fein Intend 'Once and For All' Action." *Times* (London), 5 August 1971

Chichester, Michael, and John Wilkinson. *The Uncertain Ally: British Defence Policy, 1960–1990*. London: Gower, 1982

Clare, John, "Ulster Premier Refuses to Call in Troops." *Times* (London), 5 August 1969

Coffman, Edward M. "The Long Shadow of the Soldier and the State." *Journal of Military History* 55, no. 1 (1991): 69–82

Conflict Archive on the Internet. *A Chronology of the Conflict*. Entry for 12 July 1969. http://www.cain.ulst.ac.uk/othelem/chron/ch69.htm, accessed 27 January 2014

Cost of the Troubles Study. *Final Report*. Belfast, 1999, http://www.incore.ulst.ac.uk/publications/pdf/cottreport.pdf, accessed 10 September 2015

Craig, Tony. "Laneside, Then Left a Bit? Britain's Secret Political Talks with Loyalist Paramilitaries in Northern Ireland, 1973–1976." *Irish Political Studies* 29, no. 2 (2014): 298–317

Critchley, T.A. *The Conquest of Violence: Order and Liberty in Britain*. New York: Schocken Books, 1970

Crossman, Richard. *The Diaries of a Cabinet Minister*. Vol. 3. New York: Holt, Rinehart and Winston, 1977

Cunningham, Michael. *British Government Policy in Northern Ireland, 1969–2000*. Manchester: Manchester University Press, 2001

Davis, Jon. *Prime Ministers and Whitehall, 1960–74*. London: Bloomsbury, 2007

Deane-Drummond, Anthony. *Riot Control*. London: Royal United Services Institute for Defence Studies, 1975

Desch, Michael C. "Soldiers, States and Structures: The End of the Cold War and Weakening U.S. Civilian Control." *Armed Forces and Society* 24, no. 3 (1998): 389–405

Dockrill, Michael L. *British Defence since 1945*. Oxford: Blackwell, 1989

Donoughue, Bernard. *Downing Street Diary: With Harold Wilson in No. 10*.
London: Jonathan Cape, 2005

– *Prime Minister: The Conduct of Policy under Harold Wilson and James Callaghan*. London: Jonathan Cape, 1987

Douglas-Home, Charles. "British Troops May Become Targets, GOC Says."
Times (London), 19 August 1969

Edwards, Aaron. "A Whipping Boy if Ever There Was One: The British Army and the Politics of Civil-Military Relations in Northern Ireland, 1969–1979." *Contemporary British History* 28, no. 2 (2014): 166–89

Elliott, Sydney, and W.D. Flackes. *Northern Ireland: A Political Directory, 1968–1999*. 5th rev. ed. Belfast: Blackstaff Press, 1999

English, Richard. *Armed Struggle: The History of the IRA*. Oxford: Oxford University Press, 2003

Eveleigh, Robin. *Peacekeeping in a Democratic Society: Lessons of Northern Ireland*. Montreal and Kingston: McGill-Queens University Press, 1978

Farrington, Christopher. "Mobilisation, State Crisis and Counter-Mobilisation: Ulster Unionist Politics and the Outbreak of the Troubles." *Irish Political Studies* 23, no. 4 (2008): 513–32

Faulkner, Brian. *Memoirs of a Statesman*. London: Weidenfeld and Nicolson, 1978

Feaver, Peter D. "Crisis as Shirking: An Agency Theory Explanation of the Souring of American Civil-Military Relations." *Armed Forces and Society* 24, no. 3 (1998): 407–34

"Field Marshal Lord Carver." *Guardian* (Manchester), 12 December 2001

"Field Marshal Lord Carver." *Telegraph* (London), 11 December 2001

Finn, John E. *Constitutions in Crisis: Political Violence and the Rule of Law*. Oxford: Oxford University Press, 1991

Fisk, Robert. *The Point of No Return: The Strike That Broke the British in Ulster*. London: André Deutsch, 1975

Fox, Captain K.O. "Public Order: The Law and the Military." *Army Quarterly and Defence Journal* 104, no. 3 (1974): 298–305

French, David. *The British Way in Counter-Insurgency, 1945–1967*. Oxford: Oxford University Press, 2011

"A Gamble for Peace in Derry." *Guardian* (Manchester), 15 August 1969

"General Sir Frank King." *Herald Scotland* (Glasgow), 3 April 1998

"General Sir Frank King." *Times* (London), 2 April 1998

Geraghty, Tony. *The Irish War: The Hidden Conflict between the IRA and British Intelligence*. Baltimore: Johns Hopkins University Press, 1998

"Government Decides on Firm Policy against Ulster Strikers at Crisis Meetings." *Times* (London), 25 May 1974

Hamill, Desmond. *Pig in the Middle: The Army in Northern Ireland, 1969–1984*. London: Methuen, 1985

Heath, Edward. *The Course of My Life: My Autobiography*. London: Hodder and Stoughton, 1998

Heather, Randall W. "The British Army in Northern Ireland, 1969–72." MA thesis, University of New Brunswick, 1986

Hennessey, Thomas. *The Evolution of the Troubles, 1970–72*. Dublin: Irish Academic Press, 2007

– *A History of Northern Ireland*. New York: St. Martin's Press, 1997

Higley, Lorin D. *Civil-Military Relationships: Theoretical Parameters in the Era of the 1990s. A Classified and Annotated Bibliography and Reference List*. N.p., n.d.

Hoffman, Bruce. *Anonymous Soldiers: The Struggle for Israel, 1917–1947*. New York: Alfred A. Knopf, 2015

Hoggart, Simon, "Bogsiders' Bitter Condemnation." *Guardian* (Manchester), 1 February 1972

Howard, Michael. *The Central Organization of Defence*. London: Royal United Services Institution, 1970

"How Long a Stay for the Troops?" *Guardian* (Manchester), 15 August 1969

Huntington, Samuel P. *The Soldier and the State: The Theory and Politics of Civil-Military Relations*. New York: Vintage Books, 1957

Jackson, Harold. "Army Says Shooting Began before Paras Acted." *Guardian* (Manchester), 1 February 1972

– "Mr. McAteer Calls for Help from the Republic." *Guardian* (Manchester), 11 August 1969

Jackson, Harold, and Simon Hoggart, "Stormont Back Today; Eire Calls for UN." *Guardian* (Manchester), 14 August 1969

Janowitz, Morris. *The Professional Soldier: A Social and Political Portrait*. New York: Free Press, 1960

Johnson, Franklyn A. *Defence by Ministry: The British Ministry of Defence, 1944–1974*. New York: Holmes and Meier, 1980

Jones, Tim. "Mr. Faulkner Makes Appeal to Stormont Rebels." *Times* (London), 16 July 1971

Jordan, A.G., and J.J. Richardson. *British Politics and the Policy Process: An Arena Approach*. London: Allen and Unwin, 1987

Keithly, David M., and Stephen P. Ferris, "Auftragstaktik, or Directive Control, in Joint and Combined Operations." *Parameters*, 29, no. 3 (1999):

118–33. http://strategicstudiesinstitute.army.mil/pubs/parameters/Articles /99autumn/keithly.htm, accessed 13 February 2016

Kennedy-Pipe, Caroline. *The Origins of the Present Troubles in Northern Ireland*. London: Longman, 1997

Kissane, Bill. "Defending Democracy? The Legislative Response to Political Extremism in the Irish Free State, 1922–39." *Irish Historical Studies* 34, no. 134 (2004): 156–74

Kitson, Frank. *Low Intensity Operations: Subversion, Insurgency, Peacekeeping*. London: Faber and Faber, 1971

Krulak, Gen. Charles C. "The Strategic Corporal: Leadership in the Three Block War." *Marines Magazine* (1999). http://www.au.af.mil/au/awc /awcgate/usmc/strategic_corporal.htm, accessed 12 September 2015

Lafree, Gary, Laura Dugan, and Raven Corte. "The Impact of British Counter-terrorist Strategies on Political Violence in Northern Ireland: Comparing Deterrence and Backlash Models." *Criminology* 47, no. 1 (2009): 17–45

"Lord Mason of Barnsley Obituary." *Guardian* (Manchester), 20 April 2015

"Loyalist Strike Called Off." *Guardian* (Manchester), 16 May 1974

"Major Chichester-Clark Indicts Eire." *Times* (London), 18 August 1969

Marshall, Rita. "O'Neill Defends Police Action." *Times* (London), 8 October 1968

Maudling, Reginald. *Memoirs*. London: Sidgwick and Jackson, 1978

McCleery, Martin J. *Operation Demetrius and Its Aftermath*. Manchester: Manchester University Press, 2015

McIntosh, Malcolm. *Managing Britain's Defence*. London: Macmillan, 1990

McKittrick, David. *Despatches from Belfast*. Belfast: Blackstaff Press, 1989

McKittrick, David, and David McVea. *Making Sense of the Troubles: The Story of the Conflict in Northern Ireland*. Chicago: New Amsterdam Books, 2002

The Military Balance, 1968–69. London: International Institute for Strategic Studies, 1968

Moloney, Ed. *A Secret History of the IRA*. Toronto: Penguin Canada, 2002

Mounter, Julian. "Peace Talks at Stormont." *Times* (London), 19 August 1969

"Mr. Fitt and the Misfits." *Guardian* (Manchester), 7 October 1968

"Mr. Heath Returns to Hold Watching Brief for Commons Clydeside Debate." *Times* (London), 1 August 1971

"Mr. O'Neill Praises Police but Blames Extremists." *Guardian* (Manchester), 6 January 1969

Neumann, Peter R. *Britain's Long War: Britain's Strategy in the Northern Ireland Conflict, 1969–98*. Houndmills, UK: Palgrave Macmillan, 2003

"No Union with South, Mr Faulkner Says." *Times* (London), 27 May 1974

"Obituary: General Sir Harry Tuzo." *Independent*, 18 August 1998

O'Dochartaigh, Niall. *From Civil Rights to Armalites: Derry and the Birth of the Irish Troubles*. Cork: Cork University Press, 1997

"Official Statement." *Times* (London), 15 August 1969

O'Halpin, Eunan. "'A Poor Thing but Our Own': The Joint Intelligence Committee and Ireland, 1965–1972." *Intelligence and National Security* 23, no. 5 (2008): 658–80

O'Leary, Brendan, and John McGarry. *The Politics of Antagonism: Understanding Northern Ireland*. 2nd ed. London: Athlone Press, 1996

"O'Neill Defends Police Action." *Times* (London), 8 October 1968

Patterson, Henry. "The British State and the Rise of the IRA, 1969–71: The View from the Conway Hotel." *Irish Political Studies* 23, no. 4 (2008): 491–511

Perlmutter, Amos. *The Military and Politics in Modern Times: On Professionals, Praetorians and Revolutionary Soldiers*. New Haven, CT: Yale University Press, 1977

"Petrol Bombs Used in New Ulster Riot." *Times* (London), 4 August 1969

"Police Hold 18 in Belfast." *Guardian* (Manchester), 27 May 1974

Prince, Simon Peter. "5 October 1968 and the Beginning of the Troubles: Flashpoints, Riots and Memory." *Irish Political Studies* 27, no. 3 (2012): 394–410

"Questions for Ulster." *Times* (London), 7 October 1968

Raghaven, Srinath. "Protecting the Raj: The Army in India and Internal Security, c. 1919–39." *Small Wars and Insurgencies* 16, no. 3 (2005): 253–79

Report of the Bloody Sunday Inquiry. 10 volumes. London: Stationery Office, 2010

"Right to Be Cautious." *Times* (London), 8 October 1968

Rimington, Stella. *Open Secret: The Autobiography of the Former Director-General of MI5*. London: Hutchison, 2001

"Riot in Derry as 1,000 Paisleyites Are Besieged." *Guardian* (Manchester), 4 January 1969

Roberts, Adam. "The British Army and Politics: A Historical Perspective." *Armed Forces and Society* 3, no. 3 (1977): 531–56

Sanders, Andrew. "Operation Motorman (1972) and the Search for a Coherent British Counterinsurgency Strategy in Northern Ireland." *Small Wars and Insurgencies* 24, no. 3 (2013): 465–92

Sanders, Andrew, and Ian S. Wood, *Times of Troubles: Britain's War in Northern Ireland*. Edinburgh: Edinburgh University Press, 2012

Schiff, Rebecca L. "Civil-Military Relations Reconsidered: A Theory of Concordance." *Armed Forces and Society* 122, no. 1 (1995): 7–24

Smith, Adrian. "Command and Control in Postwar Britain: Defence Decision-Making in the United Kingdom, 1945–1984." *Twentieth Century British History* 2, no. 3 (1991): 291–327

Smith, Brian. *Policy-Making in British Government: An Analysis of Power and Rationality.* London: Martin Robertson, 1976

Smith, M.L.R. *Fighting for Ireland: The Military Strategy of the Irish Republican Movement.* London: Routledge, 1997

– "Fin de Siecle, 1972: The Provisional IRA's Strategy and the Beginning of the Eight-Thousand Day Stalemate." In *Political Violence in Northern Ireland: Conflict and Conflict Resolution,* ed. Alan O'Day, 15–32. Westport, CT: Praeger, 1997

Stanhope, Henry. "Army Adopts New Role with Swoop on Ulster Terrorists." *Times* (London), 24 July 1971

Strachan, Hew. "The Civil-Military 'Gap' in Britain." *Journal of Strategic Studies* 26, no. 3 (2003): 43–63

– *The Politics of the British Army.* Oxford: Clarendon, 1997

"A Sustained Campaign of Violence." *Times* (London), 17 July 1971

Sutton Index of Deaths. www.cain.ulst.ac.uk, accessed 10 September 2015

Taylor, Peter. *Loyalists: War and Peace in Northern Ireland.* New York: TV Books, 1999

"13 Killed as Paratroops Break Riot." *Guardian* (Manchester), 31 January 1972

"Tough Tactics in Derry." *Guardian,* (Manchester) 7 October 1968

"Troops to Break Strike." *Guardian* (Manchester), 25 May 1974

"Ulster's Failure of Leadership." *Guardian* (Manchester), 12 August 1969

"Ulster Leaders Meet Wilson Today as Services Near Collapse." *Times* (London), 24 May 1974

"Unions Claim They Now Hold All UCS Yards." *Guardian* (Manchester), 31 July 1971

United Kingdom. *Parliamentary Debates.* House of Commons. 1968–74 http://hansard.millbanksystems.com/

United Kingdom. *Parliamentary Debates,* House of Lords. 1968–74 http://hansard.millbanksystems.com/

United Kingdom. Ministry of Defence, Defence Council. *Land Operations.* Volume 3. *Counter-Revolutionary Operations.* Part 1: "Principles and General Aspects." London: MOD, 29 August 1969

United Kingdom. Ministry of Defence. *Operation Banner: An Analysis of Mil-*

itary Operations in Northern Ireland. Ministry of Defence, 2006,
www.vilaweb.cat/media/attach/vwedts/docs/op_banner_analysis_released
.pdf, accessed 23 February 2012

United Kingdom. War Office. *Keeping the Peace (Duties in Aid of the Civil
Power), 1957*. London: War Office, 1957
– *Keeping the Peace, Part 1 – Doctrine*. London: War Office, 1963

Walles, Malcolm. *British and American Systems of* Government. Oxford:
Philip Allan, 1968

"What the Troops Mean." *Times* (London), 15 August 1969

"What Way Out for Ulster?" *Guardian* (Manchester), 16 August 1969

Whitelaw, William. *The Whitelaw Memoirs*. London: Aurum Press, 1989

Widgery, The Rt. Hon. Lord. *Report of the Tribunal Appointed to Inquire into
the Events on Sunday, 30 January 1972*. London: HMSO, April 1972.
www.cain.ulst.ac.uk, accessed 14 May 2015

Wilson, Harold. *Final Term: The Labour Government, 1974–1976*. London:
Weidenfeld and Nicolson and Michael Joseph, 1979
– *The Governance of Britain*. London: Weidenfeld and Nicolson and Michael
Joseph, 1976.
– *The Labour Government, 1964–70*. Harmondsworth: Penguin Books, 1971

Wood, David, "Forces Facing a Long Stay." *Times* (London), 16 August 1969
– "Wilson in Talks with Callaghan." *Times* (London), 15 August 1969

Yardley, Michael, and Dennis Sewell. *A New Model Army*. London: W.H.
Allen, 1989

Young, Thomas-Durell, "Military Professionalism in a Democracy." In *Who
Guards the Guardians and How: Democratic Civil-Military Relations*, ed.
Thomas C. Bruneau and Scott D. Tollefson, 17–33. Austin: University of
Texas Press, 2006.

Ziegler, Philip. *Wilson: The Authorised Biography of Lord Wilson of Rievaulx*.
London: Weidenfeld and Nicolson, 1993

Index

Bloody Sunday. *See* operations and
plans. *See also* Saville inquiry
into; Widgery inquiry into
Bloomfield, Kenneth, 79, 247n128
Bogside. *See* Londonderry
bombings. *See* violence
border (between Northern Ireland
and the Republic of Ireland), 54,
82, 122–4, 144, 146, 168
Bowen, Desmond, 219
Brennan, Lt. Col. Clive, 108, 115. *See
also* intelligence: interrogation-in-
depth
Bridges, Thomas Lord, 189
Britain's Long War, 6, 20, 206
British Army
– formations and units of: British
Army of the Rhine, 28, 163, 169,
173, 196, 221, 260n58; 8 Brigade,
120–1, 125, 128, 129; 1st Battalion, Prince of Wales' Own Regiment, 54, 68, 70, 228n1; 1st Battalion, Light Infantry, 181–2; 1st
Battalion, Parachute Regiment,
118, 128–30, 134–5, 136; 1st Battalion, Queen's Regiment, 182;
Headquarters, Northern Ireland,
17, 32, 71, 83, 84, 85, 103, 106,
108, 112, 113, 127, 129, 141, 162,
163, 164, 169, 171, 172, 191, 195,
201; 39 Brigade, 29, 53, 108;
Ulster Defence Regiment, 114,
182, 191, 222, 257n1; United
Kingdom Land Forces, 29, 169,
173, 222, 260n58
– political role of, 7–8, 15, 2–23,
30, 31, 86, 89, 110, 122–4, 136,
147, 173, 178, 182–4, 190, 192,
196, 198, 204, 209, 213, 216–17

– professionalism of, 7, 8, 29–31,
33, 124, 132, 137, 159, 175, 178,
182, 189, 198, 214–19; strength
of, 4, 28–9.
See also Baker, Gen. Sir Geoffrey;
Carver, Field Marshal Sir
Michael; chief of the general
staff; commander land forces;
Dyball, Maj. Gen. Tony; Farrar-
Hockley, Maj. Gen. Anthony;
Ford, Maj. Gen. Robert; Freeland,
Lt. Gen. Sir Ian; general officer
commanding; Harris, Lt. Gen. Sir
Ian; Hunt, Gen. Sir Peter; King,
Lt. Gen. Sir Frank; Ministry of
Defence; operations and plans;
Tuzo, Lt. Gen. Sir Harry
British State and the Ulster Crisis, The,
183
B-Specials. *See* Royal Ulster Con-
stabulary, Special Reserve

cabinet security committee. *See*
Northern Ireland, government of
Cairncross, Neil F., 78
Callaghan, James, 26, 27, 35, 41, 50,
51, 53, 55, 60, 65–9, 75, 76, 79, 91,
211, 212, 219. *See also* government, British: secretary of state
for the Home Office; Home
Office
Carrington, Peter Lord, 17, 27, 28,
94, 101, 102, 103, 105, 106, 109,
110, 115, 116, 117, 131, 139, 148,
150, 151, 161, 169, 171, 176, 211,
212, 213, 219, 224n27, 242n26,
252n83. *See also* government,
British: secretary of state for
defence; Ministry of Defence

cy committee, 31, 33, 34, 227n30; "machinery of," 10, 11, 23, 24–39, 50, 73, 74, 78, 123, 144, 162, 189, 220; minister of state for defence, 94, 103, 105, 116, 148, 151; minister of state for the Home Office, 69; minister of state for Northern Ireland, 168, 181, 190; official committee on Northern Ireland, 27, 38, 53, 55, 78, 141, 143, 222; Parliament, 8, 16, 20, 26, 27, 31, 36, 42, 49, 51, 52, 60, 65, 69, 76, 87–8, 96, 99, 104–5, 132, 133, 140, 142, 149, 151, 165, 167–8, 178, 181, 199, 245n80, 245n95; permanent secretaries and undersecretaries, 32, 34, 50, 52, 78, 147, 149, 150–2, 165, 170, 175, 195, 198, 202, 212, 226n10, 227n30, 254n24; prime minister, 8, 11–13, 14, 18, 26, 27, 28, 31, 36–8, 41, 46, 49, 50, 51, 54–6, 56, 60, 69, 77, 88, 90, 104, 113, 119, 121, 130, 132, 133, 135, 137, 138, 148, 152, 162, 165, 181, 184, 186, 188, 189, 192–5, 197, 199, 201–2, 210, 211, 212, 228n51, 245n80, 253n8; secretary of state for defence, 12, 17, 27, 28, 30, 31, 32, 34, 35, 38, 45, 46, 49, 50, 51, 54, 59, 61, 72, 84–6, 94, 97, 105, 106, 131, 139, 140, 142, 144, 147–53, 158, 159, 160, 167, 168, 172, 181, 186, 189, 193, 195, 202, 211–12, 215, 224n27, 227n30, 242n26; secretary of the state for the Home Office, 26, 27–8, 35, 41, 45, 49–51, 60, 63–6, 68, 77, 79, 83, 87, 90–4, 97, 98–102, 104, 105, 108, 109, 111,

132, 139, 140, 142, 145, 151, 176; secretary of state for Northern Ireland, 17, 27, 142, 146–8, 149, 150–2, 153, 156, 157, 159–62, 166, 167, 168, 169, 173, 175, 176, 181, 186, 189, 191, 194, 200–1, 204, 212–13, 215, 216; 10 Downing Street, 71, 72, 81, 191. *See also* Allen, Sir Philip; Armstrong, Robert; Balneil, Lord; Bridges, Thomas Lord; Cairncross, Neil F; Callaghan, James; Carrington, Peter Lord; Cary, Sir Michael; Cooper, Sir Frank; Dunnett, Sir James "Ned"; Groves, John; Heath, Edward; Healey, Denis; Hockaday, Sir Arthur; Home Office; Hooper, Sir Robin; Hunt, Sir John; Jones, Kenneth; Mason, Roy; Maudling, Reginald; Mayne, J.F.; Ministry of Defence; Napier, Oliver; Nash, K. T.; Nicholls, Nigel; North, Robin; Northern Ireland Office; Orme, Stanley; Rees, Merlyn; Smith, Howard; Stephen, Derek; Stephens, Anthony; Stopford, E.K.; Trend, Burke Baron; Whitelaw, William; Wilson, Harold; Woodfield, P.J.; Wright, Oliver

Groves, John, 201–3
Guardian (Manchester), 42, 67, 70, 76, 199, 202, 213

Hamill, Desmond, 181, 214, 228n1
Harris, Lt. Gen. Sir Ian, 45, 61. *See also* command and control; general officer commanding
Hattersley, Roy, 69